RADICALS

WHY TOMORROW BELONGS TO POST-DENOMINATIONAL CHRISTIANS INFUSED WITH SUPERNATURAL POWER

REV. DONNA HOWELL

WITH FOREWORD BY DR. THOMAS HORN

DEFENDER

CRANE, MO

RADICALS: Why Tomorrow Belongs to Post-Denominational Christians Infused
with Supernatural Power

Defender
Crane, MO 65633
©2017 by Thomas Horn and Donna Howell
All rights reserved. Published 2017.
Printed in the United States of America.

ISBN: 978-0-9981426-6-1

A CIP catalog record of this book is available from the Library of Congress.

Cover illustration and design by Jeffrey Mardis.

All Scripture quotations from the King James Version; in cases of academic
comparison, those instances are noted.

Contents

Jesus Was a Radical

By Dr. Thomas R. Horn

THE WORD "RADICAL" has meant many things to people throughout history. Some hear it and immediately think of rallies, picket signs, and violent protests. Others hear the word and appreciate its insinuation of a return to fundamental truths. But whatever imagery it inspires for each individual, there is no denying that it almost always represents an extreme when applied as an adjective describing a person's words and actions toward or against something—especially an "establishment."

I will get straight to the point: Jesus Christ, Himself, was a radical, the greatest of all, and the institution He opposed was the Pharisaic "Church" of His day—an establishment that had shaped an apathetic world culture all Christians today agree was way off the mark. "Thank God," we all concur, "that Christ came to reform and revolutionize everyone's thinking back then, or there's no telling what any post-Judeo religion would have become."

Jesus was repeatedly approached by leaders within the Church of the Law who tried to trap Him in a corner with public challenge-and-riposte rhetoric games, and every time—*every time*—He accomplished what no regular human could have done: He fulfilled the Law to the last letter whilst maintaining the highest zeal for love, compassion, and the true holiness that births from a righteous heart instead of mechanical adherence to that prized, yet cold, list of religious "rules." But, every time, He did so by meeting the challenge head-on with gentleness and wisdom, and every time, He shocked those around Him who were not only used to the calloused culture of traditions, they were so comfortable in their robes and shiny lifestyles that they didn't want it to be contested by the likes of this new Rabbi who wandered from place to place in unassuming sandals.

The Jews had waited eons for the Messiah, and many had in their heads what He would be when he arrived: a Pharisee of all Pharisees soaked with riches and impressive garments; a warrior carrying a sword dripping with the blood of revenge whose voice would echo off the mountainside a message of apocalypse for the Romans and any other oppressors of the Jews. They expected a radical, yes, but they did not foresee that the prophesied Messiah would expose the very inflated institution of self-righteous hypocrisy they had established and used to oppress and judge their own people. He was the exact opposite of the Messiah they anticipated. He did not come to lend momentum to their progressive religious takeover, but to tear it down and reform it. Those who truly understood what He was achieving while He walked the earth—those who truly had ears to hear and eyes to see the spiritual kingdom over which He would rule—denied themselves, took up their crosses daily, and followed Him (Luke 9:23), refreshed by the reformation He spoke of. Those who did not understand what He was accomplishing—those who enjoyed their station within the company of comforts and power and control—sought to silence Him by any means necessary, including death.

And He was so committed to His ministry that such a death could not and would not intimidate Him away from His message.

Jesus was the Radical of all radicals.

Throughout time and especially during spiritual awakenings, His most dedicated followers have likewise been considered radical.

I was a young man during such a time, and throughout the 1960–70s I personally witnessed and benefited from the birth of the radical "Jesus

People" movement. This was an era packed with drastic social and political activism. From some angles, a person can trace the unfolding antiestablishment counterculture of the '60s to grass roots/freedom movements earlier on. There are also those who say the counterculture was merely an extension of growing, Age-of-Fire Pentecostalism, encouraging religious people to abandon rituals and institutional dogma for dynamic Holy-Spirit-led manifestations. However, these types of facts may overlook something very important: the sovereignty of God. That is to say, God does new and unexpected things in times of His choosing, which inspires contemporary generations of radicals to depart ecclesiastical norms that can neither be organized by men nor energized by practiced methodologies, at least not in the beginning. I believe we have entered such a time again, and the evidence is reflected in familiar antiestablishment sentiments today—both religious and political. We are rapidly ripening for an awakening, and this book leaves no illusions about how that could suddenly unfold, unexpectedly giving rise to a new breed of post-denominational radicals infused with the supernatural power of God.

Using the Bible's book of James, Donna Howell reasons with unparalleled clarity, mingling the past and future into sharp relief that will keep you coming back to refresh your bearings over and over. This book is so smart, so timely, yet grounded in biblical history and revelation imbued with fierce urgency that is now.

As in her earlier work *Final Fire*, Howell is superbly positioned to bring religious historical thinking to bear on the church scene with unpretentious words that remind us how radicalism isn't always a bad thing when it comes to God—it sprouts from willing and hungry hearts unsatisfied with tradition, then shakes institutional expectations as it did in Jesus and His brother James's day.

I've told my friends, staff, and family how much the current social and cultural phenomena remind me of the days leading up to the Jesus People movement. Something very similar is definitely in the air right now, and it may only yet be a spark, but Donna Howell has convinced me that it will soon be a fire. A raging, sovereign, RADICAL fire!

So, You Want to Change the World?

AMERICA TODAY IS sensing something we cannot easily describe. We have been aching for a real connection to something beyond humanity's capability for fulfillment. We are hungry for contentment and peace on a global scale as well as on a personal level.

We see this emptiness every time we log online and see that at least half of our Facebook friends are posting memes or status updates about their daughters and sons being bullied in school; their finances tapped dry; the last time they went to church and why they will never be back; how they have been turned down by yet another medical insurance company and don't qualify for low-income healthcare; who or what they're casting their votes for and why that political personality or social movement is simply the lesser of all evils; what constitutional freedoms they believe they're being slowly deprived of; and what all of this means for future generations…

We hear of the emptiness every time we turn on the news, each station blaring updates about another economic and national downfall; devastating climate changes; earthquake, flood, and storm damage to major cities and the people suffering from these natural disasters; new parasites or viruses that have the medical world puzzled while entire regions are placed under quarantine; terrorist organizations and the threat they pose to our country's peace and welfare; shootings at public schools; riots on the street; wild protests; public figure scandals; increasing persecution of select social groups on a territory that *should* be a diplomatic nation…

We feel the sting of emptiness each time an Internet troll attacks someone else—with a boldness and hatefulness one of those trolls would *never* have the gall to execute in person—without regard to how much pain that causes another person or to how the attack ultimately contributes to this large-scale loneliness we are all feeling. We suffocate under the pressure of it each time we attend a church where a pulpit-pounder abuses his or her position through crowd manipulation and then asks for money to support the "ministry"—and those who donate to the cause feel doubt set in only days later, wondering if anything is true in the world of religion anymore. We choke against the strangling of it when we hear of another dictatorial law claiming ownership of an area of our lives that used to be protected by national liberty.

We fight: individual against individual, organization against organization, party against party, government against government, nation against nation, social group against social group, church against church. And *as* we battle against ourselves from every angle, we are many times deceived into thinking that we are fighting the "good" fight, standing for what we believe in, making a difference, changing the world, creating a "better place." What is "better" for one activist party is "worse" for another, and the bar is raised for rage mounting upon anger mounting upon discontentedness…until our energy is milked to the last drop and all we have left is to give into the same depressing demoralization to which those around us have already surrendered.

Starving to gratify this underlying feeling, this ravaging beast that claims our joy and destroys our trust in relationships and government and the world, we seek contentment and peace through *human* efforts. But can the answer to all of humanity's problems be corrected through human means in the first place? Can a nation divided against itself stand?

Jesus Christ didn't think so. (See Mark 3:24–25; Matthew 12:25; Luke 11:17.)

America, as well as many other nations worldwide, is besieged by a confusing paradox. Do we wrestle against the agendas that jeopardize the world we wish to have, knowing that a kingdom divided against itself cannot stand and our arguments only contribute to an eventual dissipation of united values? Or do we sit back silently and allow a compromise of our beliefs in the interest of peace, knowing that this, *also*, contributes to the dissipation of the values we believe are moral and upright? Do we fight until we die internally, or do we sit on our backsides until we die internally?

Don't we all long for the *Leave it to Beaver* days when white picket fences lined our hopes and dreams, our children were safe playing outside, our neighbors always had a cup of sugar to lend, and our biggest problem during the week was deciding what flavor of pie to take to a potluck on Sunday? I realize this is an oversimplification—in every historic period our country has faced challenges—but, by comparison, we are no longer one nation, under God, indivisible. We haven't been that for a *long* time. Today, we are one nation, under many principalities of darkness, and we are not indivisible but we are *divided* by every single social and political nuance every single day.

Who can satisfy the hunger we feel for amity?

What can place a salve on the wound of constant, universal dejection?

What is the ultimate answer?

I, Donna Howell, did not conceive the answer to that question within my own mind, but I do know what Book holds the answer.

So, I ask: Do you want to change the world we're living in? Do you *really* want to make a difference in a deep and lasting way, beyond simply sponsoring further discord among "we the people"?

I know of one man who did this long ago. His name was James the Just, and he was the half-brother of Jesus Christ.

Yes, Jesus Christ the Messiah *was* the first and foremost changer of the world, well beyond any other man, including James. However, Jesus came to save the world spiritually, so that "*whosoever will* believe upon Him would not perish, but have everlasting life" in heaven, with God, Himself (John 3:16; emphasis added). What Jesus accomplished led to a forever freedom beyond this lifetime for anyone who chooses to accept Him. But, Christ's kingdom was "not of this world" (John 18:36), as He openly admitted; therefore, His ultimate redemptive purpose for all humanity was not "of this world" but of the next. Christ was, is, and always will be the One who changed the world more than any other human by giving this temporal reality hope and purpose through the shedding of His blood. However, because He was also God, no man, woman, or child before or since can achieve what He has done for humanity no matter how hard one may try to do so.

Christ came for *spiritual* reformation. And He was uniquely poised to do so.

But when He died, rose again, and ascended, a great confusion spread throughout the surrounding regions of the earth that remained during the Apostolic Age (the era from Christ's ascension to the death of the last apostle), calling for a reformation of the Gospel as passed orally (and often incorrectly by those who were not apostles) from one border to another. Churches were sprouting up all over the territory claiming a belief in and obedience to the Risen Christ, but their behaviors and lifestyles showed ignorance and lack of true submission to Christ's directives. Bickering, arguing, and dissention of morality became the mounting result of those populations who were quickly turning this new "Christ-ianity" into another social or lifestyle movement with growing tension between unofficial sects. The Church of Christ was a social club. (Sound familiar? It should. It's not only what I've outlined up to this point, it's what our current Church has once again become.)

What Christendom needed in those days was a radical redirection of focus from halfhearted "religion" and social bickering to a deep relationship with the Risen Messiah.

It is an age-old truth of human nature: Morality cannot be legislated or mandated by any governing force, including Church leadership or theocracy, lest it result in mass rebellion and/or revolt. On the other hand, a true change of *heart* by the believers would result in a change of social issues, and one man understood this very well.

James, the author of the book by the same name, rose up for *social* reformation of the Christian Church. And He was uniquely poised to do so.

What Christendom needs *today*—as it did in James' day—is a radical redirection of focus from halfhearted "religion" to a deep relationship with the Risen Messiah and Yahweh. We need leaders to rise up for social reformation of the Christian Church. And *you* are uniquely poised to do so.

As such, the "where to start" and "what to do" questions can—and should—be answered by looking in Scripture, particularly at the man who brought about this radical overhaul in the first place.

Remember as you read ahead that every chapter poses the question of whether you want to be a part of the next Great Awakening…and if you do, it cannot be an idle decision.

Chapter 1

Who Was James, the Reformer of the Social Gospel?

LET US BEGIN by learning a bit of background on the book of James, beginning with the questions of its authorship.

The Author

In James 1:1, James only identifies himself as "James, a servant of God and of the Lord Jesus Christ." Although theories abound as to the authorship of the book of James, only three concepts deserve real focus, as they are the only ideas that pose any substantive connection to the timeline and development of the early Church:

1. James the Great (also "Greater"), a central apostle of Christ, brother of John, and son of the fisherman Zebedee
2. James, the son of Alphaeus
3. James, the half-brother of Christ, later a key leader of the early Church

Several valid arguments throughout the ages have strongly supported the authorship of this epistle to James the half-brother of Christ.

First, James the Great was martyred by Herod in AD 44 (Acts 12:2). The epistle was dated to circa AD 60–62. Thus, James the Great was deceased by the time the epistle was written. This leaves only the son of Alphaeus and the half-brother.

Second, however, we know almost nothing of the son of Alphaeus, and we know that the half-brother was a name on nearly everyone's lips around Palestine in that day. The simple introduction of the epistle implies that a lengthier self-identification is not necessary. Had the son of Alphaeus been the author, an identifier would have likely been given, so the book would *not* have been attributed to the half-brother of Christ, who was such a well-known and distinguished leader at the time of the book's writing that he had been called a "pillar of the church" by Paul (Galatians 1:19; 2:9). Since a description of the author is missing from the epistle entirely, it appears a valid assumption that no further explanation was necessary, for of course the half-brother of Christ and pillar of the early Church did not need a grand introduction. (James, the son of Alphaeus, was not prominent in any writings of that time, including the scriptural records. Serious scholars and theologians have largely dismissed the notion that the son of Alphaeus had anything to do with writing the epistle.)

Third, much internal and external documentation points to the half-brother:

1. The language style used in the epistle is a match for that used in the speech the half-brother gave the Jerusalem council in Acts 15:13–21.
2. Descriptions of the half-brother throughout the New Testament (c.f. Acts 12:17; 21:18; 1 Corinthians 15:7; Galatians 1:19; 2:9, 12) seamlessly agree with what is known about the writer of the epistle.
3. The epistle was written from a Jewish background, also using Hebrew idioms translated into highly educated Greek, with great

respect for the Mosaic Law, which is uniform to the upbringing and education of the half-brother.

4. Jude, the other half-brother of Christ and largely uncontested as the author of the book of Jude, began his writing with the same introductory identifier, referring to himself as a "servant of Jesus Christ"—much like a familial, household moniker—but he goes on to identify himself as "a brother of James [the half-brother of Christ]" (Jude 1), the aforementioned, well-known "pillar."

5. According to Donald Guthrie of New Testament Introduction, "There are more parallels in this Epistle than in any other New Testament book to the teaching of our Lord [Christ] in the Gospels."[1] This is significant, as theologian David Mallick says: "James is producing reminiscences of oral teaching which he previously heard for himself [from his half-brother, Christ],"[2] which is yet another familial connection—this time between Christ and His half-brother, James.

6. Alexandrian scholar and early Christian theologian, Origen, attributed the epistle to the half-brother.

7. Caesarea's Greek historian, Christian polemicist, and exegete, Eusebius Pamphili, attributed the epistle to the half-brother.

With so much evidence pointing to the fact that the enigmatic "James" of the epistle was, in fact, the half-brother of Christ, we will continue now via that conclusion. Therefore, the question that tends to surface early on is usually, "What would it have been like to be the sibling of *the* Jesus Christ?"

The Sibling

Though Catholics typically believe in Mary's perpetual virginity, scriptural evidence claims otherwise. She was certainly a virgin when the Holy Spirit came upon her and Christ was conceived, but following that, she gave birth to at least six other children.

In Luke 2:7, Scripture tells us that Mary "gave birth to her firstborn." The word "firstborn" (as opposed to "only") indicates there were other children. In Matthew 13:55 and Mark 6:3, the question is asked about Jesus, "Isn't this the carpenter's son?" and Christ's "brothers" (as opposed to "cousins" or equivalent) are named specifically—James, Joses (Joseph), Simon, and Judas (Jude; of no connection to Judas the betrayer)—as well as the mention of "sisters," which is plural (meaning at least two, equaling a total of at least six siblings and possibly more). All of these would have been half-brothers and half-sisters to the immaculately conceived Jesus Christ, the mentioned carpenter's son—not cousins or spiritual family.

Mary, Joseph, Jesus, James, Joseph Jr., Simon, Jude, and "sisters" all lived together as a family unit. Christ was around thirty when He began His public ministry, but prior to that, He shared a home life with them in much the same way any normal family would…with the exception of the fact that He never sinned, even once (1 Peter 1:18–19; 2:22; 2 Corinthians 5:21; Hebrews 4:15; 1 John 3:5).

Extrabiblical stories circulate involving how Christ as a youth purified water, made clay sparrows and breathed life into them, commanded a tree to arc its branch so He could reach fruit, resurrected a friend, resurrected a teacher, multiplied wheat, lengthened wood in the carpentry shop, stood in an assembly of predatory animals while they worshiped Him reverently, healed a woodcutter, and healed James from a snakebite wound, as well as other less popular legends. None of these stories is biblical, and we do have biblical proof that they are all the workings of uninspired, human imagination. Luke 2:40 (with its author known commonly as "the careful historian" for his unique attention to Christ's early years) states simply that Jesus grew, became strong, gained wisdom, and was bestowed with God's grace, but there is no account of childhood miracles or amazing signs and wonders. As a child running around in sandals and giving warmhearted greetings to His neighbors, Christ was like any other little boy. This is reflected in how the people of His hometown reacted toward Him in His later ministry years (Mark 3:21). (Also note that in John 2:11, the miracle Christ performed when He turned the water into wine at the wedding in

Cana was the "beginning" of His signs and wonders, so there would not have been any prior.)

Although Christ's childhood was comparatively normal, Hebrews 5:8 states that His obedience was "by the things which he suffered," so we know that He experienced suffering and sadness. He met temptation face to face on a regular basis, as any human would, "in all points [i.e., from every angle; at each turn; in every stage of His life] tempted like as we are, yet *without sin*" (Hebrews 4:15; emphasis added). From these verses and others, we have proof that the world and the people around Christ were the same kind of world and people that would surround any normal boy who was being raised in a fallen state, but He was *perfect*.

The same childishly prideful back talk toward parents that may have come out of the mouths of Jesus' playmates would have been enticing to Him as well, or else He would not have been "tempted like as we are." The same pretty eyes that would have caught the attention of the other young men would have caught the attention of Christ, or else He would not have been "tempted like as we are." The same theft, lies, deceit, egotism, vanity, self-gratification, covetousness, greed, laziness, enviousness, disrespectfulness, anger, frustration…*all* flew in front of His face every day of His life, or else He would not have been "tempted like as we are."

Despite this, Christ never entertained an immoral thought, He never had a poor attitude, He never challenged or defied His parents, He never grumbled about what was on the supper table or argued about eating all His vegetables, He never quarreled with his younger siblings, He never said a bad word, He never talked about people behind their backs, and He never squandered a second of His time on earth.

By the time Christ was the age of twelve, if not before, He understood who He *really* was after it came to Mary and Joseph's attention that He was not in the family caravan leaving Jerusalem after the Passover pilgrimage. (Boy-Jesus was not the kind of child a parent would normally have to track down, so it wasn't until a full day's journey they realized He was missing.) They located Him in the temple courts after three days of searching. He was visiting nonchalantly with the teachers there, who were astounded at His astute and learned interactions. When Mary asked why Jesus hadn't stayed with the family, He responded by asking them why they would have had to search for Him in the first place. Wouldn't they have known that He would be in His Father's house, going about His Father's business (Luke 2:41–49)?

This response was not disrespectful. Instead, it was a prodigious affirmation that Jesus very well knew who He was, calling God "My Father," and asserting to His parents that He was aware of His charge.

He didn't get in trouble for having gone missing, either, because His parents understood there was something significant about Jesus' choice to meander through the temple courts. Mary and Joseph knew that the boy was the Son of God, and as such, they knew that He would one day do something irreversibly intense to our planet—so far be it from them to hinder His progress or punish Him during the preparative steps of His youth. The Scripture simply says that, after His response, "he went down with them [His family], and came to Nazareth, and was subject unto them [He obeyed His parents]: but his mother kept all these sayings [His response about His Father's house/business] in her heart. And Jesus increased in wisdom and stature, and in favour with God and man" (Luke 2:51–52).

Even though Christ's appointment in the temple courts was an ordained moment in His life, once discovered, He was agreeably subject to the authority of His earthly parents. And for eighteen years following, Jesus remained with His family as a son and a brother.

As a parent, a perfect child would be the one we all would want to raise. As a sibling, however…

Imagine *that!*

Christ was fully God, but He was also fully human; therefore, He would have had boyish moments with James as they both grew. Many younger siblings follow the older ones around. They probably threw sticks together. They likely skipped rocks together. Jesus probably ruffled James' hair. The idea that they would have playfully wrestled around is not a stretch.

I can see several adorable scenes unfold in my own imagination at the mere thought of boy-Jesus. When I was a little girl, my older brother and I used to play "church." He would set up "pews" out of couch pillows and fill them with stuffed animals, and I was his "worship leader," playing an air piano (or the bricks near our fireplace), and as I sang, he would stand nearby strumming a real box guitar and uttering hearty hallelujahs. When the "worship service" concluded, I would take my seat in the front "pew" and listen to a two-minute sermon my brother would preach (usually the same one about obedience and faithfulness in a sinful world), and then he would ask for a raising of hands as a response to a life-changing question, which was usually a word-for-word repetition of what he'd heard given from the pulpit at the real church we attended:

"Every head bowed; every eye closed. How many of you men and women out there are ready to stop [doing such-and-such] and make a lifelong commitment this morning? I see that hand. I see that one, too. How many of you are willing to do what it takes to follow through with that commitment?… Hands all across the building. Hallelujah. You see this, Lord? Your children are ready for Your presence this morning."

And then we would have an altar call.

I remember one teddy bear I had as a girl. I had safety-pinned a hand-kerchief sling around its arm, and that bear must have been "healed" of its broken bones thirty times. I saw many a stuffed animal give its heart to the Lord in those days.

How did James and Jesus play? What did their youthful, brotherly love look like? Did they, too, play "synagogue"? Did Jesus practice His oratory skills before a congregation of James, Jude, Simon, Joseph Jr., a few sisters, some rocks, and some figs? Certainly I mean no disrespect by presenting such extrabiblical imaginings, but I believe too many folks want to abolish any idea of young Jesus playing like a regular Jewish boy would, as if He came out of the womb quoting the Septuagint. Yet, the Scripture clearly indicates that, aside from having a spotless character and leading a sinless existence, Jesus' life was normal until the wedding at Cana. Does it not make Jesus Christ even *more* endearing and lovable as a friend—a true companion to humankind—to believe that He enjoyed such playtime? (The notion of "playing synagogue" is not an outlandish idea, anyway, considering the articulate Christ of the ministry years appeared to always have an answer ready, even for the most difficult questions. Of course He was anointed, and it was from that anointing that His greatest moments beamed, but perhaps some preaching to the trees may have been a part of His development also.)

James probably challenged Jesus to races around the fields. Jesus was probably the first responder when James suffered a skinned knee. When James was sad, Jesus' arm must have been the first to land on His little brother's shoulders in comfort. When James had questions about Yahweh, there is no doubt that the astute and learned Jesus—the same Jesus who astounded the teachers of the temple courts in His youth—would have been able to provide His kid brother answers.

James was *familiar* with Jesus.

Of course, this is not to say that James never would have been challenged as the younger sibling of God Almighty. Many adults can remember a parent from their youth saying, "Why can't you be more like your brother [or sister]?"

I wonder if, or how many times, James might have heard the equivalent of this question.

Mary and Joseph never had reason to discipline Jesus, because He was the perfect child. All they could do as parents was show Him love and constant affection. From a human standpoint, that may be a contributing factor for why His brothers and sisters later rejected Him as the Messiah (John 7:5).

When the day came that Jesus had performed miracles and signs, and even the "unclean spirits, when they saw him, fell down before him, and cried, saying, Thou art the Son of God" (Mark 3:11), His brothers and friends said He was crazy, that He had cracked, that He was "beside himself" (Mark 3:21). His brothers, friends, and those of His hometown were "offended at him" when He taught in the synagogue (Mark 6:3). Jesus knew this moment would happen, and His response was, "A prophet is not without honour [i.e., "a prophet is celebrated"], but [meaning "everywhere but"] in his own country [or hometown], and among his own kin [or relatives], and in his own house [amidst his siblings]" (Mark 6:4).

Familiarity with Jesus and His perfection did not inspire James to believe in His Messiahship. James didn't find it easier to believe in His brother as the Son of God just because he had witnessed His unique character and flawlessness. No—in fact, it would have likely made it much harder. Christ was perfect, yes; but to James, He was just a brother. A sibling. A part of the family. An equal to other human men. James was the oldest son of the family aside from Jesus, so he would have had the longest time of all Mary and Joseph's children to observe his brother being a regular, non-miracle-working boy during their playtime or their hours spent carpentering. Despite Christ's ability to avoid angering His parents throughout His youth, James observed the behaviors of a regular boy. A nice boy, yes. A sweet boy, certainly. But God?! Equal to Yahweh? A *part of* Yahweh? Heavens, no…

So normal was Christ's childhood that when His twelve disciples gathered to follow Him in His mission, the people in his hometown were anything *but* believing. They all thought He was crazy. *That's* how ordinary Christ's early years were!

And James was up close and personal through every moment.

Yet, though James did not believe his half-brother's claims of being God, the day Christ bled to death on the cross in front of His mother and the Roman soldiers must have been a tragic day for James, indeed. The days of ruffling hair and wrestling around were over. The sermons in the woods to siblings and figs would not be preached again. The races through the fields were but a memory. What on earth must have been going through James' mind during that event? Did he still wholly reject the idea that Christ was Lord? Did he still believe that his brother was simply a sad and tragically misled crazy person? Or, perhaps, was there just an inkling of faith rising up within James that told him his brother was the real deal?

The world will probably never know what James felt the day Christ was crucified. What we *do* know, however, is that after Christ died and rose on the third day, He appeared to James in person (1 Corinthians 15:7). What an intense meeting that must have been! I can only imagine the previously doubting James falling on his face before his now-risen half-brother and Son of God with "nail prints" in His hands and a hole in His side from the spear (John 20:24–29), the walking proof of death defeated—the living proof that He was, is, and always will be exactly who He said He was! And James wasn't the only one of the brothers who experienced enough personal testimony to believe. After Christ ascended into heaven, Jesus' mother *and the rest of His brothers* were present among the 120 believers in the Upper Room (Acts 1:14).

That was it. The appearance of Christ changed the course of James' life, and by extension, the course of history. As a result of their coming to believe, James and his brother Jude would both go on to write epistles included in the canon of New Testament Scripture.

At this point we can see how being the half-brother of Christ would *benefit* James. How unlikely his role as a leader of the early Church seemed when Jesus was first assembling His followers. Now, though, he stood as *most* likely to understand the pure nature of Christ's mission: Well before he was confronted with talk of Jesus as Messiah, James had walked and talked and played and wrestled and bounced around with boy-Jesus during childhood. Years before James would ever see his brother taken to trial and made to answer for Himself about which kingdom He belonged to, James would have been an eyewitness to how teen-Jesus interacted with others around Him, what truth and wisdom He lovingly bestowed upon peers who were struggling with life's hard-hitting questions, and what encouragement He offered others with words no other person could offer. Before Christ ever visited His fore-running cousin at the famous Holy-Spirit-descending baptismal, James had watched as adult-Jesus poured into Scripture and Greek, produced theological conclusions with a truth no other person could accumulate through their own interpretation, formed opinions about religious authority, and approached the Jewish faith with unparalleled fervor and revitalization at every turn.

Every day James had observed how Jesus responded to the world around Him: what made Him laugh, what made Him cry, how He reacted when questions of this earthly existence arose, what He found inspirational versus what He saw as blasphemous, whom He saw as truly righteous versus whom He saw as pretenders in robes...*what made Him tick*. The very familiarity that made James the unlikeliest of believers came full circle to make him the most likely of crucial early Church leaders! For who else on earth—except only Mary, Joseph, Joseph Jr., Simon, Jude, and "sisters"—would have had the privilege of living in such close proximity to God, Himself, in human form? Every reaction that Christ the Son of God had as a human—by nature of the Trinity—was precisely the same reaction that the Holy Spirit and Creator Yahweh would have had, and James had a front row seat! James had seen the literal God in action every day of his life for thirty years, and as such, his perspective was now enlightened to distinctively understand Christ's nature and purpose. James' authority is overshadowed by Paul's much of the time today because Paul wrote a significant portion of the New Testament, but having God in human form as a sibling for three decades, refusing to believe, then coming to believe—all this would have placed James in a position to speak with massive influence and authority in his day.

And *oh* did the early Church need a leader like James...

After the day the Christian Church was inaugurated when the Holy Spirit came upon Christ's followers at Pentecost, the twelve apostles went out to the surrounding territories to spread the Gospel. Many other key figures in Christ's circle also scattered from Jerusalem after observing the stoning of Stephen. A void was left right there in the middle of Jerusalem—the heartbeat city of God's people. Without a voice to reach the Jews with the truth about Jesus as Messiah, the most vital historical location of all would have been lost. So James stayed there and ministered to the people, and almost overnight became the bishop of the city, the pastor of the people, the shepherd of the flock.

- James was present the day Paul came to meet secretly with the leadership of the local church in Jerusalem to tell them of his conversion (Galatians 1:18–19).
- James was listed as one of the first recipients Peter commissioned the believers who had prayed for him to testify to regarding the account of his miraculous escape from prison (Acts 12:17).
- James was a head advisor and prominent groundbreaker in the council of Jerusalem when the question of Gentile fellowship and circumcision was raised (Acts 15). And it was at this council that, under the leadership of James and Peter, the sound doctrine of purification by faith alone (not by the observance of rituals or ceremony)—through the proof of the Holy Spirit's outpouring on uncircumcised Gentiles—was established for the Church. (More on this shortly.)
- James was still the leader of the church in Jerusalem when Paul was tried a decade later (Acts 21).

James was unquestionably positioned dead center as the principal leader in Jerusalem, and much of the early Christian Church's health and stability rested on his shoulders. Momentous accounts were to be brought to his attention directly. Not one central, early-Church issue occurred near Jerusalem without his knowledge and/or input.

He served his post faithfully, and at every turn he was active in preserving the Gospel message he believed his brother, Christ, had come to bring. Out of this unadulterated passion for Jesus Christ and His crucifixion, arising, and ascension as the Son of God, James wrote a very important letter "to the twelve tribes which are scattered abroad" (James 1:1). His letter was written to encourage the early Christians who were suffering, to correct erroneous theology about the nature of salvation, and to urge his readers to more appropriately understand the relationship between true righteousness and good deeds. The language used in his exhortation is bold, vigorous, fearless, and passionate. He did not set out to flatter believers or stroke egos, but to blast the early Church with an outcry for repentance and righteous living. He wrote with the authority of a man who had observed God in the flesh for thirty years, and who had lived to see Him risen. He wrote to Jewish Christians who were dispersed throughout the land in hiding from the persecution of angry mobs and Herod Agrippa with the same wisdom flavor as that used by the writer(s) of Proverbs. His robust call for uprightness amongst believers earned him the name "James the Just." (According to Eusebius in *Ecclesiastical History*, James was on his knees so much for his brethren that he developed rough skin like a camel's. This is why you may have heard of James referred to in pop culture Christianity as "Old Camel Knees.")

In AD 62 or 63, James was martyred for his refusal to assist the scribes and Pharisees in repudiating the legitimacy of his half-brother as the Son of God. According to early Christian chronicler Saint Hegesippus (later quoted by Eusebius), James was thrown from the temple, but he did not die from the fall. Instead, he turned his body, kneeled, and prayed in a similar fashion to Christ on the cross: "I beseech Thee, Lord God our Father, forgive them; for they know not what they do."[3] He was there stoned and beaten to death with a staff.

Thrown from a building. Stoned. Beaten.

Martyred for his faith in his sibling as the Son of God.

James was the most *unlikely* leader of the early Church because of the familiarity he had while watching his brother grow.

But James, upon becoming a believer as an eyewitness account of the risen Christ, became the most *likely* leader of the early Church because of the familiarity he had while watching his brother grow.

The Audience and Message

Not far into the expansion of the early Church, erroneous doctrine began to pollute the Gospel message. There was great confusion as to what this new and comparatively liberating theology was demanding of the people, and what it meant for Gentile believers. Circa AD 49 (around the time of Paul's return from his first missionary trip with Barnabas), an argument arose when teachers proclaimed that Christ *was* the Savior, but that faith in Him alone was not enough to ensure one's salvation. A believer also had to be circumcised and carry out selected Judaic customs from the Law of Moses, they said. What resulted was a syncretism of salvation through faith in Christ on the one hand and ceremonial tradition or "works" on the other.

The stance of Paul on this subject, according to Romans 11:5–6, was that salvation is now a matter of grace—and if it is a matter of grace, then it cannot be a matter of works, "otherwise grace is no more [or "no longer"] grace."

Thus, the aforementioned Jerusalem council was gathered to settle the issue. Paul, Barnabas, Peter, and James were all present at the meeting, though, as the pillar of the church, James served as the chief director. After "much disputing" (Acts 15:7), Peter stood to address everyone present, delivering a very wise line of reasoning: Through the recent proof of the Holy Spirit descending upon uncircumcised Gentiles who had *not* observed Judaic customs or traditions, God now "put no difference between us and them, purifying their hearts by faith"—and that to now place upon Christ's Gospel the "yoke" (burden) of such expectations was to "tempt God" (Acts 15:9–10). In such a brilliant and evidently irrefutable approach, Peter was making the point that sinners are saved, hearts purified, and spirits reunited after death to the presence of God through faith *alone*, and not through works. This he said in the presence of the presiding James, who *confirmed* Peter's sentiment of salvation through faith alone by saying, "God…*did visit the Gentiles* [He met them where they were regardless of the fact that they were not stringently following Mosaic Law or ceremony and had no intention to start doing so], to take out of them *a people for his name* [to claim them as His people]. And to this *agree the words of the prophets*, as it is written" (Acts 15:14–15; emphasis added). James then quoted the Septuagint, in Amos 9, saying:

> After this I will return, and will build again the tabernacle of David, which is fallen down; and I will build again the ruins thereof, and I will set it up:

That the residue of men might seek after the Lord, and all the Gentiles, upon whom my name is called, saith the Lord, who doeth all these things.

Known unto God are all his works from the beginning of the world. (Acts 15:16–18; cf. Septuagint, Amos 9:11, 12)

James, the half-brother of Christ, was central to the early Church's acceptance of salvation by *faith alone*, and *not by works*—and he proved it with his closing remark: "Wherefore my sentence [or "judgment"] is, that we trouble not them [other translations say "don't make it difficult for them"], which from among the Gentiles are turned to God" (Acts 15:19).

However, in James' epistle penned around the same time, he poses the question: "What doth it profit, my brethren, though a man say he hath faith, and have not works? can faith save him?" (James 2:14). A few verses later, he states that faith, without "works," is "dead" (James 2:17). At the onset, if one is willing to isolate the verses from the Jerusalem council in Acts 15 and these two from James, and quote them against each other without proper exegetical context, it is easy to see a clear and present contradiction. At the council, he stood for salvation by faith and *not by works*, but in his epistle he suddenly says that *faith is completely dead and useless without works*. So to which camp does James really belong?

Over the centuries since James' epistle was written, it has been brought into much controversy regarding the "faith through works" argument. Though we will take a deep look at how each verse of the book of James applies to today, because of the confusion of the faith issue and how misunderstood James' words on this subject have been (and due to how important the understanding of these words are to the rest of this book you hold in your hands), it proves necessary to address the matter quickly here.

The error is found in the individual reader's interpretation of the word "faith" and what that word means to a follower of Christ.

To some, religious faith only means believing that something exists—much like a child might believe in something or someone he or she can't see, like fairies or the bogeyman—or that it means that one "belongs to the faith," as a member of a church or religious organization. To this, James states, "Thou believest that there is one God; thou doest well: the devils also believe, and tremble" (James 2:19). In contemporary language, he is essentially saying, "You claim to believe in one God. You're doing well up to this point. Good job, guys. However, even the demons of hell believe in one God, but they will not live in heaven for eternity. How could they? They're demons! They tremble at the very thought of God!"

If faith *only* meant believing a thing that you can't see exists, then an evil man (much like the demons just mentioned) could go about killing, pillaging, stealing, and creating worldly havoc in the name of Satan and still be taken to heaven when he dies, merely because he believed that Christ existed as the Messiah. Such a man would not even need to invite God into his life, say the sinner's prayer, repent, be a good person, pray, have a relationship with God, or even have the remotest respect for God. Merely by believing a thing exists, this man would be saved even though his life is dedicated to the workings of God's greatest spiritual enemy. Heaven forbid that salvation would work that way! This man would "believe in" both Satan and Christ, but his "works"—and by extension his "faith through works"—would be satanically opposed to God. To the concept of faith being separated entirely from works, James says, "Show me thy faith *without* thy works, and I will show thee my faith *by* my works" (James 2:18; emphasis added). Today, we might reword this: "Show me this religion of yours that has nothing to do with how you live. Then I will let you see how I live, and by my lifestyle you will know my religion." Christ, Himself, said similarly, "Ye shall know them by their fruits.… Even so every good tree bringeth forth [or "produces"] good fruit; but a corrupt tree bringeth forth evil fruit" (Matthew 7:16–17).

James chose a different set of words than his brother Jesus, but he ultimately made the same statement: Our lifestyle and decisions produce the fruit by which we will be recognized as a "good tree" or a "corrupt tree."

Yes, faith—and faith *alone*—brings salvation. But *real* faith, *true* faith, is only genuine when our choices reflect our belief with action.

I once had a pleasant conversation with a friend regarding the frequently misunderstood "once saved, always saved" doctrine. She explained that many errantly assume this means that you can say the sinner's prayer and then sin the rest of your life, because once you are saved there is no going back spiritually, despite how you live on this earth. Although I do not entirely agree with all the theology surrounding this doctrine, I greatly respect her summary of it. "Basically," she said, "we believe that once a person makes the choice to invite the Holy Spirit into his or her heart, *if the decision is sincere*, then that person will always be saved, because through the Holy Spirit's assistance he or she will continue making the choice to live for the Lord righteously. If a person goes through the motions of conversion but does not follow that event with righteous living, then the person was never sincere in the first place and, thus, was never truly saved in the first place." I do believe that many have sincerely given their hearts to the Lord and later fall away, and as such, I struggle with accepting this doctrine, but I can appreciate and respect the idea that a heartfelt conversion experience should produce a permanent change of heart and lifestyle for the confessor.

God told the Old Testament prophet Hosea to marry a prostitute as a symbol of God's relationship with His people, Israel. Israel still "believed in" Yahweh, but their "works" opposed God, because they made sacrifices to pagan idols. As Hosea knew all too personally, some aspects of God's requirements regarding faith and works can be easier to grasp when compared to marital infidelity: If a man repeatedly cheats on his wife, but he still believes in her, we still call him an "unfaithful spouse." In this context, faith is seen as a devotion. A duty. A kept promise. A covenant. Being "faithful" in a marriage requires the "works" of fidelity.

Consider this comparison:

- A "faithful" spouse stays true to his wife even when he is tempted by the opposite sex to do otherwise, and should he fall into an affair through weakness (or have unhealthy thoughts or habits that place a strain on the marriage), the right thing to do is confess his sin to her, repent, and restore the relationship by striving to be the best husband he can be—whilst continuing to bear public witness of his devotion and love for her.

- A "faithful" Christian stays true to God's Word even when tempted by the world to do otherwise, and should the Christian fall into sin through weakness, the right thing to do is confess the sin to God, repent, and restore the relationship by striving to be the best possible example of God's graceful and redemptive nature—whilst continuing to bear public witness of devotion and love for the Lord.

James' epistle says we will know whether our faith is real or counterfeit based on whether we back our faith claims with behavior that proves it—the behavior that produces corresponding fruit. If we have true faith in the Lord, then the Holy Spirit will be within us. And if the Holy Spirit is within us, then we must endeavor to behave as if He is.

Yes, James said, salvation is through *faith alone*, and not through circumcision or the sacrificing of animals on altars. But when James began to hear of Christians who were embracing debauchery and still considered themselves saved simply because they believed something existed, he brought further definition to the word "faith," alerting the green believers that faith and works are equivalent and indistinguishable.

Faith is a verb.

Fruit in Today's World

Having brought clarity to this matter, understand that the charge of righteousness underlying the word "faith" is in no way all that James' epistle has to offer, and the scattered Jews and early Christians were by no means the only audiences who would draw great, life-changing truths from his Holy-Spirit-inspired writings. Contrarily, his book lifts off the page like an orchestral hit, a "pow" in the ears of those who will hear, a call to action for those who care enough to play their part in making the world a better place, a timelessly applicable cry for reformation in every age from his forward until Christ returns.

James' words ring just as true today as they did then, and they pertain to our modern world more today than ever.

No one can do what Jesus did. However, anyone with a true anointing on his or her life and the willingness to speak can do what His little half-brother did, should the Lord so choose to use him or her in that way. James was an unlikely reformer because of his circumstances, but it was because of those same circumstances that when he believed, he became the most obvious and trustworthy reformer of his arena and one of the most powerful men our planet has ever documented. Never believe the lying words, "God cannot use me because of [this or that]," for it is *because* of "this or that" that you are the most likely to be used in your arena.

Aside from Christ, a perfect person has never existed. He was useful to the souls of mankind because of His perfection and position as the Son of God. We are useful to the souls of our fellow man because of our imperfections and position as associate sinners.

Now, let us turn our attention to the modern world, and see how timeless James' instrumental advice really is today.

Do you want to change the world?
Do you want to play a part in the next Great Awakening?

Open your heart and mind now to the teachings of the man who assisted in reforming the "social Gospel" back to the sincere Gospel of Christ.

Chapter 2

Trials Are Not Easy, They're Necessary

JAMES 1:1–3

ONE OF THE beautiful things about Scripture is that it can timelessly and seamlessly apply to each of our personal lives, those we know, our own trials, temptations, and culture. It is a Word with power that will never fade. It never stops making sense. It never stops being true. It never stops breathing life into the weary and providing profound answers to those who cannot find answers anywhere else.

And it never stops being misinterpreted.

How many times have you heard someone say that the Bible is filled with contradictions? How many times have you heard people isolate one verse and apply it as a doctrine over their family and their congregations— and all the while you suspect there's something not quite truthful about how they are using it? It happens all the time. And it's tragic. The greatest power in the Word is when the whole truth, and nothing but the truth, is understood from it. Then, suddenly, all apparent contradictions disappear, and all manipulations of Scripture pop out as uncannily obvious.

I won't spend too much time on this particular study, because this book is not a "how to study the Bible" guide, but I feel a tremendous need to outline here and now how James' epistle will be reflected upon throughout the rest of the book. Because we are applying words written thousands of years ago to a completely different world and time, we must take a moment to comprehend the process of getting information out of an ancient culture and making it relevant to our modern lives. James' message could not be more important right now in this world that is starving for peace, revival…a Great Awakening. I believe he saw potential and value in those society had disregarded, and I believe this next movement of God is going to involve people groups nobody sees coming. In fact, some of the things I plan to point out in subsequent chapters will sound so unorthodox and radical to our current Christian worldviews that I fear this book will offend some if I don't explain where and how I'm getting my information. The Bible is a great source, but both leaders and laypeople within the Church carry out a great deal of verse-dropping, misquoting, misunderstanding, and misinforming regarding what the Book actually says. There has been a many-decades-long trend of speaking authoritatively about the stories and advice from Scripture without even thinking about background of the Scripture, and without completely studying what the words *really* meant by those who wrote them.

Even well-meaning ministers of the Gospel are capable of inadvertently misleading their listeners. Unfortunately, they are also able to initiate a great wave of skepticism and dismissal for those who hear and later question this unanointed teaching.

People have understandably complained for years that Church leaders take Scripture out of context, and they frequently do, but *why* does this happen?

Proper exegesis is not taught to the extent it should be.

The Word is alive because its truth is anointed by the Holy Spirit. However, even in the most powerful teachings, when Scripture is twisted to mean something it didn't mean originally, the truth isn't presented. It is not anointed. When the source of such material is corrupt (the source being the human who teaches it, not the Word, itself), it only renders a greater public disregard for any information of the Word that *is* true. And when the true facts are later represented, those who were jaded by the first wave of confusion aren't interested in being confused or misled again, so they ignore the truth entirely, assuming everything is erroneous—they throw the baby out with the bathwater, so to speak. It is then possible that they would hear a more accurate sermon or witness and close their mind to it because of the damage the misinformation of the past has caused.

This tragedy becomes far worse when other preachers and teachers pick up on the trendy form of ministering and repeat the offense. An entire religious and cultural worldview becomes skewed around popular forms and formulas. Young, sincere preachers stand at pulpits and repeat familiar lessons they've learned from their mentors involving verses that were taken out of context in the first place, and as a result, generation after generation becomes so familiar with the newer (but less truthful) concept of the verse that the truth is gradually sapped. (I believe our Church is very caught up in this, and has been for as long as I have been alive.) This type of teaching becomes what the world views as "church," but it means little more to secular minds than an establishment of rituals while the living, breathing Word is cast to the wayside in trade for a performance and showmanship. This becomes mounting "evidence" to the lost that the entire Word—and *all* the claims therein—is based on the product of wild imaginations.

We have to accept the fact that when the injury of misinformation is piled atop a Church that has for so many years accepted unanointed teaching because it's the religious ministry practice to which they're accustomed, we arrive at an equation that spreads distortion like a brushfire. Add to this years and years of the public's cultural familiarity with and acceptance of the skewed ministry concept, and we arrive at a day when any teaching that challenges that norm is marginalized or written off as the ramblings of a nonconformist radical—despite how much truth might be presented in the message. It's an age-old social science: When people have largely adopted a way of thinking into their society and slowly built a universal worldview around it, they will not easily receive modifications to that worldview—even when it is based on inaccuracy. They don't want to hear the truth because it means letting go of all they've known or believed up to that point, so they hold on to what's familiar, what's comfortable, always referring to the others in their support group for confirmation of a path that is biblically wrong.

So, let us take a minute to go over some standardized study points, and then we will dive into precisely how the book of James is relevant to us today.

Throughout my college studies, I have found that these are the most important questions to ask when reading any of the books of the Bible:

1. What literary genre does the material fall into?

The books of the Bible have been separated into literary genres by many scholars in order to aid study. If a reader doesn't know what genre applies to a text, they cannot understand what the original text was meant to convey. Most popularly, the canonical list of books within today's Holy Bible fall into eight categories: historical narrative, law, wisdom, poetry, prophecy, apocalyptic, gospel, and letters (epistles, such as that of James).

A reader wouldn't take in a science-fiction novel involving a lot of futuristic medical information the same way he or she would digest a modern medical textbook at a university. Both books feature heaps of information about medicine within their pages, but because they belong to different genres, the material exists for different purposes (one entertains, one educates). Likewise, we cannot approach apocalyptic Scripture in the same way we would read a historical narrative (one warns, the other informs). Doing so causes confusion and leads to misinterpretation of the text.

2. Who was the author?

In every conversation—whether between myself and someone else, or between two other people talking on television, at church, or wherever—when I hear someone speak, I consider who the speaker is in order to understand the meaning of his or her words. A person's speech or written works cannot be separated from his or her identity. Two people can be involved in the same cause, but come from completely different angles. Knowing who they are is as important as hearing what they say.

When you go to church and listen to a sermon delivered by a pastor you have known for some time, you grasp his words better than you would grasp those of a total stranger. You may have heard this pastor share testimonies, make the congregation laugh by telling silly stories about his home life, and open up his heart passions every Sunday. At times, you even know what he's going to say before he says it, because you know his personal convictions and you're used to his oratory style. You're familiar with him.

All the writers of the books in the Bible were involved in one central cause: bringing truth to the world. But many of them came from different angles in their approach to this cause. Paul had a different purpose for writing his letters to the early Church than Moses had when he documented ancient history. Knowing what Paul went through on the road to Damascus is crucial to understanding the passions behind his letters. Knowing what Moses went through during the Exodus helps us understand his anger toward the Israelites when he descended Mt. Sinai. *If you don't know the man behind the text, you won't understand the author's voice and intentions.*

3. Who was the original audience?

Just as with the author, the original audience cannot be separated from the purpose of a written text. New Testament letters address the false teachings, anxiety, persecution, and theological confusion of the early Church that was forming from Jews and Gentiles alike throughout Palestine and the rest of the world when Christ was no longer corporeally present to teach. Who these people were is just as important as understanding the identity of the writer. If we simply take in the text without understanding who was originally benefitting from the material, we cannot understand *how* the material was beneficial. As such, we modern readers will find it much more difficult to render that text personally beneficial in what we are going through.

4. What were the circumstances that made the writing a necessity?

Knowing what was going on in the world or culture at the time of a writing is crucial to understanding the purpose of the writing. We have to consider what is being addressed and in what social/cultural setting in order to properly apply those lessons to our own culture/society. Paul's advice to the churches sprouting up across Palestine after Christ's ascension may at times seem similar in intent or meaning to the words of an Old Testament prophet just before the Babylonian and Assyrian exiles, but they weren't addressing the same events. We cannot apply all of Paul's words to the ancient Israelites, and we cannot apply all of an Old Testament prophet's words to the early Church of Paul's day. In the same trail of logic, responsible readers will look for how the circumstances of our current modern world or individuals within it parallel the circumstances at the time of the original writing before making assumptions on how a verse applies to anything or anyone today.

5. What was the cultural language style in use at the time of the writing?

This is one of the most important, yet frequently overlooked considerations when studying Scripture. Culture is embedded in language, and language in culture. The two cannot be separated. The way we speak in America is different from how Chinese people speak in China, even when the languages are translated from one to another. For example, I might say, "It's raining cats and dogs outside." To an American, that means the rain outside is heavy. To foreigners, I have just stated that canines and felines are falling out of the sky. If they take my word as gospel, they will apply some kind of meaning to canines and felines being in the sky—whether literally or allegorically—and, to them, that would never relate to heavy rains. This example was of an idiom: a group of words that sound like one thing, but mean something else, based on cultural use, acceptance, and familiarity.

From Genesis to Revelation, there are examples of idioms, rhetoric, grammar fluctuation, syntax variations, and semantics that, if taken out of their culture, do not mean what the original author intended. Since no culture today perfectly operates like those existing at the time of scriptural writings, it can often be difficult to understand what we've read when we dive into the Bible. Therefore, trying to understand the cultural language at the time of the writing seems like a tedious endeavor, but it is well worth the effort when the consequence otherwise is misinterpretation.

6. What does the surrounding text say?

Lastly, once we have, to the best of our ability, figured out the genre, author, audience, circumstances, and cultural language (and commentaries are helpful if we get stuck), we must consider what is being said in the verses before and after any passage, as well as farther out to the whole book's message. Isolating one verse without considering its context is very dangerous, and leads many people to adopt faulty creeds.

Take, for example, the popularly quoted Jeremiah 29:11: "'For I know the plans I have for you,' declares the Lord, 'plans to prosper you, and not to harm you, plans to give you hope and a future.'" Many well-meaning Christians have taken this as a promise that no matter what happens, they will eventually be prosperous. But reading the surrounding text reveals that this verse was never meant to be dropped in a social setting to inspire a climb up the corporate ladder, to land an audition at a major theater, or have an old car come back to life if we just keep sitting on this verse and hoping the clunker will start. Looking at the broader context, we see that the "you" in this verse refers to a collective people: the ancient Israelites. This was a message given from the Lord, Himself, through the prophet Jeremiah to the future of Israel.

However, that doesn't mean that this verse has no relevance to Christians today. It absolutely does—more today than ever! If we properly consider the genre, author, audience, circumstances, and cultural language behind the verse, and then consider it within the surrounding text, we come up with the following equation: The "you" in this verse—the parallel of that "you" from the ancient writing to today—is the Church, all the people of the Lord. God knows the plans He has *for the collective Body of Christ, the Church*; He has plans to prosper *the Church*.

With all of this said, we are ready to begin the study of James' epistle verse by verse and consider how his words apply to us now—most immediately, how the world never seems to change…

Trials of the Ancient World and Today

> [1]James, a servant of God and of the Lord Jesus Christ, to the twelve tribes which are scattered abroad, greeting. [2]My brethren, count it all joy when ye fall into divers temptations [diverse/various kinds of troubles]; [3]Knowing this, that the trying of your faith worketh patience.

The first verse in the book of James is a greeting from James, the half-brother of Christ, to the twelve tribes of Israel, who at this time have been scattered abroad after the Babylonian and Assyrian exiles drove the chosen people to the far ends of the earth. As we can see from verse 2, James wasted no time in getting straight to the point by openly acknowledging the reality of harsh spiritual living conditions. Readers are then told to "count it all joy" ("rejoice") when we meet with trials of various kinds, knowing that faith and obedience to the Word will test our patience—but in this test, our patience and faith will grow if we remain vigilant in trials.

Today's Christians from all over the world face many trials every day. As believers, we're required to confront these issues—as uncomfortable as that may be at times—while remaining accountable to carrying out the loving behavior Christ modeled. Certainly, we each have tests and hardships unique to our own circumstances. For one among us, a great trial might be to temper that lying tongue; for another, it might be to remain true to a spouse when his or her marriage is on the rocks. For yet another, a daunting challenge might be to place the right priority on praying and reading the Bible more often in such a busy and hectic schedule. These trials are personal, and do not apply to everyone. Many books have already been penned that help people overcome personal struggles, and that is not what this book will do. Because James' epistle was written to the Church and for use by the Church, we will treat it as such herein.

There are trials that apply to everyone on a national and global scale, and Christians are required to respond to these issues, *again*, as uncomfortable as that may be at times, while still being held accountable to carrying out the loving behavior Christ modeled. Some in the Body of Christ believe that because He didn't come to enact social reform or get involved in politics (since His kingdom was "not of this world"), we should only be concerned with spreading the Gospel and remaining uninvolved in all social and political issues in order to follow His example. This is a valid point, one to which I give much heartfelt respect. Others believe that we aren't really following Christ if we're not attempting to radically reform our country into a nation that pleases God and propels us farther toward His blessing. Again, this is a valid point, and one I respect.

However, I believe that both of these viewpoints, when adopted as extremes, are wrong. To remain silent and peaceful always and hope that an opportunity to witness will come along by itself is wrong when we have been commanded to "go and preach to the whole world" (Matthew 16:15–16) and to "rebuke and exhort" wickedness (2 Timothy 4:1–2). To shove your belief system down someone else's throat with the expectation that such an act will reform anyone or anything is also wrong when we have been commanded to love others above any other agenda (Matthew 22:39; 1 Corinthians 13:13). But somewhere in the middle of these extremes, we find a sweet spot—that's the goal we must strive toward.

Politics. Racism. Abortion. Homosexuality. Social justice. Immodesty. Addiction. Abuse. Violence. Suicide. All of these issues and so many others are modern trials facing members of today's Church, the Body of Christ as a whole, and to which today's Church should be responsive.

When James said we should "count it all joy" when trials come at us, he didn't mean that we should rejoice at immorality that surrounds us, but that we should rejoice about the fact that we are being given the opportunity to grow our faith and our patience, and ultimately to become stronger *as we are responding to* the immorality (our response being our "works"). The natural human response to trials is despair. Thus, considering it a joy to have trials placed on us is not natural or easy, and therefore requires a conscious effort. Perhaps, then, knowing that we have a duty to respond to the issues of our day, and to count it as joy while doing so, we should take a closer look at the problems facing the early Church in order to harvest the utmost wisdom in how James' advice applies to us contemporarily.

The Trials of the Early Church

The following is a list of trials James discussed throughout his epistle. Although limited to what James addressed, it mirrors many of the same issues as most of the other apostolic writings. However, since this book focuses on the meat of James' words, we will stick to his list.

Dissension and Fighting

As mentioned earlier, as the early Church was in its initial phases of development, there was much arguing amidst Christ's followers about what exactly was expected of the believers. Many people incorrectly assume that the early Church worked together peacefully and in union of thought and mind from one church or gathering to another. (In fact, I have heard full sermons preached on this notion more than once, whereupon the speaker suggests fervently that we should return to the attitudes and passion of the first-generation Christians.) However, this could not be farther from the truth. Because James wrote the epistle to address problems facing the early Church in the first place, we have to assume its members were committing all the grievances he tackled:

- Social class (rich, poor, popular, etc.) was the deciding factor in how a person was treated upon entering the church (James 2:1–13).
- Believers, including the "teachers," were rude and slandered each other with loose tongues (James 3:1–12).
- "Bitter jealousy" and "selfish ambition" among believers resulted in "unspiritual, demonic…disorder" (James 3:13–18; ESV).
- Listed in the "fights among you [believers]," we see that they committed murder out of greed (see later notes about "murder"), quarreled out of envy of one another's possessions, lived "double-minded" lives (lived for God while at church and hypocritically engaged in sinful acts and bickering the rest of the time), and spoke evil against each other (James 4:1–12).
- They arrogantly boasted about their lives and successes (James 4:13–17).
- They hungered for money and fancy clothes (James 5:1–3).
- They fraudulently cheated the laborers they hired to help them with their fields by withholding promised pay, while they themselves lived in luxury and self-indulgence (James 5:4–6; but see notes later on about the laborers representing more than simple field workers).
- They made promises and oaths that they did not keep (James 5:12).
- When believers wandered away from the truth, we can assume by James' choice to address this that the other believers didn't appear to care (James 5:19–20).

False Teaching

Besides the tension among the believers, their false doctrines and theologies were also being introduced to the early Church at a rapid pace. Unlike today, the early believers did not have the ability to fact-check someone's belief system by turning to the New Testament, because it did not exist at that time. Apostles who knew Christ, walked with Him, heard His teachings, and knew His purpose were writing letters and documents of instruction specifically to tackle issues facing the early Church, and it was from those letters and documents that the New Testament was formed. Prior to that, however, just about anyone could wander into a church and claim to have all the answers, and the people were vulnerable to their counterfeit gospels.

- There were those claiming that you had to be circumcised and continue to follow certain Judaic rituals in order to be saved, and this was greatly opposed at the aforementioned apostolic Jerusalem council (Acts 15). Additionally, some preached that salvation was achieved *only* by works of righteousness (rituals, tithing, ceremony, etc., much like the Pharisees modeled). These individuals became known as "Judaizers," but frequently today, such personalities are referred to as "legalists."

- Some believed that salvation by faith alone meant merely believing that God existed and that Jesus was the Messiah, or attending church service, and that your lifestyle and choices outside the walls of the church were all but irrelevant (James 2:14–26). Today this is referred to as "antinomianism" (remember this word for later study within this book).

- Throughout the New Testament, many verses point to the reality that primitive Gnostics were infiltrating the early Church and syncretizing Christianity with other false doctrines and theology (such as the "scriptures" found in *Nag Hammadi* in Egypt). These teachers intermingled with the Christians and spread their own version of the gospel that promised a higher level of enlightenment, wisdom, and spirituality. Paul's epistles were instrumental in refuting these false doctrines, most notably in his messages to the Romans, Galatians, and Colossians.

- A great emphasis was placed upon healings after the miracles of Christ had been witnessed. After the Day of Pentecost, the apostles saw miracles occur even when Christ was not present. Therefore, healing became one of the key focuses of the early Church. However, because of the religious syncretism and Gnostic gospels, many Gentiles were introducing healing doctrines based on heathenistic invocations, magic, and pagan ceremony. One verse that tackled healing through correct channels was James 5:15, which noted that it is only through a prayer of faith that one will be healed.

Persecution

Jesus foretold that His followers would be persecuted for their faith in Him as Messiah. In the writings of the New Testament, as well as in extrabiblical/historical documentation, we see that this persecution was indeed carried out to the extreme. Persecution included social harassment, political liberties/rights disputation, torture, and martyrdom. This caused an extreme issue for early Church leaders because believers were scattering out of fear, leaving the Church, and renouncing their faith. (The epistles of Peter heavily dealt with this issue.) Therefore, it was difficult to establish and maintain a solid church body. The following list is in no way exhaustive, but these names refer to the most well-known martyrs of the Apostolic Age in the first century. (Note: The destruction of Jerusalem by Emperor Nero was in AD 70, so some of these martyrs were connected with this event.)

- **Saint Stephen** (Acts 7:54–60): After delivering his speech to an angry mob, Stephen looked up, saw Jesus Christ standing at the right hand of God, and told those surrounding him what he saw. This claim was considered blasphemy by unbelievers, and he was immediately killed. Saul of Tarsus (later the apostle Paul) was present at this stoning and approved of it; this event preceded Paul's further persecution of Christ's followers. As such, Stephen's death was paramount to the scattering of believers, as the threat of martyrdom was now very real to early Christians. The most likely date of Stephen's death is AD 34–35.

- **Apostle James, the son of Zebedee** (Acts 12:1–2): James was beheaded by the sword at the order of King Herod Agrippa in AD 44–45.
- **Apostle Matthew:** Matthew was beheaded at Nad-Davar in Ethiopia circa AD 60–70.
- **Apostle James, the half-brother of Christ:** As discussed earlier, James was thrown from the temple in Jerusalem, then he was stoned and beaten to death when the fall did not kill him. His death is dated to AD 62–63.
- **Apostle Peter:** Peter died by an inverted (upside-down) crucifixion in AD 64, according to tradition. The inversion was done upon Peter's own request (according to Eusebius), as he did not consider himself worthy to be crucified in the same way Christ had been.
- **Apostle Simon, also known as "Simon the Zealot":** Many violent and conflicting accounts of Simon's martyrdom exist. The most popular one depicts him being sawed in half, and this is why he is seen in many art pieces holding a long saw. The year of his death was most likely AD 65–74. Some records claim he was martyred alongside Jude, but the location is unknown.
- **Apostle Paul:** Paul was beheaded by Emperor Nero in Rome in the year AD 67, according to historical records.
- **Mark the Evangelist:** Coptic tradition states that a rope was tied around Mark's neck and he was dragged to his death throughout the city of Alexandria, Egypt, in AD 68.
- **Apostle Andrew:** Hippolytus' record indicates Andrew was bound to a cross with rope rather than nails on the *crux decussata* (X-shaped cross), now referred to as a "Saint Andrew's Cross," in the town of Patrae, Achaia, in Greece in AD 70.
- **Apostle Thomas:** Tradition states Thomas was stabbed with pine spears, tortured with fire-heated plates, and then burned alive in India in AD 70.

- **Apostle Matthias, the replacement of Judas Iscariot:** Conflicting accounts state that Matthias was beheaded, crucified, and/or stoned. Most accounts cite the year of his death circa AD 70–80.
- **Apostles Philip and Bartholomew:** Although, again, there are varied accounts of their deaths, the popular but anonymously written *Acts of Philip* states that both men were tortured and then suffered inverted crucifixion together in the city of Hierapolis. Other accounts suggest beheading. Yet other sources hold to the historical interpretation that Philip was evangelizing in Phrygia when he was tortured and then crucified by the Jews in AD 54, and that a similar fate befell Bartholomew in AD 70. It is said that Philip continued to preach even while he was bound to the cross.

The Trials of Today's Church

As you read through the trials facing today's Church, note the strikingly precise similarities to the trials just listed within the early Church.

Dissension and Fighting

Today's Christian Church—and especially in the USA—is as guilty as ever of dissension and fighting, and in similar ways as the early Christians. We still don't seem to understand what is expected of believers, and tragically, this stems from a massive lack of biblical knowledge, understanding, and correct exegetical interpretation. Not only do we fight amidst our own people—essentially divided against ourselves, which Christ made clear was a pattern for great downfall—we fight with the secular world, which anymore seems to view us as judgmental, narrow-minded verse-droppers who twist Scripture to flatter our own interests and agendas. Whereas the list below absolutely does *not* apply as a blanket statement over all Christians, because there are many very sincere people in the Church today, as a whole, we face the same problems James was addressing.

- Social class (rich, poor, attractive, popular, etc.) is often still the deciding factor in how we treat those who enter our churches.
- Believers among us, including the "teachers," are frequently rude, judgmental, and slandering toward each other with loose tongues.
- "Bitter jealousy" and "selfish ambition" amidst our fellow believers certainly rear their ugly heads today, and we need to heed the warning that this will still result in "unspiritual, demonic… disorder."
- Similar to the items listed in the "fights among you [believers]" in the prior bullets, we even now continue to feed our greed; roll our eyes, bicker over, or covet what other believers possess; live "double-minded" lives, living for Christ on Sunday and for self the rest of the week; and speak evil gossip against each other.
- Many of us still arrogantly boast about our lives and successes, even while in the presence of those we know who have so much less.
- Most of us still hunger for money and fancy clothes, and this hunger modernly extends to automobiles, electronics, big homes, gadgets, etc.
- Too many among our church memberships still fraudulently cheat others (bosses, employees, neighbors, taxes, etc.), both monetarily and through lies we tell about how our time is spent, while living the comfiest and most self-indulgent lifestyles we can simply because it's the desire of our flesh to do so, and we don't have the strength to resist.
- Too many of us still make promises and oaths that we do not keep.
- When believers wander away from the truth, we don't always appear to care; in fact, our attitudes at times escalate to the point that we think we are a better, stronger Body of believers without them…a "taking out the trash," so to speak.

False Teaching

Today, much like in James' day, a growing list of false doctrines and theologies are being introduced within the very walls of our churches on a global scale. This is, in my opinion, a greater grievance than it was for the early Church, because we have the canon to rely upon, all the answers at our fingertips—yet we squander that precious tool daily. We now have in every Christian home (hopefully) the very letters and books written by the apostles who died violently to spread them.

What might these leaders of the early Church say if they knew that, two thousand years after their efforts, we were still tolerating false doctrine? No longer should "just anyone" be able to wander into a church and claim to hold answers for a higher enlightenment through religious syncretism and counterfeit gospels because we have the very Word that refutes it. This should not be a vulnerability for the Church to the degree it is today… And yet, we encounter it repeatedly! False teaching is *rampant*, improper exegesis is *rampant*, and the brand of resistance the Church is putting up against it is largely ineffective (as we will discuss in more depth in later chapters).

- *Many* people today place conditions upon salvation, and not just the "live righteously" faith-works that James addressed, but legalistic, Pharisaic, "you're not really saved unless you live the way I think you should" type rules and regulations. As a child in church, I many times heard the equivalent of, "If you don't agree with my theology or doctrine, then you need to pray for your soul." This approach to our Christ-ian duty strips the Gospel of its redemptive purpose and grace, makes God seem like an angry dictator who lives to oppress His people, and drives away sincere people. It also serves to represent us in poor light to the lost.
- Some still believe in lawlessness as acceptable—that salvation by faith alone means merely believing God exists and that Jesus is

the Messiah, or attending church service, and that our lifestyles and choices outside church are all but irrelevant. This gospel of "antinomianism" is very alive in our current Body.

- Gnosticism and religious syncretism in Christianity appear to be at an all-time high. Our tolerance is imbalanced. So as not to offend and drive away the unsaved masses, we have declined in calling sin what it is; we have allowed doctrines and theologies outside the Bible to enter and pollute the Gospel. As a result, sin is being daily redefined to widen the boundaries of what is now considered acceptable. Certain social movements have filtered Scripture to suit their causes and have built entirely new, so-called Christian organizations out of opposing principles. We are still being promised a higher level of enlightenment, wisdom, and spirituality through the ideologies of self-proclaimed Christians whose beliefs are primarily pagan. Add to this the fact that so many Christians today don't even know what the Bible says—and are therefore vulnerable to the darts of false doctrine—and we see that even sincere, heartfelt, and obedient churchgoers are celebrating a religion that at best only vaguely resembles the conservative Christianity of previous generations.

- There are not as many healings, signs, and wonders visible at the time of this writing as there were in the development of the early Church—*or* even as recently as the great revival during the Age of Fire in the 1950s (involving the famous ministries of Katherine Kuhlman, Oral Roberts, and Billy Graham, just to name a few). However, that hasn't stopped many within the Christian Church to focus on bizarre, physical manifestations of the Holy Spirit through ungodly, heretical, and even blasphemous means. As we will discuss later, I personally have witnessed more than a few events that can only be referred to as heathenistic invocations, magic, and pagan ceremony—none of which had even the slightest inkling of biblical support—and those events occurred in the midst of people who were enacting such rites "in the name of

Christ." Yes, it is possible that miracles can transpire within these settings—and they have—but as "Satan himself is transformed into an angel of light [frequently "appears as an angel of light"]" (2 Corinthians 11:14), the emergence of miracles, signs, and wonders does not automatically equate the presence, will, and/or endorsement of God.

Persecution

In the previous pages, we discussed the persecution of the early Church leaders, and in our modern world, persecution of Christianity is raging. According to Open Doors USA, a nonprofit organization established in 1955 to fight Christian persecution (now active in over sixty countries throughout the world), "Each month, 322 Christians are killed for their faith, 214 churches and Christian properties are destroyed, [and] 772 forms of violence are committed against Christians."[4]

Later on the website, we read: "Beatings, physical torture, confinement, isolation, rape, severe punishment, imprisonment, slavery, discrimination in education and employment, and even death are just a few examples of the persecution [Christians] experience on a daily basis."[5]

Brutal and violent murders are taking place in lands across the globe. Due to the gory and disturbing details of the most recent ISIS headliners, and because this book is not a report on global persecution of Christianity, we will not list the details of the tragic deaths of those whose lives have been lost as casualties of a great warfare.

However, I want to give my deepest and most heartfelt condolences to the family members who remain. I cannot even begin to tell you how much of a light your sons, daughters, brothers, sisters, mothers, and fathers were in these darkened times. Their lives will never be forgotten, their legacies of faith will always stand as the greatest of all examples of passionate Christianity, and for countless generations their message of belief in Jesus Christ will inspire others to remain diligent and steadfast in their devotion.

And with Trials Come Tests

Having compared the trials of the early Church with the Church of the modern world, we must now turn our attention to the tests that will apply as we face those trials. Those around us who are thirsty to drink from the living waters that only God can provide need the Christians of the world to stop in their tracks, *really consider* whether we want to be Christians, *know* what it means to be Christian, and *choose* to do what the Bible commands us to do.

Unfortunately, though this sounds obvious, it is not an easy thing. With trials, which are devastating enough by themselves, come tests.

Follow with me in the next chapter as we consider an overview of the tests James outlines for us in his letter.

Do you want to change the world?
Do you want to play a part in the next Great Awakening?

Count your trials as "joy." Expect them so they do not surprise you and demoralize you when they appear. Know that if you remain diligent throughout the trials, you will have greater strength when the personal tests come to haunt...

Chapter 3

Just When You Thought You Were Comfortable...

JAMES 1:4–27

IF THIS NATION—if this globe—is about to experience another Great Awakening, and I believe it is, then it's time to stop playing church while, daily, thousands around us are passing from this life into eternity. This not only means counting all of our trials as joy, but buckling down and enduring the tests that help fortify us as the stronghold both the Church and individual Christians need to be. For every trial that we triumphantly withstand, another brick is laid. For every test we surmount and come out of as victors, another layer of mortar is applied. We do not become conquerors the day we invite the Lord into our lives. It takes great spiritual sweat and grit and determination to not only see tests for what they are, but to celebrate each one as they, like trials, shape us into a secure battalion of power that no devil in hell can stand against when the winds of revival blow.

Understand that although they are difficult, tests are mandatory. They serve to separate the boys from the men. They call upon those willing to mature and put away childish things. They find us in our most vulnerable moments and needle us into deciding to be true ambassadors of Christ or to become irresponsible and lackluster followers of a lifestyle code we claim to belong to—but the values of which we ignore.

Those of us who want to be a part of the next great movement of God must reconsider the level of commitment we plan to put into it. Anyone who wishes to see atheists, homosexuals, prostitutes, drug addicts, liberals, delinquents, adulterers, and transgressors from all secular spheres fall on their knees and accept Christ at the head of their lives must learn to be *doers* of the Word—and not simply hearers who casually drop verses into a conversation with a lost sinner when it suits us and call it our good deed for the day. If we really want revival, if we are truly and deeply passionate for it, if it resonates in our spirit and we find ourselves constantly consumed by thoughts of it, then it's time to glove up and apply the elbow grease, because it isn't going to be easy.

We have now discussed that faith is a more complicated verb than we may have thought—an *action* birthed from choices in living and not simply believing that something exists—and comparing the trials of the early Church with the trials of today's Church, let us now consider what James says about the tests of faith in the midst of these trials.

Patience

The first clear and present test of the faith by works that James considers is patience.

> [4]**But let patience have her perfect work, that ye may be perfect and entire, wanting nothing.**

One should never expect that a "perfect work" will come around before its time, and every step of a process requires delicate procedure for a work to deliver excellent results. As an example, consider the process of baking a cake.

Anyone can bake a cake from a pre-boxed, "just add water" product, but it will always taste like a substandard dessert. *Gourmet* bakers, on the other hand, carefully consider each ingredient—i.e., they determine exactly what size and type of eggs are needed, decide whether to sift the flour, and select the best type of sugar to use, etc. From there, the bakers place the ingredients in a bowl and whisks with exactitude for a certain length of time as decided by their experience. Once they add the mixture to the pan, the experts in the kitchen know precisely what temperature the batter must be baked at and for how long, whether to place it in a regular or convection oven, where any hot spots might be in the oven, and whether it needs to be moved or turned midway through baking. Then the bakers watch to ensure that the cake is achieving the desired results while it's under the heat, sometimes poking it in the middle to test the progress. When the cake is ready, the gourmet bakers draw the masterpiece from the heat and set out to cool. They know that the frosting will melt if it is applied too soon, so they must be patient while the yet-unfinished cake release its internal temperature into the air.

Once cooled, the bakers become artists, first adding a foundational layer of frosting and then approaching with special decorating tools. Every stroke is a matter of high concentration, as even the slightest tremor of the wrist could create an irreversible gouge or blunder in the tender frosting and wreck the entire appearance of the work.

When the cake is completed and ready for sale or a catered event, it is "entire," and the bakers and their completed confections are left "wanting nothing," because the reward is in knowing that the recipients of the effort will be pleased. However, had the bakers used the wrong sugar, the flavor would be inferior. Had they removed the cake even a minute too early or too late, the texture would be ruined or the cake would be burned. Had the frosting been applied incorrectly, the flavor or texture wouldn't matter, because the product would not be appealing. If any step is taken without true patience throughout the process, the cake is not worthy of the asking price, and it does not stand as a creditable representation of its potential. In some cases, the cake must be discarded and begun again, resulting in a waste of time.

So are we the bakers, or the cake? In this analogy, the Lord is the Master Baker, and the cake is our ministry—our potential for His use here on earth. Every true Christian is a minister. No credentials are needed to minister to someone in need, whether that need be financial, physical, or spiritual, etc. (Note, however, that although every Christian is a minister, not every Christian is a public teacher/preacher; we will discuss that specifically in later chapters, including how the responsibility differs.) For some, our ministerial position is behind a pulpit, but for countless numbers, it is as a neighbor, a colleague, a friend, a son, a daughter, a mother, or a father. It breathes wherever our boots carry us, whether that is on a bus, into a library, at the restaurant we cook in, in a nursing home, or at the local tack shop. I will say it again: Every true Christian is a minister. Every true Christian has a ministry. And *every* Christian, while he or she is maturing in the ministry, will meet trials.

God knows this.

God allows this.

God uses this.

It is not easy to remain patient through the entire ministry-baking process. If we take our roles in daily ministering seriously, then that ministry becomes a part of us—to the core. To the very heart. When our works on this earth toward the goal of the Kingdom face trials, we feel the sting of it as well.

Let us consider a step-by-step comparison:

Ingredients for later purpose: We must endure seasons of waiting while the precise ingredients are chosen to make our ministries into what they will ultimately be baked into. We must resist the temptation to jump into the bowl too quickly. Doing otherwise might jeopardize the quality of our ministerial purposes later on. Once a cake is baked, brown sugar cannot be exchanged for cane.

A new believer with little knowledge of the Word can be called to preach, but without holding the ingredients of biblical understanding, he will never be prepared to respond correctly when challenged by the whisk. He cannot jump into a time machine and exchange the ill-informed and heretical sermon he preached in his untrained youth—and the damage that sermon did to his reputation as a minister—for an anointed sermon.

He cannot go back in time and undo the damage his heresy caused to the listeners. His life as a minister of the Lord certainly does not end if he is sincerely committed to restoration and continual growth, but he jumped into the bowl too fast, so the Master Baker must whisk out a lot of uncomely lumps to make the batter useful again. Because of the young minister's impatience, the entire mixture has unwanted ingredients that cannot be removed. These ingredients must be lived with unless it is so polluted that the procedure must begin again (which is possible, but not ideal), and by plodding ahead before the Master Baker willed, the minister has only *slowed* his journey to the bowl.

Being whisked for later strength and texture: We must withstand as we are placed in the mixing bowl and our ingredients are pounded and knocked around. Without full comprehension of the ministry the Master Baker is designing, we have moments when we don't understand the level of precision that has gone into choosing our ingredients just to see those beautiful ingredients thrust about wildly and smashed so that they don't even resemble the pieces the Baker meticulously chose to begin with. We sometimes tend to believe that we were put together so that we would live as pretty elements in a silver bowl forever. We have "arrived," or so we think, and we stand proud of every granule of sugar. But to the Baker, a bowl of fixings is useless and raw, it could never be baked in that state, and if it lies stagnant for much time at all, it spoils, and the ministry fails completely.

Being whisked is uncomfortable, and in a way it can weed out the serious ministers from those who are not truly committed. The serious minister not only allows the Master Baker to do His work, he "counts it all joy" that the whisk brings strength, accomplishing what will later become a "perfect" texture left "wanting nothing." The uncommitted minister resists the whisk until he spoils; his only options are to give up entirely and let go of his useful purpose unto the Kingdom or start again as a new creation—in which case he *still* has to face the whisk when it comes. A perfect cake, a great minister/ministry, only comes after trials are counted as all joy and embraced with an attitude that holds full confidence in the strength that is promised on the other side of the corresponding test of patience.

The heat of the oven for tempering: The whisk disappears, and we are given a moment to breathe. The trusting minister knows it's not over. Others of us, however, because we cannot see the Master Baker's design, wonder what it's all been for. We think about how we waited patiently while our ingredients were chosen, and how we waited patiently when we withstood getting hammered, and now here we are, a puddle of gooey mess that doesn't taste good to the people around us; our ministry is at a low point. Our precious ingredients are all jumbled up, and nothing looks familiar.

Then we see the hand of the Master Baker lift us from that spot, and for a season we are encouraged as we are carried across the kitchen, resting in the knowledge that even though *we* can't see the ultimate fruit of our work, He has a plan to bring us to fruition, because when the Baker begins a perfect work in a minister, He is faithful to complete it (Philippians 1:6). We are poured lovingly into a mold, a new shape, and we feel encouragement and celebrate the new direction we're being taken in.

But it is *then* that the doors of the oven are opened wide and waves of heat penetrate our utopian fantasies.

Many great ministers have jumped ship by this point. How could a loving God do this to them? Haven't they waited patiently for long enough? Haven't they trusted Him even when they didn't understand what He was creating? Haven't they always been faithful, trusting that the Baker knew the plans He had for them, that they would prosper and not be harmed, according to Jeremiah 29:11? Isn't that what that verse means? (Again, another example of why it is so important to consider the context of each biblical promise before misapplying it, because otherwise it will lead some to believe the promise of God for their lives was abandoned…)

And now He's placing them in the thick of the heat? Perhaps they don't need to grow beyond this point. If they have to suffer the heat of the oven, then forget it. They risk eventually rotting out of their useful-ness and allowing their ministry to be tossed in the wastebasket, but that is the last straw. The camel's back can take no more. They now exist in a cold, refrigerated ministry that only appeals to a minority who happen to enjoy raw cake batter in passing until their ingredients spoil—and they will—and after such an experience they are far less likely to ever attempt ministry again. They are content to accept the fact that they will never truly feed the expecting masses the sweet course they could have offered. Not if it means the oven. They will *resist* the oven.

For those willing to weather the intense, blistering temperature trial, the point at which the maximum volume of patience is required, internal change happens almost immediately, and it's not a change they asked for. Their batter gets hot and the ingredients begin to finally give way to a tex-ture that entirely dismisses the beauty they once held. They feel at times that the Master Baker is far away, busying Himself with other cakes. They believe they are alone, forgotten. And even in those moments when they look through the door and see the Baker gazing in at them, from their perspective, it appears that He wanders away again.

Then finally, the door of the oven opens and they watch as the Baker's hand reaches in, but their hopes of relief are shattered when they realize it's not to rescue them from heat, but to poke them in their center. He speaks clearly, lovingly, and from His own experience as the Master…but the words He gives are the hardest they have yet to hear…

"You're not ready yet" (cf. 1 Corinthians 3:2; John 16:12).

The door closes again, and the heat surrounds them.

How can this be happening?! How much more can one take?

The Baker knows that it's almost over, that the minister has nearly become his definitive potential product for His Kingdom's use. The min-ister, however, only has the option of sitting still, waiting, and *trusting*.

The minister who has fostered anger in his heart toward a God who would allow these things to happen to him will resist the hand of the Baker and choose to live in his misery oven until he is burned forever: He doesn't like what's happening to him and views God as one that continues only to confuse him and do him harm, so he suffers ministerial burnout and decides that reaching the lost is simply "not his calling."

The faithful and obedient minister, on the other hand, will celebrate the moment the Baker returns to retrieve him from the oven for the next step, choosing to believe that through the heat, he and his ministry have been tempered.

The frosting as a dressing for success: The Master Baker opens the door, reaches in, and lifts the faithful minister from the heat. The Baker's words to His creation are now the best of all…

"Well done. You made it. You are a good and faithful cake. You made it through these trials, you trusted in Me as your Baker, and I will frost you as a royal dessert" (cf. Matthew 25:21, 23).

The minister is placed on a platter and the hot mold is removed, bringing immense relief. While the minister is cooling, he watches as the loving Baker collects His instruments for dressing. And then comes that long-awaited moment when the final touches are spent upon the minister, and his ministry appears as something with a purpose. He had not been capable of fulfilling his crucial role in the Kingdom at any moment prior, but now it is evident that the Baker has shaped him into a masterpiece.

He is a "perfect cake," left "wanting nothing," and the Baker is no more intimidated by multiplying that cake's potential into the ultimate fruition than He was with the loaves and fishes. The minister who refused to hide his light under a bushel in the midst of confusion and heat is now "blessed" (Matthew 5). He can allow the fruits of his labors to be divided, multiplied, and magnified for the Kingdom.

A "perfect cake" baked by the Master Baker is never devoured. It is *savored*. It leaves "nothing wanting," and its taste leaves an impression on those who experience it well after it is gone.

But a "perfect cake" requires patience.

When James instructed that patience must have its perfect work that we may be entire and our potential left wanting nothing, his comment was not limited to pastors of churches. Each and every Christ-ian has a duty to wait for the loving hand of the Master Baker to do His work in us as people in His service, in every area of life, because it is only after the process of development that we can reach the zenith of what we are called to do as individuals. As servants.

I know what kind of cake I want my ministry to be to this uncertain world, and I know what kind of impression I hope my life will leave on those who have experienced knowing me while the world remains a turbulent place. I pray that I am obediently patient during each step of the way, and I pray that my ministry—whatever that will ever be in this life—is multipliable.

Wisdom

The second test of faith by works is wisdom. Here, James gives what are the most crucial, yet seemingly most overlooked, pieces of advice for those of us who wish to reach the lost.

> [5]**If any of you lack wisdom, let him ask of God, that giveth to all men liberally, and upbraideth not; and it shall be given him.**

This faith-test is fairly self-explanatory. True wisdom regarding the will of God (as opposed to philosophical conjecture) in all situations can only be given by asking the One who holds the wisdom. The Word says that God gives wisdom "liberally" (generously, without withholding) to "all" who ask for it—and He "upbraideth not," which means He doesn't shame or rebuke such a request. In fact, God is *pleased* by prayers of dependency.

Consider God's fulfillment of Solomon's request for wisdom. After Solomon offered a thousand offerings to the Lord upon the bronze altar at Gibeon, God approached him and allowed him to ask for anything. God didn't immediately promise to give Solomon whatever he asked for; instead, God gave Solomon an opportunity to ask for whatever he wished, and then He listened to Solomon's request. Godly wisdom was all Solomon wanted, and as we see in 2 Chronicles 1:11–12, God saw the humility and dependency of the wise man's prayer, and the request was granted:

> And God said to Solomon, Because this was in thine heart, and thou hast not asked [for] riches, wealth, or honour, nor the life of thine enemies [revenge], neither yet hast asked long life; but hast asked wisdom and knowledge for thyself, that thou mayest judge my people, over whom I have made thee king, wisdom and knowledge is granted unto thee; and I will give thee riches, and wealth, and honour, such as none of the kings have had that have been before thee, neither shall there any after thee have the like.

Not only did God give freely the wisdom that Solomon sought, but He also rained riches, wealth, and honor upon him with an abundance that no king had seen prior or would ever see again—all this because Solomon approached the Lord with a request for wisdom to carry out His almighty will through His servant. God did not tell Solomon that any-thing he asked for would be granted; He told him he had the opportunity to ask for anything he wanted. Had Solomon asked for riches or political control, the story would have played out selfishly on Solomon's behalf, and there is no telling what the Lord would have granted. In being given the opportunity to ask for *anything he wanted*, Solomon cast aside all earthly cares—politics, social status, wealth, women, power—and sought wisdom: a building block upon which good works for the Kingdom could begin. In response to Solomon's request for wisdom, the Lord also granted the riches Solomon didn't openly seek, entrusting that the riches would be wisely used…but wisdom had to come before riches.

It is for good reason that Solomon has since been known as the wisest man who ever lived, *and* the richest.

The truth is, every person willing to speak to God has a right through the gift of free will to approach the throne of God and ask for *anything* he or she wants. Nothing is guaranteed, but the right to ask for anything is present for all. This is not to say that no request is capable of offending

God. If we ask for wealth, fame, power, sex, or some other corrupt and fleshly benefit, we are approaching the throne out of selfish ambition, and we cannot expect God to operate like a celestial Santa Claus who gives us whatever makes our lives more exciting and comfortable, especially when that desire is purely our own, and has nothing to do with His will. (More on this issue later.) These are, of course, extreme examples that many Christians already know are inappropriate prayer requests, but there are other examples of wants that seem at the onset to be completely sincere and harmless, but which have selfishness at their root.

Not all prayers of self-promotion are innately selfish or evil, such as when a man hopes to get a better job so he can provide for his family. But when the root of the prayer is self-promotion, *and the gift of wisdom has not been sought first*, the heart of the asker is intrinsically in the wrong place.

Consider this example:

- Dave wants to make more money so he can pay medical bills for his family.
- Dave, not having sought wisdom, and believing he has the answer to his problem already, asks the Lord to provide a job at a different company where he can obtain better income, since he sees himself getting nowhere at his current one.
- Dave doesn't know that Jared, his boss, has secretly been taking notes about his skills and plans on placing his name at the top of the list for a position in another department with a sizable raise after the next board meeting.
- Dave continues to pray for a different job, and even spends his hours off the clock actively and aggressively applying for positions at competitor companies. He grows weary waiting for the Lord to provide, weary that he is turned down at every interview elsewhere, weary that his "cake" has not finished baking in the timeframe he expected, and as a result, his attitude at work starts to become bitter. His work performance declines.

- Jared discovers that Dave has been applying elsewhere, takes note of the change in his attitude and performance, and reconsiders submitting Dave's name, since it appears that his heart is no longer in his work. When he approaches Dave about his stability at the company, Dave tells Jared the truth, because Dave is a good Christian man who believes in honesty…but it is the truth *as he sees it* without godly wisdom: He believes that he is no longer supposed to be at this workplace, and that he needs to work for someone else eventually.
- Jared gives Dave his blessing, but understandably now views Dave as a short-term employee who is on his way out, and who would not be the best candidate for a raise in a new department.

Prayer for something we want without seeking wisdom from the Lord first is the same as telling the Lord that we already know what is best for us, and letting Him know that we simply need Him to make it happen the way we see it playing out. Without wisdom, God becomes the hand-out guy only, instead of the Divine Will behind our plans. Now consider this scenario:

- Dave wants to make more money so he can pay medical bills for his family.
- Dave, believing that only God knows the best path for his life, prays that the Lord will provide him wisdom in the coming days at his place of work. Wisdom behind every action he performs. Wisdom in every interaction between himself and the other staff members. Wisdom in every financial decision he makes. God's divine wisdom and will behind every moment of his day. He prays that if he is in the wrong place, the Lord will make him wise to seek work elsewhere, also.
- Dave doesn't know that Jared has secretly been taking notes about his skills and plans on placing his name at the top of the list for another department with a sizable raise after the next board meeting.

- *After seeking wisdom*, Dave prays that if he is, in fact, in the wrong place, the Lord will provide another job, and in Dave's off hours he applies for work elsewhere, meanwhile continuing to seek wisdom and utilizing the first faith test from the book of James (patience) to move forward with every interview. As he is turned down time and time again, he counts it all joy that his trials are making him stronger. He trusts the Lord completely and embraces the whisk and the oven, knowing that the Master Baker is beginning a good work in him. At the center of his prayers remains the determination of seeking wisdom, wisdom, wisdom.

- Jared discovers that Dave has been applying elsewhere, but he is confused about this: He has only ever seen Dave work very hard with a good attitude. He had therefore assumed that Dave was happy at this workplace. Jared places his plans to take Dave's name to the board on hold so he can speak to him personally. When he approaches Dave about his stability at the company, Dave tells Jared the truth, because Dave is a good Christian man who believes in honesty. After having sought wisdom in every aspect of his life, Dave explains to Jared that he was looking for another job only because he needed more money for family medical expenses. But, he adds, he is happy to be wherever the Lord wills him to be—even if that means staying where he's at while the Lord is working to make him strong and wanting of nothing.

- Jared gives Dave his blessing if he chooses to leave, but his confidence in Dave's stability in a new department with a sizable raise is now strengthened as he sees all Dave's needs being met by offering him the new position. Jared believes that Dave will be with the company for many years if he can get Dave this raise, and the benefit will be mutual because Dave is perfect for the job. It's a win-win.

- In the next board meeting, Jared makes the recommendation, and Dave gets a raise.

If the all-knowing God knows a man wishing to provide for his family must stay right where he is for a time until his boss gives him a huge raise and places him in the department that best suits his personality and gifts, then asking the Lord to provide a completely different job at another company—*without first asking for wisdom*—is selfish. This is true even when the original motive is pure, because he is, again, telling God he already knows what's best for him and God simply needs to use His almighty power to gift what Dave thinks he needs. In both scenarios, Dave actively applied for other jobs. In the second, however, because he chose to seek wisdom while applying the lesson of patience, Dave gains respect and is awarded with a raise.

Seeking wisdom from the Lord first, like Solomon, tells the Lord that our deepest desire is to become a building block upon which any blessing can be properly spent or utilized once given. Then perhaps some Dave out there, like Solomon, will not only get the wisdom he asked for, but the riches of the new job as well.

(Understand that this anonymous Dave illustration is simply one example out of billions. It is not a fail-proof plan, nor should it be considered any kind of mystical formula that will apply in every circumstance. It is merely a modernized and loose parallel of the Solomon prayer story to help bring a fresh perspective on the lesson that can be learned from Scripture.)

Wisdom "shall" be given to those who ask.

[6]But let him ask in faith, nothing wavering. For he that wavereth is like a wave of the sea driven with the wind and tossed. [7]For let not that man think that he shall receive any thing of the Lord. [8]A double minded man is unstable in all his ways.

As you can see, there are some qualifiers to James' words. We have to ask in faith that the request will be fulfilled. We can't pray with genuine humility and dependency if we secretly believe that although the Lord *could* give it, He will not choose to do so. We are therefore a double-minded person (belonging to two schools of thought or behavior at one time; in many biblical cases "double-mindedness" refers to holiness on one hand and worldliness on the other, and it is the epitome of hypocrisy) if we do such a thing, and our request bounces around like waves of the sea. Some come to the throne of God with a request, but their internal thoughts reflect the following: "I believe You can, but I don't believe You can...I mean, I believe You *could*, but I don't believe You will... Well, what I mean is, You did it for that guy, but maybe You won't for me, or can't, or, I don't know. I'm confused!"

Waves. A moving back and forth from one human conclusion to another, never settling. It's all just chaos. We're confusing even ourselves regarding our very own belief system. We either believe He can give wisdom, and therefore *will* give wisdom to "all" who ask in humility—as promised in the Word—or we don't. Double-minted people aren't just unstable in asking for wisdom, James says; such people are unstable in "*all* [their] ways": in everything they say or do. Not only will these people *not* receive wisdom, they will *not* receive "anything from the Lord," according to James! Though this sounds harsh, the logic is very simple: Nothing you ask for will be given to you if you ask without faith in receiving.

I wish I could promise that the rest of this book will flatter readers with warm fuzzies, but that wasn't the ministry James stood for. He didn't aim to flatter; he aimed to *reform*. If we truly want wisdom from God in these troubling social and political climates, we have to get the chaos of tossing, double-minded waves out of our heads, ask the One who gives divine wisdom, and believe that He will do it.

Pride or Reliance in Material Possessions

Beginning in verse 9, we reach the third test:

> [9]**Let the brother of low degree rejoice in that he is exalted:**
> [10]**But the rich, in that he is made low: because as the flower of the grass he shall pass away.** [11]**For the sun is no sooner risen**

with a burning heat, but it withereth the grass, and the flower thereof falleth, and the grace of the fashion of it perisheth: so also shall the rich man fade away in his ways.

This faith-test harmonizes with Christ's words in Matthew 19. A rich young man approached Christ, asking what he had to do to inherit eternal life. After the young man promised that he had made good on upholding the Ten Commandments, Jesus said, "If thou wilt be perfect, go and sell that thou hast, and give to the poor, and thou shalt have treasure in heaven: and come and follow me" (Matthew 19:21). The rich man walked away sorrowful, because he was unable to comply with the order to release his material possessions. His pride was tied to the ownership of "things," and his lifestyle relied on the earthly and temporary rewards those materials provided.

Following this, Christ's disciples asked what reward *they* would receive as a result of having given up every material possession and comfort in order to follow Him. His response was that "every one that hath forsaken houses, or brethren, or sisters, or father, or mother, or wife, or children, or lands, for my name's sake, shall receive an hundredfold, and shall inherit everlasting life" (Matthew 19:29). Jesus went on in the next verse to explain the poetic truth that "many that are first shall be last; and the last shall be first." In other words, "Many who live for their own gain in this life—including Christians—will be at the bottom of the totem pole in the next life, and those who cast aside worldly riches and wealth in this life to follow Me at all costs will be recognized for that sacrifice in eternity."

However, let us not mistake this verse, as many have done in the past, to mean that any earthly material possessions, wealth, or comforts are immoral. The Bible says *many* times that the Lord wishes to pour blessings upon us…even earthly ones. The issue lies in the heart.

As we discussed only pages ago, God saw that Solomon had humility and dependency on Him, and instead of asking for riches, he asked for wisdom. God then showered earthly riches upon Solomon, so any claim that earthly possessions are evil are in error. It is a matter of the sacrifice one is willing to make in order to please God. For some, like the rich man in Matthew 19, whose dependency was placed on money, the sacrifice *will* be riches. Others may have to sacrifice time, energy, relationships, opportunities, and so on. Had Matthew 19 featured a poor but lazy man, Christ's words would not have been about wealth (because naturally, that wouldn't have made sense), but they might have been something like, "If you want to be perfect, leave your current life and follow Me, knowing that this will mean you have to get out of bed in the morning and can't lounge around all day anymore."

Christ, in Matthew 19, and James, in 1:9–11, were not singling out material ownership as immoral. They were addressing a matter of heart for the follower of Christ, bringing attention to the truth that if our satisfaction or reliance is on "things," then our satisfaction and reliance will naturally not be on Christ. *Nothing* we "store up" (Matthew 6:19) on earth is anything to brag about.

James is making the point in 1:9–11 that the brother of "low degree" should "rejoice that he is exalted," but the man who places his trust in earthly treasures, electronics, fancy cars, or big homes will be "made low," because when he dies, he cannot carry any of his possessions with him, and his legacy is tragic. His epitaph may as well read, "Remembered for his collection of shiny things." It will all pass away like the withered grass and dead flowers, and all that he considered fashionable, sparkly, or impressive will perish.

One test of our faith is in the direction in which we place it. God is eternal. Possessions are temporal. Nothing is wrong or evil about living comfortably. *Everything* is wrong and evil about placing possessions and/or our reliance upon them above the call of following Christ.

Temptation

We now arrive at a test that no one has ever completely conquered:

[12]Blessed is the man that endureth temptation: for when he is tried, he shall receive the crown of life, which the Lord hath

promised to them that love him. [13]Let no man say when he
is tempted, I am tempted of God: for God cannot be tempted
with evil, neither tempteth he any man: [14]But every man is
tempted, when he is drawn away of his own lust, and enticed.
[15]Then when lust hath conceived, it bringeth forth sin: and
sin, when it is finished, bringeth forth death. [16]Do not err, my
beloved brethren. [17]Every good gift and every perfect gift is
from above, and cometh down from the Father of lights, with
whom is no variableness, neither shadow of turning. [18]Of his
own will begat he us with the word of truth, that we should be
a kind of firstfruits of his creatures.

The faith-test of temptation is one that, unlike those already discussed, applies to every living soul on earth. I have known a lot of good, Christian people who don't outwardly struggle with patience, as they appear to have it aplenty and in every situation; the same can be said of those precious seekers of wisdom. Still others are humble in almost everything they do, so pride or reliance upon "things" doesn't appear to be an issue. Whereas it is rare to meet someone who has successfully conquered *all three* faith-tests previously listed, it is impossible to meet those who have completely rid themselves of this fourth faith-test: temptation.

This is why James didn't say, "Blessed is the man who has entirely defeated temptation," because if we are human, we haven't. Instead, he said, "Blessed is the man that *endureth*," giving props to those who see temptation for what it is and remain steadfast against it. To be "blessed" in this context suggests to me (and many scholars of celebrated commentaries) that a person who endures the test of temptation and triumphs will be truly happy. This doesn't infer that anyone will always triumph over temptation, for only one human (Christ) has ever done this. It does, however, mean that for those who endure the test of it, fight against it, and remain dutiful to God to the best of their finite ability, the crown of life will be the reward for showing true love for the Lord through righteous living.

The word "temptation" tends to conjure flooding imagery of people giving into easily recognizable sin, such as infidelity, murder, pornography addiction, theft, blasphemy, etc. However, other sins of the flesh are far more common among Christians on a daily basis and are far less frequently addressed from the pulpit. For instance, consider rudeness or judgmentalism. At first thought, those don't seem like a mortal sins that should be placed on the same plane as sins like murder or blasphemy, but in some cases, being rude or having a spirit of condemnation in our relationships can lead to even worse outcomes.

Kevin was a nonbeliever who was on the fence about his convictions. He had been praying for years that some "higher being" would reveal himself. Unsure about which faith is the true one, Kevin began to research and read about Christ, and decided to attend a local church to see what it was all about. Before the sermon began, Kevin observed two chatty ladies in a nearby pew. The women were talking about the "scandalous" information they had just received about someone called "Sister Betty" who, from the direction of these ladies' glances, was seated across the auditorium. Before Kevin left the property, one church member told him he needed to cover his tattoos and remove his piercings so he wouldn't set a bad example for the teen groups, and another one curtly asked him to stand farther away from the building if he was going to smoke "lung-cancer sticks."

Does this sound a bit too dramatic? Have we Christians by and large overcome this kind of rudeness and judgmentalism? Evidently not, because Kevin is a real person (though his name was changed), and this experience led him away from Christianity and into mysticism. He responded with that age-old, "If that's what Christianity is, I don't want any part of it." Who could blame him? While *in* the Church, believers tend to expect and overlook some of these moments as separate from God—because we, the believers, are also human and therefore susceptible to failing—*outside* the Church, nonbelievers hear that we are the ambassadors of Christ and that it is our creed to represent Him in all that we do, so they observe our behavior and associate it with the Man we follow. If their knowledge, understanding, and familiarity of the Gospel is in infancy and they see "the Christ-ian ambassadors" acting like snobs, what other conclusion might they come to besides assuming the Gospel of Christ is nothing more than a corrupt institution of holy rollers, and whose Leader might be—God forbid—seen as equally judgmental and uncaring? Kevin is merely one example of *many* whose souls may be lost for all eternity because that one rude or judgmental Christian gave in to the temptation of self-inflation or gossip.

Would it be worse for a Christian to click around a questionable website than to lead another into eternal separation from God? It's a hypothetical question, for sure, because we are not the Judge. *Neither* sin is justifiable, nor is it up to us to decide which sin is worse than another, but it is also not up to us to claim we understand the consequences of any one sin over another.

Sometimes the most overlooked or "small" temptations/sins can be the most harmful to the others we're commissioned to reach.

James says we should not claim that God, Himself, has tempted us. At the onset, that sounds ridiculous, because Christians know that God is only holy and therefore does not have any reason to tempt us. Yet, since the very first human and forward, we have done this. As soon as God questioned Adam and Eve in the Garden of Eden regarding the forbidden fruit, Adam's first response was, "The woman whom thou gavest to be with me, she gave me of the tree, and I did eat" (Genesis 3:12). In other words, "God, You gave me this woman, and she is the one who led me to sin. *You're* the one that put this temptation here!" How many times do we suggest that we have been tempted beyond our threshold by something that God allowed into our lives with a "why would You let this happen" concept?

Some adhere to the idea that because God created the world and everything in it, He is responsible for creating sin. If that were true, then we could appropriately claim that God has placed temptation in our lives as well, knowing we would be led to it. But when God created the world and humans, He saw that His handiwork was "very good" (Genesis 1:31), meaning that it was the opposite of sin or evil. According to many respected scholars and Bible commentators, He *did not* "create sin." He *did* create mankind with free will so we would not be mandated into any specifically pre-delegated, lemming-like, mechanical existence. And it was that free will that Adam and Eve rebelled against, polluting the sinless and perfect world God created. If God provides a computer and Internet access for a man who needs to do research for his job, he cannot claim later on that he became addicted to online pornography because God blessed him with access to the Internet. If the Lord provides a single mother the money to care for her children, she cannot claim later on that she spent all her money at the bar because God blessed her with the money that tempted her to drink it all away. And this could go on forever, but at the end of the day, we need to act like adults and take responsibility for the wrong actions we carry out.

Noteworthy to this deliberation, 1 Corinthians 10:13 says, "There hath no temptation taken you but such as is common to man: but God is faithful, who will not suffer you to be tempted above that ye are able; but will with the temptation also make a way to escape, that ye may be able to bear it." More simply, "The temptation you face is not unique to you. Everyone has been tempted in these ways. God will not allow you to be tempted to the point that it is outside of your capability to resist. As hard as it may feel, you *will* have the power to resist, and God will make sure there is a way out of that situation so you can." He's on our side when we face temptation, and we can believe with full faith that He will point us to the escape tunnel when sinful temptation is coming at us with full ramming speed.

James goes on to say, "Do not err," but by this he doesn't mean, "Do not make any mistakes," because that is unfeasible advice for any human. The "Do not err" instruction is an introductory directive for what he says next: Every good and perfect gift comes from Father God, who does not vary in His goodness. As such, "Do not err" should be perceived as, "Do not misunderstand" or "Do not be deceived," followed by the teaching that all good things come from God. We are then to be "a kind of first-fruits of his creatures." A "firstfruit" in the Old Testament times referred to the best yield produced at a harvest. This piece saved from the grower's crop would be offered as a sacrifice to Yahweh (Exodus 23:19; Deuteronomy 26). Comparatively, then, Christians—as a people the ultimate Grower has planted on earth—are to strive to resist temptation so that we may be seen as the best yield of the crop, and our lives and lifestyles should be offered in sacrifice to Him.

Hearing and Living the Word

The last faith test is challenging, but essential:

> [19]Know this, my beloved brothers: let every person be quick to hear, slow to speak, slow to anger; [20]For the anger of man does not produce the righteousness of God. [21]Therefore put away all filthiness and rampant wickedness and receive with meekness the implanted word, which is able to save your souls.
>
> [22]But be doers of the word, and not hearers only, deceiving yourselves. [23]For if anyone is a hearer of the word and not a doer, he is like a man who looks intently at his natural face in a mirror. [24]For he looks at himself and goes away and at once forgets what he was like. [25]But the one who looks into the perfect law, the law of liberty, and perseveres, being no hearer who forgets but a doer who acts, he will be blessed in his doing.
>
> [26]If anyone thinks he is religious and does not bridle his tongue but deceives his heart, this person's religion is worthless.

As simple as these words are, they might be some of the most important ones we can ever apply to our daily behavior as Christians. I believe that nearly anyone can read these words and know their meaning, but for some reason the passage appears to be ignored daily by many Christ-ambassadors.

The very nature of trials tempts any person, Christian or otherwise, to do the exact opposite of the first of these verses. When we feel stress, worry, anxiety, or any serious, negative emotion, it is only natural to be slow to listen and quick to speak. If a man has a stressful day at work, facing trials of various kinds, and then comes home and takes out his aggression by barking at his family, it's not because his family has done something to deserve that treatment, but because he is quick to speak, slow to listen, and quick to anger. If a strain such as a financial burden already exists in a relationship, then every time the subject of money comes up, the husband and wife must both strive against their natural, fallen flesh in order to show the restraint James speaks of. Without restraint, this behavior becomes an all-consuming habit that is even harder to fight against as time goes on, and it manifests itself in all areas of life and in unrelated social interactions with others.

Once entertained and fed, that hiccup could apply at the worst of times, such as when someone is given an opportunity to share the Gospel.

Though I would not say this applies to all Christians, I have known many who have been given this very opportunity, and instead of listening to what or whom someone else believes, *truly* hearing what they believe so that their response can be relevant and respectful, they argue their position over the other's the second the speaker stops to take a breath (or just interrupts them entirely and takes over the conversation). Forceful witnessing is simply not effective. Aggressive conversational dominance is not a trait endorsed in the Word anywhere. And yet, because Christians are called to be witnesses, and because the Church preaches that this should be done with passion, this, for some, automatically equates vehement proselytizing.

Although there certainly are times when we should witness with our mouths, a more clear and present witness to all around us is when we live kindly and respectfully, and allow our lives to be a witness, a light, to all who are around us (Matthew 5:16). Then, once we have gained the trust of others who are searching for truth, we have the chance to witness with our mouths—but even then it should be done "with gentleness and respect" (1 Peter 3:15).

Note that it is not just about the quantity or quality of these virtues that James writes about, but the *speed*. Be *quick* to hear: Do it immediately. Do it before anything else. Be *slow* to speak: Don't talk over people. Don't cut them off. Don't only listen for a minute and then wait for their lips to close and come back with a retort. Listen first, *then* speak. And throughout the conversation—whether as a witness of Christ, a husband talking money, or a mother after a stressful day at work—be *slow* to anger.

This is the roadmap to the kind of conversation that will not only bless those around us, but also will result in our words being heard more often and more effectively. My own husband is a quiet man, and he is always quick to listen and slow to speak and become angry. He is never the head speaker at any social event, but those closest to him know very well that when he *does* speak, everyone listens quietly and respectfully. He *gives* respect, a listening ear, a closed mouth, and a patient spirit before he ever expects to *receive* these things. But in return, as I have observed thousands of times, he receives these virtues from others again and again and again through the object of mutual respect.

By this, my husband has become a *doer* of the Word. He practices what he believes in, and his works, alongside his faith, are alive. He is not a perfect man, but I can't count the number of times I have been approached by people who have been sincerely touched by their interactions with him.

James' comment about the "mirror" has led to confusion at times. However, if we take a moment to study several scholarly commentaries, the meaning is revealed. This is an example of James using the illustration of a mirror to symbolize self-reflection. By using the words "he is *like* a man who…" we know that James isn't referring to a literal looking glass, but to a metaphorical comparison relevant to the surrounding text. Those who hear the Word, but who do not follow up what they have read with a dedicated practice (by being a doer), fail the test of self-reflection. They hear the Word and study themselves, like in a mirror, but do so superficially, without assessing the spots or wrinkles their internal reflections show. They walk away, forgetting what they saw, and neglect to improve themselves. But those who hear the Word, reflect upon who they really are, commits to correcting the spots and wrinkles by obeying the commands of Scripture and becoming doers of the Word, their "doing" (works, efforts, witnessing to others, relationships, etc.) will be blessed.

If we claim to be religious, but are unwilling to obediently do what the Word instructs, our religion is *worthless*! Absolutely and completely without value.

[27]**Religion that is pure and undefiled before God the Father is this: to visit orphans and widows in their affliction, and to keep oneself unstained from the world.**

A pure and undefiled religion is defined here as to befriend "orphans and widows." But this is not at all limited to children who have lost their parents or women who have lost their husbands. That would be silly. Most immediately, it would cancel out men who have lost their wives or parents who have lost their children. But the meaning of this passage goes deeper than that, also. James didn't intend to lift these two afflicted people groups above everyone else; he simply used the most recognizably neglected people groups of his time and culture to point to a bigger picture.

In James' day, in a patriarchal society that praised men and bowed to religious authority, widows and orphans were considered low in priority. But so were the poor, the diseased, the homeless, some elderly, and anyone who didn't fit into one's religious circle. A rampant in-group/out-group mentality dominated the social order of the New Testament culture, so much so that anyone who wasn't an honored member of that social circle was forgotten. Abandoned. Left for dead, for all they cared.

James made it very clear throughout his epistle that he respected *all* people groups, and that God sees all people as equally important. Therefore, pure and undefiled religion calls for lifting up those society has deserted—*and*—those who don't fit into our circle. Simply limiting his words to widows and orphans saps the power right out of them, especially in today's world, where numerous ministries already respond to the needs of these two groups. If we take "orphans and widows" exclusively, it would be easy to say, "Well, someone else is already taking care of that, thank goodness. My job is done."

James is not saying we have to devote our time on Saturdays to visiting retirement homes or take in a couple of foster children. These are wonderful things to do, without a doubt! But James' charge is loaded with so much more information that can easily be unpacked by a simple study of the relationship between language and culture in New Testament times. Widows and orphans were the archetypal persons of distress, according to the canonical law of this era (Deuteronomy 10:18; Psalm 68:5, 82:3; Isaiah 1:17).

As a pillar of the early Church, and by choosing the two demographic parties that were the most heavily neglected at that time, James was beseeching the early Church to reach out to those who were not being reached, and to those whose status in society is not always flattering to our own. When exegetically compared to the rest of his epistle, we can easily determine that this passage means we should reach out to those who are *spiritually needy* as well. (Consider James' remarks about the prostitute Rahab in chapter 2, which we will discuss later. If he saw fit to lift her up and go as far as calling her "righteous" or "justified," then we can safely conclude that James was the radical reformer we know him to be, one who would not limit his statement here to only those who have lost parents or husbands.)

Do we limit this to a social-needs matter? Should it not also be spiritual?

We can support the poor, visit the sick, donate to charitable causes, and accomplish so many other pure and undefiled endeavors, but if our hearts abandon those who are spiritually needy, are we not contributing to a neglect that has *eternal* implications? Who are the archetypal persons of distress today that the Church is neglecting to reach?

What, then, of the atheist who lives next door to you? What of the homosexual you see every morning at the coffee shop? What of the mystic who delivers your mail? What of the violent child who bit your own son at church last Sunday? What of the prostitute you saw selling herself when you last visited Las Vegas? Are these people members of your "in group"? Probably not… Do you find them as important as those who are? I know Someone who values them every bit as much…

We are not called to "hang out with" those whose lifestyles or spiritual views conflict with our own. We are, however, called to "love" them and respect.

Keep yourself unstained by the world by equipping the tool belt James has given us in this, his first chapter. Understand that the trials of the early Church are very real today. The Master Baker is preparing you every step of the way to be used for His purpose. Slow your tongue, quicken your ears, embrace peace with others, and allow your light to be present to all people.

Do you want to change the world?
Do you want to play a part in the next Great Awakening?

Understand the trials go hand in hand with the tests of faith. Know that you must be fully committed to the changes God wants to see in you before your usefulness will ever be perfect and wanting nothing.

Chapter 4

The Body's Favoritism of Today's "Rich Man"

James 2:1–13

As DISCUSSED EARLIER, the proper interpretation and application of Scripture from an original author to a modern audience involves: 1) considering the original culture, society, and context; 2) understanding the modern issues of today's society and culture; and 3) honing in on how the context from the original writing parallels our own time and issues. As we move into James chapter 2, we see a forthright and powerful condemnation of favoritism within the Church, and it's one that I think we are guilty of right now, every day, inside literal church buildings as well as in the menial interactions of the collective Body. I believe James' words make demands on our ability to note the obvious interpretation, as well as to expand our understanding of what those words would have meant in our modern society.

James' attack on favoritism can and should apply to cultural phenomena we face in our society, even though his words don't address them specifically, because the art of applying Scripture to a contemporary world involves the process of allowing it to come alive and breathe beyond the confines of its dated application. If we didn't allow this, then the Bible would not be the great Guidebook that it is for all nations, for all peoples, throughout all time on earth. It would have only applied to the people

75

to whom it was written, and its truth would be finite. The Word of God is infinite. Allowing the Word to speak to issues that did not exist at the time of its writing is not the same as twisting or adding to Scripture; it's a matter of common sense and good exegesis to see what a biblical author was addressing in his day and compare it to related grievances of our day. With that said, there are a number of ways to apply James' concerns about how people are accepted within the Body, the most obvious being a quick-judgment reaction upon a first impression.

Quick Judgment

The second chapter of James begins with the following:

> [1]My brethren, have not the faith of our Lord Jesus Christ, the Lord of glory, with respect of persons. [2]For if there come unto your assembly a man with a gold ring, in goodly apparel, and there come in also a poor man in vile raiment;
>
> [3]And ye have respect to him that weareth the gay clothing, and say unto him, Sit thou here in a good place; and say to the poor, Stand thou there, or sit here under my footstool: [4]Are ye not then partial in yourselves, and are become judges of evil thoughts?
>
> [5]Hearken, my beloved brethren, Hath not God chosen the poor of this world rich in faith, and heirs of the kingdom which he hath promised to them that love him?

The words in the first verse here are translated more simply by the English Standard Version: "My brothers [and sisters], show no partiality as you hold the faith in our Lord Jesus Christ, the Lord of glory."

Show no partiality.

As you hold faith in Christ.

Do not *discriminate!*

James goes on to give an example, saying that if a rich man in fancy clothes comes into a church and is celebrated, treated with honor, and given the best seat in the house while the poor man in gross clothes is made to either stand or sit on the floor, then something wicked has taken place; the ones guilty of carrying out this treatment have become judges over their fellow man and have entertained "evil thoughts." James doesn't just say this is uncouth or impolite; he blatantly states that it is "evil." He then directs the attention of his readers to the eternal implications: The poor of this world are rich in faith; those who are rich in faith will inherit the promised Kingdom. In its proper context, this means we have to understand that this issue is bigger than who has the most or the least money or fancy clothes—and that those issues aren't appropriate gauges of the quality of a person's spiritual commitments. James used an example about the poor, because they represented the lowest societal rank of his day, *and* were the people in the most need of help.

By this, we are told not to turn away those who are in the greatest need of assistance. Why? Not just because we are to clothe and feed the poor (which we are commanded to do by Christ, Himself), but because the Gospel is for *all mankind.* The message of Christ is not just for the rich, prosperous, or shiny people we like to look at and hang out with—it's for *all* humans. The needs of the poor man in James' epistle are spiritual as well as physical, and if he is turned away from the Church based on his physical attributes, he cannot get the teaching he needs to feed his spirit. It's not just about allowing the poor to mingle with the rich, it's about reaching the lost, *all* the lost, whoever they may be, with the life-breathing truth of the Gospel. This includes the most despised archetypal individuals of New Testament culture (such as the poor man James wrote about), certainly, but it also includes today's archetypically despised men and women.

Even when they have money and nice clothes.

We're not to discriminate against the *spiritually* needy, which refers to *anyone,* regardless of how we're rubbed by their social status or how their lifestyle differs from our own.

How often are we guilty of doing this?

James, of course, uses only one example. (Had he used all fathom-able examples, his book would have been hundreds of pages long.) But again, that shouldn't mean we limit our understanding of favoritism in the Body of Christ to this singular example of financial stability, because James was responding to his culture, and so must we. It's a matter of social preconception. Just as James makes it clear that the poor man in vile rai-ment is equally as important as the rich man with the gold ring, if we apply the lesson of his culture to our own, we learn that nobody should be turned away, made to sit at a proverbial footstool, or shamed because he or she doesn't fit into a social image we celebrate—even when that person appears, from every angle, offensive to us.

James was ministering in a time when people were hated on a very real and literal level based on the roles they were born into: social class, ethnic-ity, nationality, religious background, and for having defamed (or been associated with anyone who had defamed) their public honor. People were considered more or less important based on whether they were Jew or Gentile, rich or poor, slave or free—and whether they had embraced Hellenization (Greek culture) brought about by Alexander the Great. It wasn't a matter of what was in people's hearts, but of how they were viewed by the world. It didn't matter if they were repentant souls lost in a spiritual wilderness with so much sincere hunger that they would have arisen as great leaders of the Church if they had been given a chance. They merely needed to represent a group that had historically irritated those in a church setting to be thrown out.

James, by instructing that a poor man should be welcomed with *equal* enthusiasm as a rich man, taught that we should abandon all social rules at the door in exchange for a free Gospel of equality for all. This concept was unheard of. It was madness. It was radical. That a slave would be accepted in the same way as the free or the Gentile as a Jew or a Hellenist as a staunch Hebrew. Unadulterated madness. The readers of such instruction would have to force their brains out of a social standard that had existed for eons in their culture to do such a thing.

And so must we.

I think at this point in our diverse world, much less of this type of discrimination is going on than was occurring in James' day as it relates to subjects like ethnicity, nationality, and wealth. A few churches out there might reject a foreign man at the door with tattered clothing and a skin condition, but as a whole, we have largely come to understand that this kind of exclusivity is sinful and unjust, thanks to the fact that we have the New Testament to instruct us otherwise. But because James' culture did not have the same kinds of diverse people groups as we do, he couldn't have addressed who we see coming through the doorway of a church building today who would give some of our churchgoers the same kind of fright as the poor man at the footstool did to the early Church.

What about the heavily pierced and tattooed biker in black leather? The teenage boy with a mohawk and guyliner? The woman with the low-cut top and miniskirt? Are their souls any less important than anyone else's because they don't appear the way we imagine an "upright Christian" should?

Perhaps our overt reactions to these types of people is because we fear danger. Maybe the man in the black leather will lose his cool and hurt someone. Maybe the teenager will lead our own teens to trouble. Maybe the woman in the miniskirt is getting a little too close to our men. These are all very real concerns that should be considered carefully and treated on a case-by-case basis. An honest and Holy-Spirit-led gut-check about anyone should not be ignored—but that is true wherever we go, inside or outside the church building. Yet, assumptions and social preconceptions about people who look or act differently than we do is a great sin. Except for those who deliberately walk into a church with the specific intent to exploit and destroy (and they are out there), people don't enter a church in the first place if they're not responding to a deep inner voice prompting them toward internal, permanent change and eternal redemption. This voice within them is likely coming from the Holy Spirit. To turn them away or respond negatively to their presence in this case would be to go against God directly, and it is, as James said, "evil."

I happen to know of several mold-breakers off the top of my head.

One of our acclaimed and beloved small-town ministers here who pastors a respected church is a serious biker—black leather and the whole nine yards—who frequently appears like a "tough guy" when you pull into church. It's given me a few chuckles in the past to watch the visitors' reactions as he blares his Harley Davidson into the parking lot, gets off his bike, takes off his helmet and cutting-edge sunglasses—and then walks straight up the steps into the church, past all the pews, and greets his home congregation from the front of the sanctuary with the warmest and sincerest smile a person has ever witnessed. Anyone in the crowd who has never heard him speak might be skeptical about the pastor at first, but ten minutes into his truly anointed (and often emotional) sermons, everyone's guard is lowered. Whereas he is well accepted in his own church and social circles (and a known pillar of this community), if he were to travel to a new city as a visitor to another church and walk in looking the way he does, there is a very real chance that he would be written off immediately as a divergent "sinner." Nobody would know he's actually an incredible preacher of the Gospel of Christ.

This preacher, this "tough guy," is going to be used greatly in the upcoming Great Awakening.

I have also known several teenagers with a true, heartfelt love for Christ and share it with the world around them while sporting skater chains, spiked bracelets, mohawks, and yes, guyliner. One young man named Ben whom I worked with for several years on the West Coast invokes some stares now and again. Often, his Facebook page is riddled with images of him all up in the camera with hip or "emo" facial expressions and hand gestures (none obscene, however) that one might assign the word "punk" to. His skater-style approach to life, his "ah-haw, dawg" and "waddup G" banter, the '90s-flare rap music he blares from the car, and his choice clothing all place him in a position to be considered by first impression to be the kind of young man many people might tell their children not to hang around. However, past the first impression, one learns that Ben is a licensed youth pastor (in one of the largest and most respected Christian organizations in the world) alongside his wife, and he has several well-produced Christian rap CDs on the market. The lyrics of his music touch *very* deeply, reflect a man who is completely and totally sold out for the Gospel, address all kinds of hard-hitting topics (such as teen suicide, loneliness, temptation, premarital sex, peer pressure, etc.), and always point back to Christ as the answer to life's problems with real and tangible application. Why rap music, you might ask? Because Ben can't sing, he says, but he knows "how a song can get stuck in your head," and when you need it, "the Truth is always with you." When someone jokingly commented a couple years ago that he "will never grow up," Ben's response was that he thanked God for that, because hurting youth need buddies. You never can tell…

And when the Great Awakening starts, we will need young people just like Ben to lead the youth of this generation into passionate ministry.

I mentioned a woman with a low-cut top and miniskirt because I have seen that example the most, and I want to spend a minute on it, because I've dealt with this issue personally. Judging a woman's character based on what she is wearing is often quite unfair, because two women can wear the *exact* same outfit with very different results. The clothing might look modest on one woman and immodest on the other, simply because the materials and hemlines land differently on their varying body shapes. I have observed many very thin females wearing skimpier clothing to church without anyone seeming to notice. However, when a buxom lady wears the same top, it's shocking. And when that same woman laughs a little too jovially, she's "flirting."

In 2013, after several years of doctors' advice, I finally agreed to have a body-altering surgery that would help the strain my natural skeleton was under and give me a much higher chance of not developing a hunch-back and postural issues later on. (Skeletal and postural issues are just the tip of the iceberg. I was physically miserable a great deal of the time regarding other symptoms that need not be mentioned here. The surgery was for medical purposes only, not for appearances, but my experience in church for the twenty years prior to that surgery is relevant to this discussion.) I won't go into detail, but I *could not* find "church" clothing that fit the body I was born into. When something fit me in one area, it didn't fit somewhere else, and maintaining modesty was a fierce challenge. Just short of paying a custom tailor to design my clothing (which I never could have afforded), there was no such thing as "shopping for church clothes."

Once in a while, I managed to find something that would fit my measurements, but then I would get stares or comments because my clothing was "too tight" or "too loose," my dress was "too short" or my top was "too low," or someone thought I was trying to "look sexy." (If you know me, even for five minutes, you will understand how little I care about adjectives like "sexy" having anything to do with any public presentation of myself.) Or, and this happened often, the clothes I found that fit well were designed for the elderly. Invariably, someone thought I was being flirtatious when I would interact with anyone, even though my personality on that day was identical to the personality I had in jeans and a T-shirt. So eventually, fairly early on, I gave up on wearing what a "girl" or "woman" ought to wear at church and started attending in oversized hoodies and jeans with sneakers. At least that was modest, right? And the *guys* were wearing it, right?

But that didn't please them, either.

I remember being asked (this rings so ridiculously to me, even today) if my casual clothing would "please God." If God would be happy with my attendance in "His house" while wearing my jeans and camouflage hoodie. If I thought Jesus Christ, Himself, would wear something like that to worship His Father. (I didn't think Jesus Christ, Himself, would wear the dresses they were wearing either, for that matter, but I kept that to myself.) I got so used to my appearance being commented on that I came up with the following answer: "Would it be better that I'm here in His house learning about Him in my hoodie? Or that I'm out there in the world on Sunday searching for a dress that fits me modestly?"

Usually this response stopped the conversation, though it was almost always followed by a humiliating moment when they (usually women) would drop their eyes to my body and study my outline, taking a few seconds to discover the real reason behind why I "treated church" as such an informal affair.

Today, as a side effect of a medical procedure that adjusted my physical outline, I can wear almost anything I want to church and nobody complains. The same clothing that would have made them balk years ago gets the "you look nice today" comment.

A similar quick judgment happened to my best friend, also. She is, from head to toe, Hollywood-level gorgeous. Her personality does not reflect a person who is aware of that, though, as the way she conducts herself with others is polite and reserved. At a youth camp a summer or two ago, she followed dress code immaculately, wearing the same thing to the poolside as the other women. Because she was naturally given a body and face that turn heads, however, she was asked to return to her cabin and change. When she asked how she had disobeyed the dress code, she was told that her clothing wasn't actually in violation at all, but that she simply "looked too good," and it was making everyone uncomfortable.

The quick judgment of females is raging in our current Church. If women dress too casually, they aren't being respectful of the house of God. If they dress in pretty clothing, they are often seen as flirtatious or brazen. If their clothing is out of date, they are the subject of gossip. And because Walmart Supercenters don't have a "trendy monk robes" section, women are naturally subject to continuously suffer greater judgment regarding outward appearance as men if they aren't committed to shopping for the latest modest clothing in a world that doesn't believe in modesty in the first place.

This is not to suggest that every woman who wears problematic clothing to church is facing what I faced and having bungled shopping trips. But what of the woman who grew up in a household where "that kind" of clothing was "just how ladies dress" or "what a woman ought to wear"? Or worse, what if she really *is* dressing in a way that catches attention because she wants attention? At the core, that likely means she wants love. Who better to show her proper love unrelated to her blouse than the Church? So many women have been failed by the Body because they are feared or hated when they don't drape themselves in acceptable fabrics.

I want to state as strongly as I possibly can here and now that I am not arguing in favor of immodest clothing in church. First Timothy 2:9a states that women (and men, for that matter), "should adorn themselves in respectable apparel, with modesty and self-control." But when people first enter a church, they can't be expected to already know what dress is most appropriate, and that head knowledge may take some time to accumulate while their hearts are spiritually developing. If men or women enter a church and are embraced for who and what they are from the beginning, it's likely that their appearance will come to reflect a respect for church-appropriate attire—once they can reflect upon the respect Christ-ambassadors have shown them first.

Consider, too, how easily the "concerning appearance" thing can be the opposite of what one might anticipate. In *Redeemed Unredeemable: When America's Most Notorious Criminals Came Face to Face with God*, a book I co-wrote with Tom Horn a few years back, we did a lengthy case study on seven deadly murderers. *All* of them dressed in regular, respectable clothing, none of them had wild hair or piercings or tattoos, and they all appeared to the people around them (even in church) as very safe, sane people. The one who surprised everyone the most because he always came across as just the nicest guy you'd ever meet was serial killer and rapist Ted Bundy, the all-American law student and smiling superhero who "was really going places." His rampage was so vicious and so fast that even *he* did not know how many women he killed. Jeffrey Dahmer, the "Milwaukee Monster," was a homosexual cannibal who murdered seventeen young men. On the outside, however, he appeared to be a normal guy. Quiet, yes—but based on looks alone, he could be compared with any other youthful, American, Caucasian male in jeans and a pullover.

There is a lesson here, however. Six out of the seven murderers featured in that book had *repeatedly* given others around them strange feelings. (Karla Faye Tucker was the only exception, and her case was very different from the others.) This was especially true of Bundy, who is documented as a man who scared girls to the core merely by making eye contact with them from across the room well before they had properly met. People to this day still talk about the heebie-jeebies they got when they looked at David Berkowitz back in the 1970s when the "Son of Sam" serial killer was at large in New York. Peers at school were noticeably spooked by the teenage parent-killer and Satanist Sean Sellers. Schoolmates of Jeffrey Dahmer to this day speak during interviews of how the "quiet kid" freaked them out for reasons they have a hard time putting into words.

Apart from these impressions, which very well could have been Holy-Spirit-led gut-checks, there were numerous accounts when the internal red flag went up after getting to know these people for a while, or during early conversational exchanges with them. So, there *are* times when we need to pay attention to how we feel about a person and proceed with extreme caution, but that is a separate issue entirely from treating others with a soul like dirt because they don't fit a social image that matches the cultural standards of a church.

Regarding the quick judgment, we must never be guilty of this lest we go against the will of God and commit pure "evil." For God so loved the world, and every human in it, so much that He gave His Son that *anyone*—so that "whosoever will" believe in Him—will inherit the same Kingdom as a Christian with the right hemline length and hairdo. "We the Church" claim at every turn that we are not guilty of this, that we *want* strange people to wander into our places of worship so we can love on them and share the Gospel with them, but I have personally witnessed the quick judgment more times than I can count in ten lifetimes. I can't apologize for calling a spade a spade. It is *well past time* that the "Christians" become Christ-ians and give a genuine smile to the "whosoever will."

Past that smile, the kind treatment *must* continue if the Body has any interest in serious revival.

The Gradual Judgment

The dismissal of a person's equality or value, sadly, isn't not limited to how he or she looks or acts at first glance. Members of the Body often heap an abysmal, "I love you, you're perfect, now change" mentality upon others when a personality quirk rubs somebody wrong or the person's theology or lifestyle isn't what Christians think it should be. It is as if newcomers are welcomed with open arms, then placed on some quiet trial and watched to see how long it will take for them to completely conform to the expectations of a congregation. If they fail to adapt in a certain amount of time, they are rejected, and *then* they are told it is because of their own failings that they were rejected, instead of being told that the Church has failed them through legalistic expectations.

A sign should be hung outside some churches that says, "Welcome one and all for at least two weeks, whereupon your value and behavior will be reassessed for attendance consideration." This kind of judgment can be even more harmful than the quick judgment, because at least if it happens quickly, those being judged are getting hit hard and fast and know where they stand with a congregation. They may have interest in trying again elsewhere. However, when they have been welcomed and loved, then rejected when they don't instantly conform to behavioral or social expectations of a congregation, that hurt may manifest itself in a cynical dismissal of Christianity as a whole.

Some of the reasons we have to reject others are extremely superficial.

A man laughs too loud and takes the wrong parking spot. A woman is always late getting herself and her six children to service. Sister Bertha is a Pentecostal, but she doesn't agree with Brother Ned about speaking in tongues during service. The newcomer Elizabeth just got a divorce, and Kathy thinks she should have hung in there if she really cared about what the Bible says. Sarah was seen at a restaurant last Saturday, and Suzie is pretty sure that rose-colored liquid in the glass with the little umbrella on top wasn't the virginal pink lemonade. Eddie skips services every third Sunday because he has the audacity to place "fishing with the boys" above worshiping the Lord. Frank said a curse word. Billy smokes. George went to a bar.

The list of potential reasons for making other people feel uncomfortable in God's house—or worse, *outside* of church while in the company of another Christian—is endless. Whereas it is true that the Body should expect upright behavior amongst its members, we need to remember that it is not based on our own ideologies of uprightness, but upon scriptural ideologies. A beautiful saying attributed to St. Augustine (but which probably originated from a German Lutheran theologian in the early 1600s) is: "In essentials unity, in nonessentials liberty, and in all things charity." When Christians *must* be united about an essential—Christ was the Son of God, He died on the cross, He rose again, and His blood has provided redemption for all mankind—then it is our duty to ensure that the essential is upheld…that no false teachers change, twist, or add to that essential. When we approach a nonessential—one person thinks drinking alcohol is a sin based on the many verses regarding the sinfulness of being a drunkard (1 Peter 4:3; Ephesians 5:18; Proverbs 20:1; and several others), and another believes it is fine to drink in moderation based on the many verses that refer to enjoying the wine God's earth produces and its health benefits (1 Timothy 5:23; Ecclesiastes 9:7; Psalms 104:14–15; and several others)—liberty of the individual must be allowed…and squabbles that cause strife in the Body are evil. But in *all* things, charity and love for others who may or may not agree with what we believe must be sustained.

What leads a person to permanent change, anyway? If people are living in a way that the congregation sees as unpleasing to the Lord, and they happen to meander into a church, they *should* be able to say they've come to the right place to find assistance in making adjustments so their lives will eventually become pleasing to the Lord. Sadly, it is so often the opposite. At the onset, they are given a list of all the things they have to do to please the *people* (usually involving legalistic demands from the nonessential group). People don't walk into a church because they are seeking to feel bad about who they are, but because they have heard the whispered promise that there is a God out there somewhere—One who will love them *just as* they are. The Church promises a "come just as you are and worship" creed, but that creed is abandoned when our perceived values are threatened by the "sins" of a finite member whose presence might tarnish the shiny toys that represent what our faith has become.

When belief systems or lifestyles do go against an essential, when people are living in a way that is an outright affront to Scripture, they should not be expected to change overnight. In a recent meeting with the president of the Royal Family Kids Camp organization, when our staff was in training to accommodate the young troubled kids who will be coming to our facilities, we were given this gem: "People will not care about what you know—until they know about how you care." Caring about people's souls and eternity *must* come before blasting them with Scripture verses that reveal what is wrong with how they live or what they believe. We cannot truly expect anyone will listen to us and digest our words if we haven't first shown that we care about them, and are willing to treat them with dignity and respect. People must experience God's love and grace before they should be told to bend to His will.

When people who are spiritually and emotionally bleeding enter a church, we, as genuine Christ-ians, must make a choice: Are we medics, or are we sharks? Do we see the bleeding, rush in with salves and ointments, and love the "whosoever will," placing their needs at the top of the triage and see to the wounds despite their race, gender, ethnicity, lifestyle, or belief system like a hospital would treat a patient? Or do we smell the blood and follow its trail to our next meal, devouring those people and making their emotional and spiritual pain greater, all the while pretending we've rejected them in the name of cleansing the temple of all unrighteousness? Jesus called these Pharisaic and religious-spirited people hypocrites and pretenders (Matthew 23)! Do we place all people in the same impartial position of importance, or do we bring out the footstool and usher the poor man in the vile raiment to his rightful place at our feet? Once we embrace visitors at the door, do we *continue* to embrace them? Or do we let them have their happy, two-week reception period and then present them with our loophole list and "jump" commands? Do we see *ourselves* as the ultimate assessors of righteous and pleasing conduct while we hide our lights under bushels called "pious appraisal," or do we allow the Holy Spirit to do His work within His people as we let our lives be the light that guides them quietly and in love until they feel the "inner voice" convicting them to be the best people they're capable of being for Him?

Yet, for as many "amens" as this mini-sermon may receive on any given Sunday, we repeatedly ignore the simplicity of it the second we are faced with a challenge. A heavy-set minister who has completely given himself over to obesity through bad eating habits might berate a fellow man for smoking, because after all, potato salad and pizza aren't the same as cigarettes... A Sunday school teacher might get angry at a neighborhood kid for stealing a quarter out of the offering bag and then make a few shady marks on her tax papers the following January, because after all, it's only the government she's lying to... A youth pastor might chastise a teenager in his church group for making an inappropriate comment about a girl's body, then brag to his peer-circle in the back of the church with details about his marital bed unbeknownst to his wife, who would be mortified, because, after all, he's a grown-up... And here's a favorite that I have seen over and over and over again: A woman might wag an angry finger at a gossiper for talking about her behind her back, and then call all the women she knows later in the week with a juicy story of her own shrouded as a "prayer request," because after all, people need to know what to pray for...

Rejection of fellow men from members of the Body. It is, in and of itself, an outright "evil," James says, regardless of the social offense that supposedly justifies the rejection, and regardless of whether those people have been graciously embraced for a reception period.

But James has even more to say on the subject of partiality and the rich, and when compared to how our Church operates in culture today, there is far more to consider than the mere flippant dismissal of fellows.

Oppression by the "Rich Men"

[6]**But ye have despised the poor. Do not rich men oppress you, and draw you before the judgment seats? [7]Do not they blaspheme that worthy name by which ye are called?**

Again, take into account the culture and people James was referring to. In his day, the rich oppressing the poor was a serious problem. Though we do hear of it today, it takes place less frequently in a church as a result of thousands of years of Christ-followers' access to New Testament writings, at least when it involves the treatment of financially destitute people beyond the doorways of our places of worship.

However, "rich men" behind a pulpit have had a heyday in recent decades through corrupt prosperity preaching, and they have completely exploited their positions in the Church, doing great damage over time. I remember watching Christian television as a little girl and seeing a certain famous pastor's wife present a lengthy prayer in which she called upon "all the little old ladies" to "write that check" and "send in their last two coins in faith" so that they would be "commended by the Savior" as the woman in the Bible had been in Matthew 12:42. Was it not these "rich men [and women]" ministers who oppressed (and exploited) the congregants? By proclaiming through a twisting of Scripture that God wants us all to have money and stuff, and by stating that the more we give to those ministers, the more God will bless us with shiny things, people were misled into giving their last dollars to these ministries on the promise of a tenfold return—and many never saw a plugged nickel come back. As a result, the entire spreading of the Gospel was shamed by this warped doctrine for a time, and it was only through several long and rough years of correction that these ministers were exposed for the frauds they were (*many* of whom were heavily involved in illegal monetary management) and that the Church was able to recover and move on. Were these men and women not guilty in their own right of blaspheming the very Name by which we are all called to preach?

Thank goodness that, at the time of this writing, prosperity preaching has left such a sour taste in our mouths that the Church has largely weeded out these ministries. Some prosperity-Gospel ministers still preach that giving money to their cause will lead to a biblically guaranteed prosperity for the giver, or that saying certain things out loud will bring blessings into one's life, but for as many people as there are who fall prey to their doctrines, it appears that twice as many are willing to refute them. (More on this subject in later chapters.)

But where do we draw the line? Has prosperity preaching stepped aside to usher in the next wave of corrupt Gospel as it relates to flashy, gaudy, glitzy, loud, ostentatious, and flamboyant worship? Who is exploiting today's Church, and by extension, the individuals who attend? Yes, prosperity preaching has declined, but what about today's service and church buildings? What do we stand for when we go to church? What do we spread? What is our message? What are our habits?

What is our *mission*?

Is it our mission to reach the lost or put on a show? Do we reach to grasp hands with the hurting, or to grasp the dollars that buy our entry-way chandeliers?

I can't say it enough: It is a matter of *heart*.

There is nothing innately sinful about a megachurch with thousands of people and a worship service played with plugged-in instruments and spotlights and fog machines. In today's culture, there may be young people who will not know how to connect to a church where a woman in a pleated skirt and suntan nylons plays hymns on a traditional organ, interjecting the occasional "glory" between each song. Of the two options, I would personally prefer the organ church and the lady in suntan nylons, as that is the atmosphere I was raised in, and I would likely find the more modern service distracting—but I *appreciate* the diversity in churches across the nation. It is a *good thing* that there are so many different ways to bring personal talent to the throne of God in worship, including music styles that have a beat and flow through amplifiers.

Even music that sounds "worldly" to some has ministered immensely to others. I remember when Keith Green's music was called "devil worship" by certain members of the Church in the 1970s and '80s. But we need only listen to one of that man's hundreds of Holy-Spirit-anointed songs—that bring life to the Gospel for millions of people—to see that as the world turns, worship styles *must* be updated. Many reading this would agree as well, though, that Keith Green's heart was in it for the lost, and he used his bold sounds to reach the very people groups that the organ-churches were not reaching.

If God gives a sincere young man the incredible ability to play the electric guitar, then far be it from the rest of the Body to tell him he shouldn't use that gift for the Lord's purposes and design. But if that same young man is in it for show—to impress everyone with how many trills and hot licks and grace notes he's capable of executing during a solo in the middle of a praise song—then his talent is wasted on a worldly purpose. That performance wouldn't likely be anointed by God, because it wouldn't be performed for the purpose and will of God. The same would be true for any others in that church with the same motive, whether they be involved in the worship team or some other place of leadership. This is not a call to all churches everywhere to trade in the technology or electric sounds for robes and harps. I have no issue with a worship service or sermon being executed with flare. My issue is when the flare replaces the Message, and when today's "rich men" use their church buildings as a way of oppressing and exploiting the Gospel: using Christ's mission to invest in attention-grabbing spectacle.

This is why today's megachurch trend concerns me. If a church's mission statement is to reach the lost at all costs and love even when love is the uncomfortable verb, then the majority of Christians who attend that church will reflect that mission, and numbers will be saved for all eternity. If a church's hidden mission is to put up smoke and mirrors to get everyone excited about an emotional experience, then all it accomplishes is a hype that is void of any Kingdom purpose—it is not anointed—and the majority of Christians who attend that church will reflect that. They will carry the "flashy Gospel" into their daily lives at work, at home, at the grocery store, and everywhere they go. Jumping up and down in an emotionally driven *whoop-whoop* session that leaves believers feeling empty an hour after church is *not* what Christ died to conceive. It is today's "rich man's" display.

It would be narrow-minded to assume that every large church with an outwardly impressive service is guilty of committing a spiritual grievance just because it invested in colorful praise…but a *great number* of churches today are less about the Man who died and rose again and more about making the Gospel look exciting to the outside world. So people will join. So people will jump around. So people will open their purses. So people will feel thrilled, stimulated, electrified...*entertained!* It's so frequently all about sensationalism and showmanship. Like a magician with a sleight of hand. Prestidigitation. Step right up, step right up. Drawing in crowds to exhilarate and delight. Pulling in the masses with promises of praising the Creator, then switching the focus to the red velvet curtain and the tricks and gimmicks that will subsequently arouse. Eliciting the attention of those whose faith is external, fed only by lights and smoke and chaotic activity, and then releasing those people into the world to represent who Christ is and was and what He accomplished on the cross. Spreading the Word in a proverbial top hat and sequined tuxedo. Conforming the Great Commission into "bread and circuses." The "rich church" and all its pretty people of honor and grandiose Gospel—versus the "poor church" whose people belong at a footstool and whose message isn't as useful because it doesn't inspire awe.

Guess what, folks... The Gospel doesn't need us to make it look exciting. It speaks of a grand eternity. Forever and ever and ever in the presence of the King of Kings. Time without end on a New Earth with golden streets that meet gates carved from monolithic pearls and walls made of pure, precious gemstones in a city lit neither by sun nor moon but illuminated by the mere presence of God. Where there will be no more pain or hurt. Where no abominable thing will enter. Where threat to health, wealth, and stability are obliterated. When every pain—physical and emotional—that we have ever felt here on earth is naught but a memory. It's all there in Revelations chapter 21.

Ministers are not shy when it comes to orating about the fires of hell and eternal damnation, but I can't figure out why we aren't focusing more often on the glories of heaven and an eternity spent in the presence of God. Instead of appealing to mankind's fears, why not appeal to mankind's intrinsic hunger for an eternal release from the temporal pains they face here whilst living alongside a Creator that has always been and will always be their truest Friend and support? The Gospel—and the heaven it promises for those who believe—doesn't need spotlights and trills to be exciting. It's *already* exciting, whether it is preached from a stage with opulent sights and sounds or from a platform with an organ and a lady in suntan nylons.

What fruit is today's church producing for a hungry and lost world? What seeds are we planting for tomorrow's harvest? Are we spreading the Gospel or exploiting it? Do we need outward richness and luxury in order to tell people about what happened to the most important Man on the planet two thousand years ago?

To the large churches with enormous budgets and spectacular services whose mission is sincere and whose focus is truly about reaching the lost with the message of Christ, I thank you and support you. To the large churches with enormous budgets and spectacular services whose mission is to impress people, and by extension oppress the Gospel and the people truly seeking it, I ask you: Who are you really doing this for?

The Bottom Line

It all points back to this:

In Matthew 22:36–40, Jesus was asked which of the Ten Commandments was the most important. His answer was: "Thou shalt love the Lord thy God with all thy heart, and with all thy soul, and with all thy mind. This is the first and great commandment. And the second is like unto it, Thou shalt love thy neighbour as thyself. On these two commandments hang all the law and the prophets."

My six-year-old refers to this as the moment "Jesus made two commandments on top of the other ten." In a way, my son is correct, because Jesus' words are not the same as those in Exodus, and He didn't answer the question He was given by pointing to one of the original ten. On the other hand, one could argue that Christ essentially grouped all ten together with this response, and nothing He said was new information. If we follow these two commandments Christ gave in Matthew, if we follow them completely and wholly as a matter of heart, we will automatically keep the ten. For how can we love the Lord with all our heart, soul, and mind, love others as we would love ourselves, and commit murder or adultery or lie or steal or covet?

James said:

> [8]If ye fulfil the royal law according to the scripture, Thou shalt love thy neighbour as thyself, ye do well: [9]But if ye have respect to persons, ye commit sin, and are convinced of the law as transgressors. [10]For whosoever shall keep the whole law, and yet offend in one point, he is guilty of all. [11]For he that said, Do not commit adultery, said also, Do not kill. Now if thou commit no adultery, yet if thou kill, thou art become a transgressor of the law. [12]So speak ye, and so do, as they that shall be judged by the law of liberty. [13]For he shall have judgment without mercy, that hath shewed no mercy; and mercy rejoiceth against judgment.

We are all human, so we all have sinned and broken the holy Law. Every single man, woman, child, and teenager on earth has (Romans 3:23). According to James, if we break one commandment but not another, we are still a transgressor of the whole Law. We are "guilty of [violating] all." Note that in verse 8, James' focus was not on stealing, lying, or any of the Ten Commandments the Church is accustomed to quoting, but on the one Christ gave in Matthew: that we would love all other human beings as we would ourselves. Then James brings this thought to a close with the concept that we must show others mercy.

Mercy continually.

Mercy when visitors to our congregation look or act differently than we want them to. Mercy when that new attendant has had more than two weeks to conform to our lifestyle and behavioral standards, yet still isn't up to our par. If the Body will stop trying to change people and love them instead, just as they are, right where they stand in life, as Christ has and does and will, then the light we show them will have lasting impact, and they will change via the anointed whisperings of the Holy Spirit's tugging… Through our love for them beyond their looks and behavior and spotted record, they will have just the smallest taste of the love they have every day and always from heaven eternal, and when they come to know the Lord, they will have a *desire* to bend to His perfect will instead of a cold obligation to.

And regarding verse 9: If we have respect for persons, all persons, then the greatest manifestation of that respect will show itself in how we spread the Gospel, whether that be for reaching those we respect or entertaining them with showmanship.

Church services and acceptance/respect of persons is just the tip of the iceberg. What James says next poses an even greater challenge. We're about to get radical.

Do you want to change the world?
Do you want to play a part in the next Great Awakening?

Make the decision that from today forward you will be a light to those around you by refusing to praise the rich man and place the poor man at the footstool—no matter what cultural application that holds for you.

Chapter 5

Deeds of a Modern Rahab

JAMES 2:14–26

EARLIER IN THIS book, we discussed the popular misconceptions of James' "faith without works is dead" Scripture. We did not, however, discuss what he had to say about Rahab. Believe me when I tell you that those present in the New Testament Palestine culture would have had an extreme reaction to James' position about her.

Let us take a moment to revisit James' words about faith, verbatim, without any interruptions. Then we'll look at the examples he gave to his readers:

[14]**What doth it profit, my brethren, though a man say he hath faith, and have not works? can faith save him?** [15]**If a brother or sister be naked, and destitute of daily food,** [16]**And one of you say unto them, Depart in peace, be ye warmed and filled; notwithstanding ye give them not those things which are needful to the body; what doth it profit?** [17]**Even so faith, if it hath not works, is dead, being alone.**

[18]**Yea, a man may say, Thou hast faith, and I have works: shew me thy faith without thy works, and I will shew thee my faith**

by my works. [19]Thou believest that there is one God; thou doest well: the devils also believe, and tremble. [20]But wilt thou know, O vain man, that faith without works is dead?

As a quick recapitulation: James is not saying that honest faith lies in rituals, but in charity and love. Love, charity, and faith are verbs. They require action. They force us to embrace the "whosoever will," whether we like how they live or what they do or how they look.

Whereas the previous chapter primarily addressed how the "whosoever will" are welcomed in church, this chapter takes it a step farther. As you will see in the coming pages, I believe this next move of God will involve movements outside church walls and involve personalities the Body never saw coming.

And I couldn't be more excited about that.

Abraham: Model of Faith

James goes on to give his first "faith justified by works" example of Abraham, one who lived his life in such faith that his works were uncompromisingly drastic when commanded to be:

[21]Was not Abraham our father justified by works, when he had offered Isaac his son upon the altar? [22]Seest thou how faith wrought with his works, and by works was faith made perfect? [23]And the scripture was fulfilled which saith, Abraham believed God, and it was imputed unto him for righteousness: and he was called the Friend of God. [24]Ye see then how that by works a man is justified, and not by faith only.

Most will recall the story of Abraham and his willingness to sacrifice his own son, his *only* son born of his marriage to Sarah, upon the altar when God told him to do so.

Isaac was the promised son. God had told Abraham that from this child would come many nations—so many offspring in his family line through Isaac that, like the stars in the sky, they could never be counted.

Abraham and his wife, Sarah, had already goofed and disobeyed the Lord once regarding the promised son when they got impatient waiting for Yahweh to open Sarah's womb in her old age, and their human solution to bring about the promise via their own means was to have Abraham lay with their maidservant, Hagar. The result of this unsanctified union was Ishmael. Ishmael was the first son of Abraham, but he was not the son God promised to bring about through Sarah.

The pain and heartache that came about through the maidservant/ Ishmael plan was enough to teach Abraham about real faith. When God says He will do something, He will do it, and even when we don't understand how, His ways are best.

Years later, when the Lord decided the timing was right, the Lord opened Sarah's womb, and Abraham and Sarah conceived, just as God said. Despite their old age, Abraham and Sarah received the promise they had been given.

Then came the day when God put Abraham's faith to the ultimate test. God commanded Abraham to sacrifice the promised son Isaac on the altar. After all that. After all the promises of future generations through the seed of Isaac… After everything they went through to have this boy, all the years spent waiting, getting to watch him grow into a young man, teaching him the ways of Yahweh, seeing him laugh and play and sing and be precious…then God commanded him to be killed on the altar.

Abraham showed unprecedented faith by preparing to carry out this command. He took Isaac, who had no idea he was the subject of sacrifice, up the mountain. When they arrived at the place of sacrifice, Abraham built an altar, dressed it with sticks, tied Isaac to it, and lifted his knife above Isaac to do the deed. The Angel of the Lord halted him at that moment and said, "Lay not thine hand upon the lad, neither do thou any thing unto him: for now I know that thou fearest God, seeing thou hast not withheld thy son, thine only son from me" (Genesis 22:12).

After this, the Lord, Himself, provided a sacrifice when Abraham discovered a ram caught by the horns in a nearby thicket. The ram was sacrificed in Isaac's place.

Many read this story and wonder what on earth was going through Abraham's mind during all of this. Didn't he love Isaac? Why would he be so willing to kill him? Why wouldn't the story have included a subplot wherein Abraham packed a bag in the middle of the night and told Isaac to run? Why aren't we told of some lengthy argument that Abraham had with God about the seemingly useless promised child "of many nations" who would die in such bloodshed before he was ever able to have even a single child of his own?

Many are so focused on the shock of the sacrifice details that they miss one crucial verse in the story: Genesis 22:8. After Abraham and Isaac left their traveling companions behind to go up the mountain alone the rest of the way, Isaac noticed that they had wood and fire to make an altar, but they didn't have the lamb. He asked his father about this, and Abraham responded, "My son, God will provide himself a lamb for a burnt offering."

Abraham already *knew* God would, Himself, provide a sacrifice. Abraham may not have known what that providence would look like, but he believed. He had faith. It was a die-hard, revolutionary, militant faith that if God promised a son who would father a great number of descendants, then God would fulfill that promise. God was true to His word the first time, and Isaac was conceived from a womb of a woman over ninety years old. If God told Abraham to sacrifice that child, then either God planned to provide a lamb at the last minute, or He was going to raise Isaac from the dead (which Abraham believed, according to Hebrews 11:19). Either way, God promised that Isaac was going to father many nations, and Abraham *so believed* the promise that not even Isaac's death would stand in the way of fulfillment.

So, no; Abraham didn't need to help Isaac escape or argue with God. According to verse 8, he already knew he was being tested, and that his works—his obedience to the command to sacrifice his son—were a part of his faith, and the two could not be divided, as they were parts of a whole.

James used the example of Abraham to show that through the *works* of his obedience, his *faith* was made perfect. Abraham was then called "Friend of God." The early Church would have gladly accepted Abraham as the model faith-by-works prototype.

But what James says next required his original audience to have an open, *open* mind.

Rahab: Model of...Faith?

Abraham is one thing. He's venerated. He's celebrated. He's a patriarch. He's one of "the greats." His actions affected the world in irreversible and astounding ways. It is because of him that we had Israel. Through Isaac's son, Jacob, we have the twelve tribes, all their descendants, and an entire ancient world filled with Yahweh's people. All of these channels led to the birth of Christ, our own eternal Redeemer, and Abraham was central to the inauguration of the entire plan from his own seed and forward. Of course we're going to revere Abraham and lift up that one obedient moment over and over again.

Um, but...

Rahab? Wasn't she a prostitute? An Old Testament woman who sold her body for money in Jericho?

Surely James is not suggesting that *she* was a woman of faith...

The story of Rahab (Hebrew *Rachab*) is an interesting one. As Joshua's two men were secretly surveying the land (cf. Joshua 6) that God had promised the Israelites, they sought lodging with Rahab the prostitute in Jericho. (According to Josephus, Rahab's house was actually an inn, so it likely would have functioned somewhat like a brothel. However, this idea some have latched onto that the two Israelite men went to Rahab for use of her colorful services is pure, sacrilegious speculation with no biblical support.) The king of Jericho received word that the Israelite men were staying with Rahab, and he sent for her, demanding that she bring them out. Rahab had already hidden the men from danger, placing them under flax stalks on her roof. Then she told the king she didn't know who they were or where they were from, and that they had left before the city gate shut at dusk. Rahab even went so far as to tell the king to "pursue after them quickly; for ye shall overtake them" (verse 5), pretending to support him in his threat against the men. The king sent pursuers out of the gate after the Israelites.

Rahab returned to the roof and spoke to the Israelites, telling them that all of Jericho greatly feared their God, Yahweh, because they had heard of all the wonders He had done for His people. She explained that the residents of Jericho were well aware that God had promised this land to the Israelites, and that "all the inhabitants of the land faint" (out of fear) at the mention of the Israelites (verse 9). A couple of verses later (11), she expressed her faith in the Israelite God, saying He was "God in heaven above, and in earth beneath."

This prostitute, this pagan, this "harlot," was willing to believe in Yahweh and save His men from danger—despite the threat to her own life if she were discovered. As far as it has been documented, there was not one holy thing in her lifestyle, her behavior, or her spiritual life before these two Israelite men came into her home. But something deeply resonated "truth, truth, truth" within her each time she heard of the almighty power of Israel's God, so that when His men arrived, she didn't for a second think that Jericho could oppose them. She immediately reacted to a still, small voice inside that told her to respond favorably to God's will and purposes.

She only asked one thing from the men in return for her kindness and protection: that her family would be spared.

The Israelite men vowed in agreement, even to their own death, that they would protect her as she had them (14).

Because the construction of her home was part of the city wall (which would be an ideal location for a brothel or inn, as visitors to the city would see it upon entering), the two men were able to escape through the window by climbing down a scarlet "thread." (This "thread" was probably some kind of sash or scarf she had used in the past to catch the eye of her clientele, as it would not make sense in those days that a utility rope would be dyed red, or that a prostitute would have a random, red utility rope. Interestingly, many believe that the "red light" traditions of later brothels or city districts devoted to devious relations at night originated with the scarlet thread of Rahab.) Before her visitors left, Rahab told them of the pursuers and instructed them to hide in the hills for three days until the pursuers gave up and returned. The men responded gratefully and told her to tie the scarlet thread in the window so that nobody in her home would be harmed.

Later, when the march around the city walls of Jericho led to every wall crumbling under the supernaturally charged blast of the trumpets and a mighty shout, Joshua sent his men into the home with a scarlet thread at its window to retrieve Rahab and her family.

Her mother, father, brothers, and clan were all spared as a result of her acting upon a conviction from a God she didn't know and couldn't understand in the pagan life she had led. It could be described as her merely responding to a hunch that the rumors she had heard about the Israelites were true and she acted out of fear, but that would not explain her expression of faith in the "God in heaven above, and in earth beneath." It is more sensible to see that Rahab had her own Holy-Spirit gut-check, and Someone she didn't know told her to heed the men and their mission and do all she must to support them. Further support of this theory is her trust of these strangers who lodged with her. If Rahab was from a pagan city, and her life was built upon selling her body and lies and deceit and debauchery, why would she simply believe the Israelite messengers when they said they would spare her—and then *stay put* as instructed like a sitting duck to see if they kept their word? She trusted them because she was trusting in something, Someone, larger than herself and the life she was used to. Everyone else in Jericho had *heard of* the Israelite God, but only she *chose* Him.

She had faith.

Her faith was backed by works.

James saw *this* side of the story when he referred to Rahab in his epistle. After mentioning the renowned patriarch Abraham, James speaks of the works of Rahab's faith:

²⁵Likewise also was not Rahab the harlot justified by works, when she had received the messengers, and had sent them out another way? ²⁶For as the body without the spirit is dead, so faith without works is dead also.

I cannot even describe the boom this verse must have had on the people groups of the New Testament. Some today still have a hard time wrapping their brains around the idea that a pagan prostitute is revered as an icon of hospitality and repentance. But in James' day, he was using a woman with a very wicked past to glorify the concept of faith through works! He could have chosen anyone out of the Holy Word to use as an example of good works, yet he chose a woman the religious men of his day would have stoned to death. Her very name in the temple scrolls must have made the Pharisees recoil. To them, the exchange between Rahab and the Israelites would have only been a business deal: her life spared for their lives spared. She helped them, so they did the right thing—not by saving her, but by keeping a vow they made in order to save themselves. And, at the end of the day, the glory was focused on the deeds of the holy men, not on the sinful woman.

In order to understand the boldness of James' charge, we have to unplug from the modern iconography of Rahab. Today, a woman like her might earn claps and amens, but to the culture of the early Church, she was someone to be taken out into the middle of a city and brutally, bloodily killed as a public example. Just a string of years before James' epistle was written, the scribes and Pharisees had brought an adulteress to Christ outside the temple. They were planning to stone her to death right then and there in obedience to the Mosaic Law, but in an attempt to trap Christ in a word battle, they asked Him to respond to the issue. His reply, like James' words about Rahab, was shocking: "He that is without sin among you, let him first cast a stone at her" (John 8:7). So, as recently as his half-brother's final years of ministry, James had become very accustomed to women in Rahab's profession being carted out to the public square to endure inhumanely painful, humiliating, and agonizing deaths, because they were considered the scum of the earth. They were nothing to the religious people groups for centuries but a scab upon the Name of God that needed to be removed harshly and swiftly. There was no saying sorry, no making it right, no reparation for the damage upon honor that prostitution or adultery stacked upon women such as these—and anyone connected to them in any social way.

Honor was everything. Seminary professor of New Testament and Greek studies, David deSilva, wrote the amazing book, *Honor, Patronage, Kinship, & Purity: Unlocking New Testament Culture*. This book stands alone as one of the most well-researched resources I have read regarding what the world was like in the days of the early Church, but it also happens to be used as a collateral reading assignment book for many Christian universities. DeSilva begins his first chapter with the statement: "The culture of the first-century world was built on the foundational social values of honor and dishonor."[6] He goes on to say: "Honor…is viewed as the first and foremost consideration…. [W]hile honor with pleasure was a great good, pleasure without honor was the worst evil. Those who put pleasure ahead of honor were considered to be more animal-like than human…. In the first century B.C. a teacher of public speakers held up honor and security as the two primary considerations when trying to win an audience over to support the course of action the speaker promoted… [and] successful orators were the ones who could demonstrate that the course of action they advocated led to the greatest honor."[7]

Again, honor meant *everything* to the people groups of the New Testament culture, and one of the biggest slams on honor fathomable was a woman who dedicated her life to breaking up marriages and exchanging sexual favors for money, all the while desecrating her own body in pursuit of the most illicit of worldly pleasures. Her reasoning for such a lifestyle (even if she had carried it out in order to feed starving children) wouldn't have mattered to those who believed God would provide for all her needs without her having to resort to prostitution. To the Jews, Gentiles, and early Christians of James' day, as well as those remaining Pharisees, Rahab's name had no business being written down at all for any reason beyond the necessity of historical narrative and factual documentation of her dealings with the Israelite messengers of Joshua. Even suggesting she could have turned from her wicked ways and been redeemed was a stretch, and it's likely that, if it came up in conversation, people would be tripping all over themselves in a race to see who could be first to list her transgressions—*not* call her "justified by works"!

Sure, the early Church was gradually coming around to accept the idea that all could be forgiven and that Christ had died for that very purpose, but we're looking at a letter to the Church that was written in its infancy. It was a newborn. It had very little direction or comprehension beyond the Pentateuch and rabbinic writings of the Jews alongside the well-established and socially powerful force of the last-word Pharisees. The day James inked up his quill and started writing the words we just read, Rahab was just a harlot who gotten really lucky and made a smart business arrangement with the Israelites. She wasn't "a *faithful* person." She wasn't "*justified.*" She wasn't "hospitable." Nobody cared about her redemption. She was hardly a person, except when someone's name needed to be dropped for shock value. Her résumé simply read "the harlot." She was, to the first-century, religious people groups, absolutely, indisputably a worthless person whose name existed in record only, but whose value to the people of God wasn't even a question.

Yet, look at what became of her. She married Salmon and bore Boaz. Boaz was the kinsman redeemer who married Ruth the Moabite in the beautiful story of Naomi and Ruth. Ruth and Boaz had Obed, Obed had Jesse, and Jesse had—drumroll please—David.

The David.

King David. The very David from whose family line the Messiah was promised to hail.

Rahab the prostitute was Jesus Christ's great, great, great (insert many more "greats" here) grandmother.

Many reflect upon the story of Rahab as if it only relates to how God uses all who are willing, no matter their past, if they will turn from their wickedness and follow Him. Whereas her story most definitely *is* perfectly suited for such a category, for the purpose of our thread here, it's so much more than that. Today, Rahab stands as a shining example of precisely why we can, should, and *must* believe in redemption for the "whosoever will"—even when that individual's life is sinfully shocking to our core. We never know which "shocking" people out there are miserable in their sin, are looking for redemption, and whose lives might be beautifully and crucially turned around for the purposes of God.

Everyone loves the wonders of Abraham, through whose seed all generations would be blessed. But nobody really seems to stop and think about the fact that it was through Rahab's womb and the seed of her son Boaz, the kinsman redeemer, that we would eventually see the birth of the Almighty Redeemer!

To the New Testament culture, the Rahabs would have been too far gone. Too far removed from any redemptive potential to be cared about. A lost cause. The *farthest* possible human life away from the Lord's reach. The subject of a public stoning.

She treated two messengers of Joshua kindly; they, in turn, treated an indecent woman with dignity and showed her kindness (a kindness that the New Testament society would have likely never shown her)—and she was thereafter redeemed. Heralded as a hero. Chosen by God to be in the very family tree of Christ, Himself. Hebrews 11 names all the great elders: Abel, Enoch, Noah, Abraham, Isaac, Jacob, Joseph, even Moses! And right there, in the middle of all the "greats" and all the "faithfuls" is Rahab. The harlot. The prostitute. The unredeemable…

She found forgiveness through repentance and a change from an old nature to a new one.

She became a completely new creature!

If it seems too far-fetched for that to be possible, consider 2 Corinthians

5:17: "Therefore if any man [or woman] be in Christ, he [or she] is a new creature: old things are passed away; behold, all things are become new."

All old things are passed away. *All* things are new.

Take the words of James, consider the culture in which they were written, and think of how they may apply today. Who is today's Rahab? If Rahab, a woman representing some of the worst of all sins at the time the book of James was written, was remembered as "justified"— some Bible translations say "righteous"—then whose potential redemption today are we ignoring? What current Rahabs are we shunning away from the Gospel? What people groups are we so shocked by that we look the other way in their presence instead of caring about their souls? Who do we consider to be today's "lost causes"?

Rejecting the Rahabs

Any time we show people outright rejection before we show them love, it is a sin, whether we are rejecting them for something we're guilty of in the past as well or not. James said that if we have transgressed on one point of the Law, we have transgressed the whole Law (2:10), and that the greatest way to uphold the law is to love others (2:8). We don't have to partake of a specific sin to become "that kind" of sinner, because there is no such thing as "that kind" of sinner. It's all sin when any one biblical standard has been selfishly forsaken. James said that if we murder someone but we didn't cheat on our spouse, we've still transgressed the whole law (2:10–11). By that logic, if we don't kill people, steal cars, or set buildings on fire, but we still reject others, we've still transgressed. Some sins, like telling a white lie, are considered no big deal, and redemption and love are available for "those sinners," according to our Church mindset today. But other sins, such as porn addictions, prostitution, premarital sex, teen pregnancies, and youth promiscuity are harder for us to wrap our minds around.

I know in advance that the following reflections will be off-putting to some. But it is my prayer that it will cause some to stop and really think about the precious creatures of God around us that we may be hurting.

How do we respond to a woman wearing six-inch heels and fishnet stockings, standing on a street corner in a busy city, asking passersby if they're looking for a good time? Do we smile at her as if she is a person with equal eternity-value, or do we sneer and turn up our chins? What about the man at work who brags about his pornography collection? Do we look for an opportunity to be kind while we gently change the subject to something inclusive and appropriate, or do we corner him and drop a verse down his throat? When we see that young girl we've only met twice who just had an abortion, do we pray for her in secret or rebuke her in person? How about that fifteen-year-old "punk" hanging around outside the burger joint openly discussing his raging sex life—who just asked you about your own? Do you avoid answering, politely head to your car, and pray for his life to find new direction as you head home? Or do you blast him with a string of curse words and give him a reason to revel in his successful juvenile provocation?

And what about those homosexuals you know? Is there hope for them, also? Or are they the spiritually untouchables? Should they be in church on Sunday?

Before I lose you on this one, understand that we are at the cusp of a *fantastic* move of the Lord, and it will come at a time when homosexual rights and social agendas are the highest they have ever been historically. Whether or not the idea of mingling with a person who proclaims a divergent orientation makes us uncomfortable, a great number of Christians *will* be placed in this position. For this very reason, I want to spend a few pages in specific consideration of homosexuals. What will we, as individuals and as the Body, choose to do when we are placed in their path?

What a difficult situation…

Is the homosexual lifestyle an issue that falls within a scriptural "essential" as outlined in the previous chapter? I believe so, yes. It is repeatedly referred to as an outright sin and abomination in the Word, both in the Old Testament that Christ came to fulfill down to the letter (cf. Matthew 5:17–18) and in the New Testament (see: Genesis 19:1–13; Leviticus 18:22, 20:13; Romans 1:26–27; 1 Corinthians 6:9).

Homosexuality is a sin. Many Christians will say *amen* at this point in the reflection.

But so is rejection. Many Christians will pause at this point in the reflection and wonder what it is I'm suggesting.

It's actually quite sad. I have asked the "should they be in church?" question to several of my Christian friends, and their answers have been naïve. We can ask the same question about any other kind of sinner today—a drunk, a thief, a porn addict, a pregnant and unmarried teenager, almost anyone—and the answer is a resounding yes: *They* should be in church. But homosexuals? Well, only if they repent *first* and vow to forever turn from their lifestyle.

Repent *first*? Why would anyone do that? How can people be expected to commit their lives to something they haven't experienced yet or to a Deity they don't already know? Why do we continually treat their sin differently than we do the sins of others?

I am not suggesting that homosexual individuals should be allowed to enter churches and cause dissention, argue with everyone, make passes at members of the same sex, mislead people with opposing philosophies, and let their voices be heard above the Gospel. That takes the virtue of tolerance to an extreme that disrespects the House of the Lord. I am, however, saying that homosexuals should be allowed to enter churches and be treated with dignity and respect, because as humans, they are as important as anyone else to the Lord. This same truly loving treatment should *especially* be carried by Christ-ians outside church buildings and into the world where homosexuals typically reside.

A gay man must be shown either through the witness of true Christians or through the Holy Spirit's direct intervention that he is loved despite his lifestyle before he will feel the conviction to change it. A lesbian must know that she will be accepted as a human with value despite her relationship with her girlfriend before she hears anything a Christian has to say. The same goes for a drunkard, a prostitute, a thief, and every other person whose life is in conflict with what the Lord deems holy and just. We Christians tend to have open minds about drunkards, prostitutes, and thieves…then a gay person enters the room and we roll our eyes or shake our heads—or worse, openly scoff at the person. And I've *seen* this, personally. Many times.

Can't we see the sin in this?

In order to shed some balance on this issue, however, the principle of mutual respect needs to be in effect. The homosexual community has been, in recent decades, so committed to their freedom agendas that *at times* they have crossed the line from seeking legal and social equality to demanding superiority. That is not true for all, but some have become very antagonistic. So, the Church as a whole has understandably put its hands up in defense, and a raging war has ensued between "us" and "them." Instead of this war being about social equality in a secular sphere, many Christians have decided to fight secular social justice with religion and Scripture—the Scripture that a great number of homosexuals don't believe in anyway and therefore don't respect—and the result becomes aggressive proselytizing versus liberal jabs, back and forth, back and forth. Whether we stand on the side of conservative Christianity or liberal homosexuality, respect must be mutual, and if there is ever to be peace, ears from *both sides* need to be quick to listen; tongues must be slow to speak; hearts need to be slow to anger.

Consider for a moment the wedding cake fiasco a few years back. In January of 2013, Rachel and Laurel Bowman-Cryer, a lesbian couple, sought to order a cake from a shop in Gresham, Oregon, for their same-sex wedding. Aaron and Melissa Klein, owners of Sweet Cakes by Melissa, who had baked Rachel's mother's wedding cake in 2011, refused service to the women on the grounds that the Kleins' Christianity could not support gay marriage. The lesbian couple filed a complaint to the Oregon Bureau of Labor and Industries, claiming an infringement of civil rights under the Oregon Equality Act. The case went to court, and for months on end drew global attention in a messy dispute. Ultimately, the bakery shop went out of business when the state awarded the Bowman-Cryer couple a $135,000 settlement to be paid by Aaron and Melissa.

Let's take a moment to view just a couple of the facts contributing to this case, based on the court testimonies of involved parties:[8]

- The Bowman-Cryer couple met Melissa when they first bought Cheryl's (Rachel's mother's) wedding cake in 2011. It was at that point established that Rachel and Laurel were a lesbian couple. It's entirely possible that Melissa and Aaron had many clients at the time and forgot this detail by the time Rachel and Laurel were engaged later on and planning their own wedding. Nevertheless, Rachel placed the order, and the payment for Cheryl's cake, which came from the same-sex couple Rachel and Laurel, was accepted.

- In late 2012, Sweetcakes by Melissa manned a booth at a Portland, Oregon, bridal show for promotional purposes. Rachel reestablished contact with Melissa Klein and, according to her testimony, explained their upcoming same-sex wedding. Emails were exchanged regarding the appointment for a cake-tasting, in which (it is claimed that) the nature of the same-sex wedding was clear. According to court testimonies, Melissa agreed to follow up with a cake-tasting appointment via a conversation through the Internet that involved full disclosure of the homosexual wedding.

- In January of 2013, Rachel and her mother Cheryl (who had one of Melissa's cakes featured at her wedding two years prior) arrived at the Sweetcakes shop for the tasting appointment. Melissa was absent, so Aaron conducted what became a very short interview. He began by asking the name of the bride and groom. When he was provided with the name of two brides, he explained that Sweetcakes did not bake cakes for same-sex weddings on the basis of religious (Christian) conviction. Cheryl asked why Rachel and Laurel's money would have been accepted in the past for her own cake. If Sweetcakes did not support same-sex couples, then why would Sweetcakes accept money from a same-sex couple earlier on, regardless of the couple it was intended for? Cash is cash, and business is business. (His answer is not recorded in the testimonial.)

- Rachel, feeling that she had publicly shamed her mother Cheryl (who had believed that homosexuality was a sin until a couple years before this event) began to cry and repeatedly apologize for who and what she was. Cheryl escorted Rachel to the car, drove around for a while consoling her, and then returned to the shop.

- Upon Cheryl's return, Rachel remained in the car while Cheryl reentered the building and spoke personally with Aaron. She explained that she used to share his convictions, but after having raised two homosexual children, her "truth had changed."[9]

- Aaron proceeded to quote from Leviticus 18:22 (translation: he dropped a verse), and explained that Cheryl's children were "an abomination unto God."[10]

The rest of the testimony from the lesbian couple involves a lot of self-shame and questioning why God would allow someone to be born a homosexual if he or she was just an abomination to begin with. Many tears were shed, and more questions than can be counted were raised as to whether an active homosexual deserves to celebrate his or her relationship the same way a heterosexual couple would. Rachel became depressed about her identity, while Laurel grew irate. However, they found an alternative bakery that agreed to accommodate same-sex weddings, and sold the couple a $600 cake for $250. Despite this agreeable solution, the media caught wind of the story and started reporting it from one coast to the other as hate mail flooded the inboxes of the Klein couple as well as the Bowman-Cryer couple. As a result of the media exposure, familial relations ended (one particularly dramatic event involved a death threat by Laurel's aunt: She would be shot in the face if Laurel ever "set foot on the family's property"[11]). Rachel's sister contacted the Kleins to give them their support over her own sister.

Further complaints from the lesbian couple were filed involving emotional damages, while the Kleins continued to unite and post updates on their bakery windows and Facebook profiles regarding religious rights freedoms. They raised a half million dollars via the GoFundMe site to pay for legal representation. (This funding was later shut down by the organization because of a conflict in its terms of service.) All the while, Rachel and Laurel were seeing to the adoption of two special-needs children, and hate mail and social media comments made them fear for their lives as well as for the lives of their two girls. However, testimonies by the same-sex couple were seen as heavily exaggerated and questionable due to emotional distress.

On the part of the Kleins, the story is quite simple: A bride entered the building for a tasting she scheduled with Melissa, announced that the cake was for a same-sex couple, and was refused service on religious conviction. Subsequently, when questioned by the bride's mother as to why service was refused, biblical evidence was offered that backed the bakery owner's decision. From the bakery owners' point of view, nothing about their refusal of service was intended to be personal. (*It should be stated that it was within their rights to refuse service on these grounds.* Abstaining from service based on religious belief is a legal right that needs to be preserved in the current political environment.)

Today, the battle rages on. The lesbian couple lives with their two daughters (now legally adopted), who attend pride parades and gay rights activities alongside their two mothers—and because of the Kleins' appeals, the money awarded the Bowman-Cryer couple in court remains locked in a government account. The Kleins continue to fight for religious freedom, touring the country and making headlines.

Okay, where do I start with this one? Here are two naturally opposing people groups, both claiming that their freedom rights (civil and religious) were attacked. Who's the bad guy here? The Christian couple or the lesbian couple?

My answer might surprise you.

Both couples acted out of line…*and it is important that this statement is understood on the basis of moral, ethical, and eternal implications, not on politics!* While the Christian bakers had—and have—the right to decline service based on religious preferences, I believe they mishandled an opportunity to be a gentle light in a dark world. And while the homosexual couple had—and have—the right to be treated with decency and respect, I believe they mishandled an opportunity to give the same respect and freedom they were demanding.

On one hand, we have a Christian couple who claim—by default of Christ-ian conviction—to be Christ's ambassadors. Yet, by telling some-one, *anyone*, that they were an abomination within their first conversation with them, they threw away an opportunity to develop a friendship with someone who may later on seek real counsel from a believer. They com-pletely trashed an occasion to witness about the love of Christ (which, as stated earlier, likely should not be done in an initial conversation either, until after a period of showing love, because people don't care what we know until they know how we care). Rachel and Laurel weren't asking them to endorse anything, perform the ceremony, or weigh in with any opinion at all. They were asking them to toss ingredients in a bowl in exchange for money, which was the business they were in. What these lesbian women were asking for had nothing to do with forcing the Kleins to march in pride parades or raise rainbow flags. If a sinful man and a sin-ful woman had been getting married, the Kleins wouldn't have made the spiritual position of the man and woman an issue. Only when he heard the word "homosexual" did Aaron reject the sale. Likewise, if a homo-sexual had asked for a birthday cake, it wouldn't have been an issue. The phrase "same-sex wedding" was what prompted Aaron to reject the sale. Far, *far* worse than rejecting the sale was that he subsequently dropped a verse and rejected the *people*. He caused them hurt, drew a line in the sand between God and homosexuals, and represented Christianity with elitism. He went well beyond the business transaction of refusing service when he told Cheryl that her children were abominations unto God. (Not to mention, if the information that came out during the court hearings was accurate, Melissa had already known of the nature of the relationship and had agreed to a tasting, so the Kleins backed out of a sale to which they had already agreed.)

On the other hand, although the homosexual community doesn't cel-ebrate the concept of love in the same way Christians do, that community bases its entire striving for equality on the foundation of freedom in love. At the core of all the requests or demands is the yearning to be able to love whom they want, how they feel led. Whether or not Christians agree with them, homosexuals believe they were born that way, and many even say God created them to be what they are. Though Christians don't really see it from this angle, everything the warring homosexuals are trying to accomplish is central to a new concept of love and liberty. They are aware as they fight for rights that their lifestyles cause a great stir for opposing people groups, and this very moment in history could be their defining moment to make the most graciously loving, understanding, and forgiving move in a case like this, so that they might stand as a shining example of homosexuals everywhere. If they want to change the world and make it a more open-minded planet, the *last* thing they should do is sue opposing social groups and file complaints with the government when they don't get what they want. All that does is feed the flames of anger in those who would call them "abominations" to their face in the first place. Yes, the Kleins missed an opportunity to witness and share about their beliefs. But so, too, did Rachel and Laurel when they made their own form of rejection by responding to an attack with another attack.

Many Christians are not equipped to answer questions regarding *why* homosexuality is a sin; they simply state that it is because the Bible tells us so, leaving many hurting and confused souls to wonder why they must feel isolated from God's loving grace. When homosexuals feel rejected by God's people, and by extension, by God—when they partake in a lifestyle that is displeasing to God, yet God's finite messengers on earth can't tell them *why* it's displeasing—then how can we, as Christians, act surprised when they in turn regard us with disdain? And they often do. Understandably, this only leads to a battle in which now *both* sides feel like the victim, the oppressed, the attacked, and no peace offering is louder than the battle cry.

One of my best friends for the last almost-twenty years is a homosexual. For the sake of complete anonymity, let's call this person "T." I asked T's opinion about the Sweetcakes case when it was in the height of media coverage, half expecting T to stand up for the lesbian couple. My friend surprised me by outlining *precisely* what I just said above, in far more colorful words. In fact, T was angrier at Rachel and Laurel for their legal aggression and how that "made the homosexual community look like a bunch of whining children to the rest of the world in a time when we're already at the center of the worst kind of attention." I laughed at this response, and then shared that the couple that angered *me* more were the Kleins…for the same basic reason: They represented God and Christianity legalistically, and simultaneously hurt another person's feelings during a time when Christians are becoming more and more persecuted on a global level. But the interesting lesson in all of this is the fact that when T's community was at war with my community, both of us were offended by the representatives of our own "side," because of how passionate we both feel about being at peace with—and caring about—others whose beliefs and practices differ from our own.

It should never be assumed that, because I have a gay friend whom I love, appreciate, and get along peacefully with, I am in support of this person's lifestyle. It's quite the contrary, and T is aware of that. But let me share how this friendship came about in order to explain how we have arrived where we are.

It was almost twenty years ago. My roommate (we will call her simply "Roommate") and I liked to stay up late and hit the twenty-four-hour coffee shops in the wee hours with magazines while we ordered junk food, got jazzed on caffeine, and sang Broadway show tunes. One particular night, T was our server. Roommate and I were looking at a magazine when T leaned over, pointed at a model from a jeans advertisement, and told us how attractive the model was. At this moment I realized T was gay. As soon as T was out of earshot, I proceeded to tell Roommate how shocked I was by this person's lifestyle. I started dropping verses and gossiping— absolutely slandering this person whose value I couldn't see past my own grand "shining light of Christianity." I went on and on. Like a blithering idiot. A self-righteous know-it-all. Acting like I was in a position to know anything about what God thinks of this person. When T came back for another round of refills, I was all smiles and sunshine, and then again, shamefully, when T walked away, it was another thirteen rounds about "what the Bible says."

After a while, Roommate and I burst into an impromptu *Phantom of the Opera* performance. (The coffeehouse was basically empty.) T heard us singing, instantly came to the table, and grabbed a third harmony line with an impressive pitch, knowing every fast-moving lyric from one of the more obscure and complicated numbers in that score. When the three of us finished, we broke into a fit of laughter. I had never seen anything like it. I didn't waste any time searching my internal Broadway knowledge base for another song, and the first one I thought of was another that T knew from beginning to end—all the harmonies, all the lyrics, and all those difficult little modulations, crescendos, and diminuendos that make Broadway music so emotional and dramatic. Afterward, there was another song. And another. And another. The dynamic of our three voices together was an experience that defied all explanation.

We ended up staying there for hours, and because it was such an odd time of night, there were almost no other customers demanding T's attention. T continued to amaze me with responses to my interests. T not only knew just about everything I did about the scores (and I was a tough competitor in this avenue, let me tell you), T also knew the names of all the great stage performers whose careers I had been following since I was old enough to read. From the hall-of-famers like Albert Finney, Bernadette Peters, Sarah Brightman, and Michael Crawford to the lesser-known names such as Philip Quast, Lea Solonga, and Anthony Warlow, T knew them all. It didn't stop there, either. As it turned out, we had the same fascinations in books, television, movies, art, and off-Broadway musicians, as well as very similar life philosophies. We laughed, harmonized, and talked until the sun rose.

On the way home, I told Roommate—a *very* sweet and nonjudgmental girl, by the way—that I still didn't care for T's choices, but that I had just had the blast of a lifetime. Then, as if on cue, I went back into my diatribe about how the Bible says this and that and so on. Roommate put up with my narrow mind about this for days. I couldn't seem to let it go. She could bring up a subject about tacos or hairspray or clothespins, and the conversation would turn back to that epic coffeehouse trip.

On the one hand, I told her, I couldn't stop thinking about how much fun we had with T and how easily I could see us all being friends forever. On the other hand, I definitely could not see over the natural wall built by the Christianity-versus-homosexuality conundrum. It was my responsibility as a Christian (or so I thought at the time) to make sure T knew my position and understood that my convictions went against all that T was, but the more I argued within myself, the more I couldn't help just wanting to get over it, be nice, love everyone, and go back to the coffeehouse for another night of harmony. Common sense told me that sharing my opinions in person with T would nearly guarantee a burned bridge. Echoing voices from past sermons told me that I had no choice but to tell it like it is and hope the lost soul would be won for Christ as a result.

I realize now that this was a gut-check. A gut-check that lasted for days. A Holy-Spirit prompting. Telling me to love the "whosoever will." Telling me to hold my tongue and wait. I prayed about it, earnestly, and in my prayers, I begged the Lord to change T so I could have a new friend. (As if a friend is only a friend *after* the person has agreed to live the way you think he or she should...) But all the while I was asking the Lord to change T, the Holy Spirit was using my experience with T to change *me*.

The next time Roommate and I went back to the coffeehouse, T was on shift. We enjoyed another incredible night, much like the first. When the sun was coming up, I boldly asked to exchange contact info with T, and even more boldly asked if we could have lunch together sometime soon, the three of us. T agreed, and a couple days later, we were sitting in the comfy chairs of a bookstore café drinking mochas and eating cheesecake. As we talked casually, I kept praying on the inside that I would be given an incredible chance to witness about the Lord. A couple of times I started to, but something stopped me, and I took the conversation in a different direction. It wasn't because I was ashamed of the Gospel or scared to share it; I just didn't feel the timing was right. So we ate, laughed as usual, and had an amazing visit. When we were done, the three of us agreed we simply didn't want our gathering to end, so we walked outside and around the corner to the sidewalk entryway of an abandoned clothing store to talk some more.

We were only there for about twenty seconds when T noticed the acoustics of our voices were bouncing off the walls and amplifying into the street. So, naturally, we had to break into a thousand Broadway numbers back-to-back for the rest of the day. People on the sidewalks kept stopping to listen and clap and cheer, and one young man even gave us each a dollar, insisting that we take it as our first stage-performance payment. T excitedly named this location "the echo room," and it was the beginning of a two-year-long period when, at every available moment, the three of us were there, standing at our "singing spots," harmonizing.

Shortly into my friendship with T, probably our second visit to the echo room, I shared that I was a Christian. If the expression on T's face could have had corresponding audio, it would have said, "This is it, isn't it? The end of our relationship? It's over? I'm an abomination to you, aren't I? You're going to tell me I have to believe what you believe in order to be friends, aren't you?" I could just see the disappointment, the agonizing years of judgment this precious soul had endured from those in my religious people group. (Remember, this was almost twenty years ago, when being a homosexual was a different thing in society.) Nevertheless, the words T spoke were, "If you let me be me, I'll let you be you. Can we agree on that?" I nodded, and for about six months, that was the only conversation we had about it. I never tried to change T. I never argued, dropped verses, quoted Scriptures, or shoved anything in T's face about my beliefs. I couldn't bring myself to. I loved T deeply, and from some internal, spiritual place I couldn't yet understand, I was being told to wait.

Let my life be a witness, and let my tongue be slow to speak.

I prayed this continually.

However, from the moment of that announcement on, T started sharing things with me. I began to know the life story and real person behind the "homosexual" title. The things T had seen and the trials T had gone through were of a completely different world than the one in which I had been brought up. When shaking hands with T for the first time, I saw smiles and laughter. But after getting to know the heart of T, I saw pain and rejection. Depth. Character. Strength. T was a truly incredible person. T loved *everyone*. T accepted *everyone*. T went out of the way to make the world a better place through actions of peace and kindness every single hour of every single day, despite the fact that T's life road had been much harder to travel than mine. Although T didn't believe in Christ, T was doing a better job of modeling love than many of my Christian friends. When something was said I disagreed with, I kept my mouth shut and waited until I was alone later on to pray. I remained slow to speak, slow to anger, and quick to *listen*. I prayed constantly for wisdom. For direction.

The day came when I came clean and told T about how harshly I had spoken that first night at the coffeehouse behind T's back. Roommate was there when I owned up to my actions, and she nodded as I confessed my shame. I wasn't saying these things to hurt T. On the contrary, I wanted T to see that through being a part of my life, through knowing T, God had completely changed me. T had made me a better friend. A better person. A better *Christian*. If I was ever going to be a light to the lost, I needed to learn to care about all people, and what better way to learn this lesson than through submersion? Although my first instinct was to pray that God change T, by the time I told T what I had said out of earshot during that initial meeting, there was no doubt in my mind, and there still isn't, that the Lord brought T into my life to change *me*.

Almost twenty years later, T is still one of my dearest and closest friends. Throughout that time, I have been given ample opportunity to judge and criticize as hard-hitters have come into some of our conversations, but I have chosen to speak to T with respect and dignity. As a result, T has been open to hearing my opinion on the very subjects I originally wanted to address and felt the timing wasn't right. We have discussed marriage rights, politics, socialism, and even who should be allowed into what public bathrooms. T's position has remained the same for two decades, but so has mine—*gently* so.

Do you want to know the most beautiful victory in all this? I cannot count—I absolutely *cannot count*—the number of times T has come to me for my outlook…and T hears what I have to say, even when my convictions are biblical in origin. I have heard many times that I am the *only* Christian that T will listen to and talk to. How many times have we talked about the Bible? Hundreds, at least. Twice in the past, T has even asked me to pray about something (which I did, fervently).

Through T, as well as independently, I have gained many other homosexual friends—one of whom told me last year that I had played a crucial role in leading her to the Lord (she has since surrendered her homosexual lifestyle to Christ). But with all of my friends, whether they are homosexual or not, I value the *person* before I value telling him or her what I know about Scripture. I pray every day that the Lord will help me always be slow to speak, slow to anger, and quick to listen—and that I will continue to show people how I care before I tell people what I know.

By no means do I intend to compare T (or any homosexual) to Rahab, nor would I intend to suggest that their lifestyles and choices are similar, but I know that certain groups in the early Church of New Testament times would have made that connection. Many in the Church of today do. Many in the Church would pounce on the opportunity to wag a finger in T's face (and they have, *oh* they have), focusing more on the sins of a homosexual than on the soul-value God has given to every living person.

Although T is not Rahab, T was *my* scarlet thread out of Jericho. Had I stayed in that tiny mindset I had about people whose lives don't parallel my own, I likely would have spiritually died there, stunted forever in a verse-dropping, worthless religion defined by judgment and contempt.

It started with how I interacted with the gay community, as can be expected…but it quickly trickled down into every single other relationship I have ever had in my life since, which was not expected. As a conservative Christian: I have been forced into an awkward social mold many times; there is almost always an initial guard raised when a homosexual person discovers my belief system; I have watched as other Christians in my circles have immediately written me off as a liberal because of the individuals I call friends; I have silently observed the staunch disdain between homosexuals and Christians…and I have grown increasingly frustrated by the idea that an entire community of people in the Church is asleep to reaching because we cannot rise above this Jerichoic, Rahab/holy men wall.

I am reminded of lyrics from "Asleep in the Light" by Keith Green, one of the greatest and most anointed Christian songwriters in history:

> Do you see, do you see, all the people sinking down?
> Don't you care? Don't you care? Are you gonna let them drown?
> How can you be so numb, not to care if they come?
> You close your eyes and pretend the job's done....
> The world is sleeping in the dark that the Church just can't fight
> 'cause it's asleep in the light.
> How can you be so dead, when you've been so well fed?
> Jesus rose from the grave, and *you*! You can't even get out of bed![12]

How long have we been "asleep in the light" while an entire community is sinking all around us? Homosexuality is a sin, but so is homophobia and self-righteous, Pharisee-branded condemnation of others.

Do you want to know the real difference between the sin of same-sex relationships and all the other biblical sins in today's social arena? Let me break it down: It's the only one that has an enormously powerful and political lobbying group promoting, sponsoring, backing, and advocating it; it's one of the only biblical sins that a reputable psychiatric professional or counselor would embolden people to be open about, encouraging them to believe they were born that way, and that they should embrace who they really are. If a kleptomaniac sought help from a counselor about his overwhelming lust for stealing cars, that counselor would not tell him that he had been born that way and that he should embrace it. If he is logical, he would tell the man that it doesn't matter if he was born that way; he should *fight* the urge to steal because the harm he is committing to society around him is clearly and immediately present to all people groups. If, tomorrow, legislation somehow ushered in a new level of tolerance for theft, and this man became open about his kleptomania and marched down the streets with theft-pride flags, it would not change the fact that he would still be committing a sin each time he embraced what he wants, regardless of how celebrated his lifestyle had become within his social circles and the surrounding culture. But, we need to remember that with each passing day, whether we agree with and support homosexual lifestyles or not, whether we believe homosexuals were born that way or not, they have an enormous level of support—with or without our approval. To shame them and tell them they're abominations is not *saving* anyone from anything.

They are *precious* people whose souls are loved as much as anyone else's. Homosexuals will not come to know Christ through clobbering, force, judgment, and anger any more effectively than we Christians would convert to a radical Islamic faith (just as an example) through clobbering, force, judgment, and anger. We are going about all of this the wrong way.

That is true regarding homosexuals, and that is true regarding all the other treasurable lives we disdain through self-righteousness and religious spirits. I *would* say that it's time the Church makes a change to how we approach the lost, but that time is not now. Not really. That time was eons ago, and is now past due. We're so very late.

God forgive us for the lives we have damaged and the people we have hurt.

Christ Died for the Rahabs

In 2014, while working on *Redeemed Unredeemable*, Tom and I agreed that the industry description of the book would read: "Jesus said that redemption, eternal salvation, is available to everyone. No one is beyond His reach; no one falls outside the boundaries of His willingness to forgive. Anyone who calls on Him will be saved, He says. But, does that really include names like Jeffrey Dahmer, Ted Bundy, Susan Atkins, Charles Tex Watson, Sean Sellers, David Berkowitz, and Karla Faye Tucker?"

The notion that any of those people would be in heaven right now understandably angers some. Oh so many times during the compilation of my research did I run across someone saying the equivalent to, "If Jeffrey Dahmer and Ted Bundy are in heaven, then I don't want to go there," or, "Why would God give the same saving grace to such evil people that he would give to me, when I have never and would never hurt anyone? That logic just doesn't make sense." I not only understand these sentiments, I *felt them* at the darkest hours of writing at my computer in the middle of the night when images of violent crime scenes would pop up on my screen unsolicited. I was so enraged at these murderers at times—for the people they killed and the families they hurt—that I had to bow my head and ask the Lord to calm my nerves and keep me focused on the project. At moments, I felt like a hypocrite because I was writing a book about how God had broken through what we humans would conceive to be insurmountable obstacles in order to reach the worst of sinners, and all the while I, myself, didn't believe the people I was writing about deserved it. After submerging my mind into the world of serial killers and human depravity for so many months, I started to actually fear dark streets and have nightmares that my children and I were victims of gory crimes. I began studying people in public that I wouldn't have even noticed before, whose immediate appearance or conversational exchange would launch me into a momentary lapse of paranoid profiling until I could shake it off and go about my day.

Intermittently, however, between moments of fear and anger came moments of praising the Lord that His grace is sufficient even for those murderers whose lifestyles and earthly decisions are so corrupt, sinful, and horrible that we can't wrap our minds around what they have done. At these times, I understood with a personal maturity—beyond that of simply believing something that has been imprinted upon me by the Church and my parents since my childhood—that God's forgiveness is not about the extremity of our crimes, the degree of our sins, or to what level other people can wrap their minds around what anyone else has done. God's love is not extended only to the elect, the blameless, or the sinless, or we would all be in trouble, because, "There is none righteous, no not one" (Romans 3:10).

As finite humans, it is easy to put stipulations or qualifiers on whom God would forgive, whom He would love, and, most importantly, whom He would die for. When Christ, in the garden of Gethsemane, said, "May this cup pass from me," He *did not* go on to say, "but if it doesn't, here are the people I'm willing to die for." We continuously find ourselves putting a list on His prayer that night; we are tempted to add our own fine print in the margins of Scripture that says, "Note: Does not apply to [fill in the blank] sins." But at the end of the day, if we truly subscribe to a Christian theology wherein Christ was and is the Messianic Savior and the part of the Holy Trinity who died and rose again, then we are by default forced to accept that Jesus—thousands of years ago and into perpetuity, as the Son of God and therefore God, Himself—*knew* who the killers were going to be, who would be addicted to pornography, who the child molesters were, who would cheat on their spouses, who would steal, who would lie, who would take His name in vain, who would betray their parents or families, and, yes, who would be homosexual.

He submitted Himself to that cross anyway.

Jesus knew who He was dying for, and there was never a directory of qualifiers, no fine print, no addendums, and no memos later on that would ever change the truth that He died so that *all* might inherit the kingdom of God—the "whosoever will," no matter who they are, what their lifestyle is, what they have done, how they have sinned, or whether other believers think they are as eligible for this free and eternal gift. The requirement of faith that we face in order to enter the pearly gates and find our names written in the Lamb's Book of Life is identical for all of humankind. If Christ died for Jeffrey Dahmer, Ted Bundy, Susan Atkins, Charles Tex Watson, Sean Sellers, David Berkowitz, and Karla Faye Tucker, then Christ died for all. If "not even a sparrow falls to the ground without the Father's care" (Matthew 10:29), then we Christ-followers serve a truly caring and loving Father who extends His affection to even the smallest of sparrows. If "the very hairs on our heads are all numbered," yet we are told by Christ to "fear not" and that we are "of more value than many sparrows" (Matthew 10:30–32), then God, Himself, in no uncertain terms, has made it clear that *all* are *wanted* and *loved* and *cherished*.

The Church would be wise to agree.

Especially—and I believe this with my whole being—because they are about to be a part of the next Great Awakening. James lifted the deeds of a repentant Rahab. If the Body will stop being asleep in the light, wake up, care, embrace the "whosoever will," and *show their faith by their works of love*, then mark my words: There will be a day soon when we commemorate the deeds of today's repentant Rahab.

Do you want to change the world?
Do you want to play a part in the next Great Awakening?

Love. Love at all times. Show people how you care before you tell them what you know. Show the Lord that you seek wisdom first and foremost in your daily interactions with people, and that you are creating a foundation of ministry that He can build upon.

Chapter 6

The Wild Tongue of Today's Preachers

James 3

EARLIER, I SPENT a few moments comparing today's mega-church trend to the "rich man's" exploitation/oppression James addresses toward the beginning of his epistle. However, as we approach chapter 3 of James' letter, we see that his attention becomes focused entirely on the ministers of his day as he gives a serious warning.

> ¹My brethren, be not many masters, knowing that we shall receive the greater condemnation. ²For in many things we offend all. If any man offend not in word, the same is a perfect man, and able also to bridle the whole body. ³Behold, we put bits in the horses' mouths, that they may obey us; and we turn about their whole body.

In the ESV, this is stated, "Not many of you should become teachers, my brothers, for you know that we who teach will be judged with greater strictness. For we all stumble in many ways. And if anyone does not stumble in what he says, he is a perfect man, able also to bridle his whole body. If we put bits into the mouths of horses so that they obey us, we guide their whole bodies as well."

I have seen people become confused when verse 2, regarding the "perfect man," is isolated. James knew as he wrote this that there had never been and never would be a "perfect man" other than his half-brother; he acknowledged that in his previous sentence ("For in many things we offend all" KJV; "For we all stumble in many ways," ESV). But remember, isolating one verse and applying it out of context to the surrounding texts and overall message leads to misinterpretation.

So, what did James mean by this mentioning of perfection?

First, consider the "who" that James is referring to: teachers, preachers, and ministers of the Gospel. Second, consider the "what" that James is referring to: the tongue; opening one's mouth to teach, preach, and minister to listeners, and the relationship between what a minister says and what he does. Third, consider what James said about the dominion a man has over a horse with a bit in its mouth, how he guides that horse where he wants it to go, and how that relates to a teacher of the Gospel over his own actions. Add these together, and we arrive at the following equation: "Not many of you should become teachers, my brothers and sisters, because those who teach will be held to a higher standard than those who only listen, and the judgment they will face later on for transgressions will be more severe. Everyone sins, certainly, but the man who perfectly practices what he preaches will be able to perfectly steer himself and his body away from the sins he preaches about, much like a man who guides a horse has full control over the horse's body and direction." The focus here should not be on whether any man or woman achieves literal perfection in his or her actions, but on the role that wild tongue plays. If a pastor preaches one thing and does another, he's not perfectly steering himself. James is shedding light on the sin of a preacher who sticks to proper teaching from the Word and then lives in a way that's contrary to that. (Every minister who preaches love and then turns his nose up at people from different social networks than his own is guilty of this.)

Barnes' Notes commentary sheds further light on this section of Scripture:

The particular thing, doubtless, which the apostle had in his eye, was the peculiar liability to commit error, or to do wrong with the tongue. Of course, this liability is very great in an office where the very business is public speaking. If anywhere the improper use of the tongue will do mischief, it is in the office of a religious teacher; and to show the danger of this, and the importance of caution in seeking that office, the apostle proceeds to show what mischief the tongue is capable of effecting....

[James means] Perfect in the sense in which the apostle immediately explains himself; that he [the teacher] is able to keep every other member of his body in subjection. His object is not to represent the [teacher or preacher] as absolutely spotless in every sense, and as wholly free from sin, for [James] had himself just said that "all offend in many things;" but the design is to show that if a man can control his tongue, he has complete dominion over himself, as much as a man has over a horse by the bit, or as a steersman has over a ship if he has hold of the rudder. He is perfect in that sense, that he has complete control over himself, and will not be liable to error in anything. *The design is to show the important position which the tongue occupies, as governing the whole man....*

And able also to bridle the whole body—To control his whole body, that is, every other part of himself, as a man does a horse by the bridle. The word rendered "to bridle," means to lead or guide with a bit; then to rein in, to check, to moderate, to restrain. A man always has complete government over himself if he has the entire control of his tongue. *It is that by which he gives expression to his thoughts and passions; and if that is kept under proper restraint, all the rest of his members are as easily controlled as the horse is by having the control of the bit.*[13]

A teacher of the Word harnesses his tongue and forces his body to match what he says before expecting to teach anyone else anything. It's not about being perfect, it's about *not* being a hypocrite. It's about *not* preaching false doctrines or a gospel of antinomianism so that a preacher can live in a way that opposes Christ from his position behind the authoritative pulpit.

The same lesson carries into the next verses:

> ⁴**Behold also the ships, which though they be so great, and are driven of fierce winds, yet are they turned about with a very small helm, whithersoever the governor listeth.**

I have heard a few sermons in my short time here on earth that claim this verse is referring to the helm as the pastor, and the ship as his congregants: An entire congregation could be swept about by the raging winds at sea, but thanks to a solid preacher at the helm, the congregation is better controlled, and the people lead more righteous lives. To a degree, such an analogy is applicable, because every church needs wise leaders who pilot their "ship" (the ministry, its leadership team, and the entire congregation) toward proper treatment of the Gospel in the interest of righteous living all around. With those who have interpreted this verse that way, or those who have chosen to apply it in this way, I don't specifically have issue. I don't intend to suggest that this verse is void of any underlying meaning regarding the helm (teacher) leading the ship (church), because by James' writing this portion of his epistle to potential teachers within the early Church, there is a connection to leadership by default.

Even *Gill's Exposition* uses James' analogy in this way:

> And so, though the tongue is to the rest of the body as a small helm to a large ship, yet, like that, it has great influence over the whole body, to check it when it is carrying away with the force of its appetites and passions; and so churches, societies, and bodies of Christians, which are large and numerous, and are like ships upon the ocean, tossed to and fro with tempests, driven by Satan's temptations and the world's persecution, and ready to be car-

ried away with the wind of false doctrine, yet are influenced and directed aright by those that are at the helm, the faithful ministers of the word, who say to them, this is the way, walk in it.[14]

However, it remains my opinion that although these two concepts are connected, James is specifically referring to the helm as the tongue of its ship, the teacher/preacher. It's about a preacher of the Gospel learning to control his tongue, lest his flapping lips render him a hypocrite or mislead a congregation. *Gill's Exposition* is correct in stating that a preacher is in the position to lead the church, but left void in that interpretation is the concern that the preacher might be leading his church *wrongly*. In order to appreciate a Scripture referring to a preacher as a helm and a ship as a congregation, one must first address what *direction* the preacher will lead the congregation, which naturally travels back to the first interpretation, that the helm is the tongue and the ship is the preacher before the preacher with an unruly tongue becomes the helmsman of a church traveling in the wrong direction.

Let us look at *Barnes' Notes* on this:

A ship is a large object. It seems to be unmanageable by its vastness, and it is also impelled by driving storms. Yet it is easily managed by a small rudder; and he that has control of that, has control of the ship itself. So with the tongue. It is a small member as compared with the body; in its size not unlike the rudder as compared with the ship. Yet *the proper control of the tongue in respect to its influence on the whole man*, is not unlike the control of the rudder in its power over the ship....

And are driven of fierce winds—By winds that would seem to leave the ship beyond control. It is probable that by the "fierce winds" here as impelling the ship, the apostle meant to illustrate the power of the passions in impelling [the preacher/teacher]. Even a man under impetuous passion would be restrained, if the tongue is properly controlled, as the ship driven by the winds is by the helm.[15]

When children are unruly, some blame the children, and others blame the parent(s). Yet one contributing factor cannot be separated from the other, because children are in control of their own actions, but those actions are largely a result of parental influence. Generally speaking, to remove either factor—the children's own will, or the parental role in shaping them—from the other would be circular and faulty logic when a behavioral grievance is noted. By that same logic, if the congregants of a church aren't reflecting true Gospel values, they are held personally responsible for the brand of light they are shining into the world because they are in control of their own actions—but if their actions are heavily influenced by a preacher/teacher, then the man or woman who opens his or her mouth to guide the flocks should be an important contributing factor in determining the origin of a behavioral grievance.

Whereas some see the helm/ship analogy as a reference to a preacher's own self-control in teaching, and others see it as a reference to a leader and his flock, eventually, both analyses still support the idea that one interpretation naturally flows into the other.

Why, then, would I care so much which interpretation "wins"? Because human nature is quick to seek justification for what one wishes to do in the flesh. Children cannot choose their parents, but adults *can* choose their pastor. If people are not flattered by what they hear being spoken behind a pulpit, they will "church shop" until they find that one human authority who says that what they're doing and how they live is justifiable based on loose or twisted reading of the Word.

Consider what 2 Timothy 4:3–4 says: "For the time will come when they will not endure sound doctrine; but after their own lusts shall they heap to themselves teachers, having itching ears; And they shall turn away their ears from the truth, and shall be turned unto fables." The ESV renders it this way: "For the time is coming when people will not endure sound teaching, but having itching ears they will accumulate for themselves teachers to suit their own passions, and will turn away from listening to the truth and wander off into myths." Contemporarily, we arrive at: "The time will come when people will go from teacher to teacher to teacher, rejecting sound doctrine in trade for a gospel that tells them all the pretty things they want to hear. They won't hear truth no matter how many times it is presented to them. Only the fairy-tale gospel will satisfy their itching ears."

People are always excited when they hear a verse that justifies living however they want or believing in whatever ideologies about God suit them, and if they can say they are merely obeying the helm that steers them (the helm they sought out who preaches what they want to hear), then they pass the accountability test in their own minds. If they were to be caught or questioned while abusing this loophole, they rely on the "I couldn't help it, it was the helm" rationale to pass the blame. That's why I fear it is more crucial to stick to what James really meant here, even though the other interpretation does have merit. If the helm/ship is all about the preacher and his tongue, then he is accountable to his own words, and the individuals in his congregation are accountable to their own decisions, not as a ship being steered by someone else.

James started this trail with: "Not many of you should become teachers." His entire focus here is who should and who should not be teaching people, based on the quality of their tongue restraint. In the past, we only had literal and physical church buildings within our locality to choose from. Now, however, there are "churches" all over the world that anyone can "attend" through the television or the Internet. Technology has proven to be an excellent tool for spreading the Gospel, but it is a double-edged sword. All kinds of warped theologies are float-ing around in cyberspace that can, will, and *do* justify all kinds of evil "in the name of Christ," so church shopping and justification for sins of the flesh as prophesied in 2 Timothy has just become a lot easier. James didn't know about the Internet and television when he was writing this letter, but he had the wisdom to understand that a flock or congrega-tion—and the direction they are traveling—cannot be addressed until their preacher learns to guide his own body/ship through proper use of his tongue/helm.

The power of the teaching tongue is great, as James goes on to say:

[5]Even so the tongue is a little member, and boasteth great things. Behold, how great a matter a little fire kindleth! [6]And the tongue is a fire, a world of iniquity: so is the tongue among our members, that it defileth the whole body, and setteth on fire the course of nature; and it is set on fire of hell.

This "little member" of the human body is capable of so much. It "boasteth great things" by default of it being the one physiological communicator of the brain. Our hand cannot speak; neither can our knee. Both can be used through "body language" to communicate, but only to emphasize what the mouth is saying. Our tongue can "boast" that it is capable of "the greatest" carrying of thoughts from the brain and out into the world around us. Through the tongue, a teacher/preacher can ignite a fire that destroys the body and all the Kingdom purposes that body might have been assigned to deliver. The tongue that is employed in iniquity is set to defile; it is set on a course toward the fires of hell.

I love what *Barnes' Notes* says on this one:

With all the good which it [the tongue] does, who can estimate the amount of evil which it causes? Who can measure the evils which arise from scandal, and slander, and profaneness, and perjury, and falsehood, and blasphemy, and obscenity, and the inculcation of error, by the tongue? Who can gauge the amount of broils, and contentions, and strifes, and wars, and suspicions, and enmities, and alienations among friends and neighbors, which it produces? Who can number the evils produced by the "honeyed" words of the seducer; or by the tongue of the eloquent in the maintenance of error, and the defense of wrong? If all men were dumb [literally mute], what a portion of the crimes of the world would soon cease! If all men would speak only that which ought to be spoken, what a change would come over the face of human affairs!...

And it is set on fire of hell—Hell, or *Gehenna*, is represented as a place where the fires continually burn.... The idea here is, that that which causes the tongue to do so much evil derives its origin from hell. Nothing could better characterize much of that which the tongues does, than to say that it has its origin in hell, and has the spirit which reigns there. The very spirit of that world of fire and wickedness—a spirit of falsehood, and slander, and blasphemy, and pollution—seems to inspire the tongue. The image which seems to have been before the mind of the apostle was that of a torch which enkindles and burns everything as it goes along—a torch itself lighted at the fires of hell. One of the most striking descriptions of the woes and curses which there may be in hell, would be to portray the sorrows caused on the earth by the tongue.[16]

Regarding these verses, *Matthew Poole's* commentary states that "the tongue, being the fire, the devil, by the bellows of temptations, inflames it yet more, and thereby kindles the fire of all mischiefs in the world."[17] *Gill's Exposition* states, "the tongue is influenced, instigated, and stirred up by Satan, to speak many evil things, and it will be hereafter set on fire in hell."[18]

[7]**For every kind of beasts, and of birds, and of serpents, and of things in the sea, is tamed, and hath been tamed of mankind:** [8]**But the tongue can no man tame; it is an unruly evil, full of deadly poison.**

The tongue no man can *tame*. Note that James doesn't say that the tongue cannot be brought under control. If a wild animal—whose nature it is to bite and inject venom into whatever it can reach—is tamed, then generally speaking, that is a permanent change. Save for some special circumstances (rabies, subsequent abuse, or what have you), once an animal is tamed, it's tamed. It is no longer "wild." But the tongue will always be wilder than even the most poisonous of snakes and, James says, it is deadly.

To read James' concerns about the tongue and then misquote 3:8 as justification for why a person "couldn't control" his or her words is a serious offense to God and Scripture, as well as to the people who are hurt as a result. The tongue *can* be brought under control, and it should be, but it will *always* require a continual effort.

Like a serpent that backs off from the bite but whose nature will always be to strike. A dog that hovers nearby baring his teeth, whose personality will always be aggressive and dangerous, but who must always be under the authority of the owner. A lion with claws extended, tempted at all times to go for the kill, but whose trainer must govern. An animal that cannot be tamed no matter the circumstances, and whose temperament will always be to harm, but whose handler must always be in control. That is the tongue. There is no taming it, and it is always proficient for use as a deadly poison. But it is also always capable of falling under the dominion of its possessor, and it must, if any teaching is going to be just.

> [9]**Therewith bless we God, even the Father; and therewith curse we men, which are made after the similitude of God.** [10]**Out of the same mouth proceedeth blessing and cursing. My brethren, these things ought not so to be.**

Hypocrisy. From the same mouth flow blessings and curses. From the same mouth flow sermons and gossip. From the same mouth flow support and backstabbing. From the same mouth flow good theology and heresy. From the same mouth flow gratefulness and grumbling. From the same mouth flow "welcome to our church" and "your kind is not welcome here."

This "should not be so," James wrote. If he says the tongue is more impossible to tame than any wild animal or beast of the field, *and* he says that teachers will be "judged with greater strictness," then how careful must ministers be when opening their mouths both behind the pulpit and away from it when giving instruction? If the "bless you" falls from the same mouth as the "curse you," we are guilty of this hypocrisy. If a pastor gives all smiles and sunshine to one member of a congregation, then slams another with vile hatred or self-righteous judgment, he is guilty of this hypocrisy. If a woman tells her Bible-study listeners that women shouldn't talk behind people's backs, and then she shrouds her own juicy tale under the title of a "prayer request," she is guilty of this hypocrisy. If we say "I'll pray for you" like the world says "let's do lunch," knowing that there is no intention of carrying out the promised act, we are guilty of that hypocrisy. The damage the minister does to the individual, the congregation, the Church, or the globe (if the audience is widespread via technology), is an "unruly evil, full of deadly poison."

James makes no bones about the fact that this is an extremely serious matter. Everything else we have addressed up to this point is related to this tongue-control concern. However, through the pure saturation of this sin being an all-too-familiar phenomenon of the modern Church, we view it with a watered-down concept that it's really not a big deal.

Happens all the time. People are people. They're bound to make mistakes. If ministers say something hurtful (and they do, frequently), if they twist Scripture (and they do, frequently), or if they approach the pulpit without spending the time it takes to follow proper Scripture-interpretation protocols (and they do, frequently), then well, oops. God will still bless *their* ministry. He will still anoint *them*, because *they* are in the "people business," spreading the Gospel of Christ to the lost. They may slander sometimes, or reject people who belong to a different social group or opposing movement, but *they* carved another notch on their belt a year or two ago when they led someone to say the sinner's prayer. They may not be taking their role as seriously as have some other ministers, but they are still mostly in this game for the right reasons. *Their* transgressions are marginal. Nobody's perfect, and at least *they* are dedicating their lives to a godly purpose.

Right?

No, no, no, no, and no.

"Not many of you should become teachers," James said. When comparing this short sentence to the rest of his convictions as shared in this epistle, this could also read, "Only those of you who are absolutely, indisputably, heart-on-the-floor passionate about taking your role as a minister more seriously than anything else in your life; only those of you who are profoundly and thoroughly committed to upholding the truth, the whole truth, and nothing but the truth of the Word of God; only those of you who are willing to take the time to *know* the Word before you *teach* it; only those of you who believe in loving the Rahabs, the prostitutes, the homosexuals, the drunks, the drug addicts, the teen moms, the "whosoever will"; only those of you who practice what you preach; only those of you who accept that your judgment for halfhearted, lackluster, lackadaisical, and apathetic treatment of your position over the Body of Christ will be harsher as a speaker than a listener, and that this judgment may be eternal…should become teachers."

Some call me, Donna Howell, a radical. My gifted friend Debbie (who has been called a "prophet" by others, but who personally shies away from that title), called me a radical. Co-staff at SkyWatch TV call me a radical. Even Jim Bakker, on a recent episode of his show while we were talking about a global Great Awakening, called me a radical. I don't know if it's true or not, and I wouldn't usually refer to myself that way, but if being antiestablishment makes someone a radical, then I must be one, because the Church has become an organized, institutionalized establishment, and I am against much of what it represents today. I cannot write a feel-good book that only serves to flatter people and encourage those in ministry who knowingly take their pulpit as seriously as one would take a job flipping burgers at a fast-food joint. Our Church has become a social, in-group/out-group assembly of lackluster, apathetic, mechanical verse-droppers who spend more time trying to accomplish a worldly endeavor and make it home by half past noon than see the lost achieve eternity in the presence of the King. As such, I apologize if what I am about to say makes anyone angry or rubs anyone the wrong way or hurts feelings, but if someone is not in it for the right reasons—if there is even an *inkling* in someone's spirit that he or she is in the ministry to toss around Scriptures with a counterfeit bleeding heart while the true Gospel of Christ is set aside in exchange for money or showmanship or social status—then that minister needs to close his or her mouth and step down before tongues spread deadly poison further.

People all around us at this very moment are hurting and dying—emotionally, spiritually, physically. Their lives and families are being torn apart. They feel the sting of loneliness and solitude in a world with so many "friends" in social media who don't know the first thing about who they really are. They see the same updates on television that we do and become lost in the whirlwind of social and political demoralization. They are hit by a very real and dangerous hopelessness every time another relationship in their life bites the dust because of the pressure of a nation divided against itself. They draw more into themselves because of the expectation that when two parties don't agree, they automatically have to pick up their swords and clash or throw up their hands and flee from a guaranteed aggression. They grow accustomed to the idea that anytime an opinion is opposed, people cannot and will not treat each other with respect and dignity, and their trust in any future relationships is gone. They have been hurt by people, so they do what they have been taught and hurt other people, just to be told afterward that they are horrible for causing that hurt. They eventually come to doubt the value of human life as God designed it and adopt the idea that God is a dictatorial and maniacal tyrant bent on designing a world that only ever causes pain to its inhabitants. They face this dejection every day of their lives, wondering what in the world it's all for.

And at the center of all of this…is the answer to all of this: Christ.

In the midst of our hectic, temporal, human life, there are people called to tell others about Him, but if those people cannot control their tongue (they do not produce right teaching, they slander, they gossip, they judge, they twist Scripture), the lost may well be lost forever.

French philosopher Pierre Teilhard de Chardin once said, "We are not human beings having a spiritual experience. We are spiritual beings having a human experience." I couldn't agree more. This life is *so* short in comparison to eternity. Eternity is forever. It goes on and on and on and on with no end. Ever.

I *should* be radical.

You should be radical.

We should *all* be radical about Christ, what He came to do, and how that accomplishment holds a power like none other to heal this planet of all hurt and pain and confusion. Radically kind. Radically caring. Radically willing to sacrifice anything and everything—as He did—to unite as a true Body against this shattering despair lost souls are being crushed under. Radically joyful. Radically committed to truth. Radically eager to be gentle when someone else isn't committed to our same truth. Radically sold out for the Gospel and all it stands for—at the center of which is love, because you can have every other fancy personality strength and speak "with the tongues of angels," but without love, it's all just "clanging cymbals" (1 Corinthians 13:1).

When John was exiled to the Island of Patmos, he received a great Word from Christ, which became what we know as the book of Revelation. It's the last, and the most apocalyptic, book of the Bible. In it, we read that John was given instructions to write letters to seven churches: Ephesus, Smyrna, Pergamum, Thyatira, Sardis, Philadelphia, and Laodicea. Each of the charges begins with Christ's words, "To the angel of [church name], write..." The Greek word *angelos* means simply "messenger," and it can be used to refer to either a heavenly messenger or a human messenger on an assignment. (For instance, John the Baptist was referred to as an *angelos* in Matthew 11:10.) In Revelation, John was instructed to write *physical* letters to these churches, and the idea that he would write a letter to a literal angel from heaven is puzzling. Additionally, since these "angels" are leaders of some churches that are openly chastised for wickedness and idolatry, this poses further confusion on potential interpretation since it can be safely assumed that an angel of heaven would not be guilty of wickedness and idolatry. Therefore, the likeliest of all interpretations of the letters' recipients is that they were the pastors or bishops of the seven churches. Many scholars have arrived at this conclusion, as have many authors of respected commentaries, which makes the words John was instructed to write quite interesting for our reflection here in a chapter on the wisdom and preaching of modern church leaders.

Some of the leaders of these churches were heralded as good and faithful, while others were scolded for their failures in pursuit of heartfelt Gospel living. Two of these churches specifically stand out to me as representations of today's collective Church: Sardis and Laodicea.

(Note that the following is not solely my own interpretation or commentary, but the interpretation of many scholars based on language studies and cultural-application lessons from five translations of study Bibles [KJV, ESV, NKJV, NLT, and NASB] and more than ten esteemed commentaries. That said, Revelation is the most highly disputed book of the Bible regarding its interpretation, and I realize that there are some who believe in a slight variation of the following analysis. My hope is that the parallel between today's Church and the following two churches in Asia has value as a warning to those with "an ear to hear.")

Sardis, the "Dead" Church

From Revelation 3:1–6:

> And unto the angel of the church in Sardis write; These things saith he that hath the seven Spirits of God, and the seven stars;
>
> I know thy works, that thou hast a name that thou livest, and art dead. Be watchful, and strengthen the things which remain, that are ready to die: for I have not found thy works perfect before God. Remember therefore how thou hast received and heard, and hold fast, and repent. If therefore thou shalt not watch, I will come on thee as a thief, and thou shalt not know what hour I will come upon thee.
>
> Thou hast a few names even in Sardis which have not defiled their garments; and they shall walk with me in white: for they are

worthy. He that overcometh, the same shall be clothed in white raiment; and I will not blot out his name out of the book of life, but I will confess his name before my Father, and before his angels.

He that hath an ear, let him hear what the Spirit saith unto the churches.

Let's begin by taking a look at some of these verses more specifically.
I know thy works, that thou hast a name that thou livest, and art dead.
The church in Sardis had a spiritually active reputation at the time of this writing. Sardis was the capital city of the ancient kingdom Lydia, and it was the oldest city in the territory, well known for its defenses and achievements in wool trade. Travelers observing the church from the outside saw a fairly peaceful congregation. It wasn't at war with any people groups, it didn't house any idols or open idol worshipers, it wasn't guilty of the "Balaam" or "Jezebel" infringements as a couple of the other churches in Asia, it held no "seat of Satan" like Pergamum, it didn't preach false doctrines, and overall it appeared successful. Its only problem was in and of itself.

It was *dead* inside.

It looked very much alive, and it "had a name" (was respected and well-known), but Christ knew that its members were spiritually asleep. Everyone who surveyed Sardis saw that it was a grand institution of upright religious folk.

Smiles. Handshakes. Bless yous. Full offering plates. Notches carved on belts.

But Christ, as He relayed to John, knew the members of the church at Sardis weren't accomplishing a thing for the Kingdom. They *were* a righteous institution, but that was precisely the problem. That was all they were. There was no fire under their backsides compelling them to reach beyond themselves and their trivial, feel-good services. The only people they were reaching with the Gospel message were themselves. Everything about their ministry was asleep.

Mundane. Routine. Commonplace. Lackluster. Lazy. Apathetic. Going through motions. Tares among the wheat. Content to remain as it was in its own monotonous and passionless gatherings.

I will remind you of Keith Green's incredible lyrics quoted earlier:

The world is sleeping in the dark that the church [in Sardis?]
    just can't fight
'cause it's asleep in the light.
How can you be so dead, when you've been so well fed?
Jesus rose from the grave, and *you*! You can't even get out of bed!

How could the church in Sardis be the "dead church" when they had been given the best gift any Man could give? How could they sit cozy, snoozing away in their comfortable lives while the early Church was in its beginning phases of development and others around them were lost and hurting and dying and giving up hope? Where was the appetite, the *craving*, to wake up, take action, and ensure that the "whosoever will" were being reached at all costs while the apostles were being martyred for this cause? Great men of God were being brutally murdered all around Sardis for their belief in the One who came to redeem the world and for their attempts to tell others about Him…and Sardis was reclining in the luxury of knowing they had already received the gift of Christ. Nothing more needed to be done, because they had already done their "duty" by believing in Him (believing a thing existed), holding services dedicated to Him, and passing out friendly handshakes to others in their in-group assembly. Surrounded by those who agreed with them. Satisfied to boil tea leaves and enjoy the sunshine on a Sunday afternoon amidst a company of like-minded, righteous-living pillars of the community. Pleased with themselves for living lives that didn't oppose God.

But by simply existing there dead, asleep, their lifestyles were in direct opposition to the Great Commission charge that *is* the Gospel. And it wasn't just because they weren't knocking on doors, jumping around the city with picket signs, or asking to be stoned. Being "radical" doesn't always mean being loud. Being "radical" can simply mean taking the gifts and skill sets we've been given and passionately doing something with it in our own arena of experience and outreach. The Sardis inactivity was an internal offense. It was a matter of heart. Its members were spiritually lethargic.

This chapter would quickly become a whole book if I took the time right now to point out the parallels of our modern Church to Sardis. Suffice it to say that I believe our Church is sitting on its laurels, watching the world die. Our ministers are more passionate about first-world problems—and bickering denominational lines in the sand and arguing about whose social lifestyles are more sinful than others and making political statements—than reaching the lost with a tangible, long-lasting, and life-breathing Gospel message. It's not about knocking on doors or fulfilling external, dry, cold obligations to "go and preach" or hand out pamphlets. It's about recognizing that one moment for what it is when a fellow human is in pain and searching, resisting the temptation to dismiss, judge, or argue, and *radically* following the love standards as outlined in Scripture.

Be watchful, and strengthen the things which remain, that are ready to die.

To those who have an ear to hear: Take heed, Sardis. Take heed, Church of today. Grasp onto what fervent passion remains amidst the Body—that passion and spiritual energy that appears to be "ready to die"—and strengthen it. Repent of apathy. Wake up. Don't give in to the temporal temptation of slumber. Whether it means preaching loudly on street corners or quietly serving as a deacon, stand for what's righteous— what's *loving*—when the moment presents itself. *Be* the people we are meant to be in Christ—as doers, and not hearers only (James 1:22).

Thou hast a few names even in Sardis…

Despite the state we are in, there are "a few names" even in our current Church—a remnant—that have held high the standards of the simple Gospel. I beseech you, preachers and teachers, strive to be one of them.

Laodicea, the "Lukewarm" Church

From Revelation 3:14–22:

> And unto the angel of the church of the Laodiceans write; These
> things saith the Amen, the faithful and true witness, the begin-
> ning of the creation of God;
>
> I know thy works, that thou art neither cold nor hot: I would
> thou wert cold or hot. So then because thou art lukewarm, and
> neither cold nor hot, I will spue [spew] thee out of my mouth.
> Because thou sayest, I am rich, and increased with goods, and
> have need of nothing; and knowest not that thou art wretched,
> and miserable, and poor, and blind, and naked: I counsel thee
> to buy of me gold tried in the fire, that thou mayest be rich; and
> white raiment, that thou mayest be clothed, and that the shame of
> thy nakedness do not appear; and anoint thine eyes with eyesalve,
> that thou mayest see. As many as I love, I rebuke and chasten: be
> zealous therefore, and repent.
>
> Behold, I stand at the door, and knock: if any man hear my
> voice, and open the door, I will come in to him, and will sup with
> him, and he with me. To him that overcometh will I grant to sit
> with me in my throne, even as I also overcame, and am set down
> with my Father in his throne.
>
> He that hath an ear, let him hear what the Spirit saith unto
> the churches.

These hot/cold/lukewarm Scriptures have continually been applied
in modern culture as referring to those "lukewarm Christians" who only
halfheartedly commit to the faith. There is some value to such an interpretation, surely, but this concept in its simplicity completely misses the
mark.

Laodicea was an industrious and successful city situated in the Lycos
River Valley, known for its wealth and prosperity. It was located a handful

of miles away from an ancient hot springs site, where steamy water flowed freely. Farther out, Colossae produced fresh, cold waters. The Laodiceans received their water from an aqueduct between these two sites, and by the time it reached them, the water supply was lukewarm in a literal sense. As such, the hot/cold/lukewarm speech used in this text was a metaphor that would have been understood by Laodicean residents on account of their location between two contrasting water supply temperatures.

Hot water is used in many drink selections, and cold water is preferred for others, but, generally speaking, nobody asks for a lukewarm drink of any kind. Likewise, hot water has many purposes unrelated to drink (cleansing, purification, heating the body, etc.), and the same can be said for cold water (to refresh, to revive, to stimulate, to awaken, to cool the body, etc.), but lukewarm water is useless, and will be "spewed from the mouth." Additionally, lukewarm water is generally regarded as a bacterial breeding ground, whereas fewer germs would survive in ice cold or boiling hot waters, so the Laodicean water supply would have been more than just undesirable to taste or use; it would have presented an element of danger to its consumer without prior purification.

Without cultural understanding of the Laodicean locality, then, it might seem like this hot/cold reference is in regard to passion or zeal. But if that were so, then wouldn't a loving God appreciate the fact that the church in Laodicea wasn't completely cold? That they cared enough to be somewhere in the middle and just hadn't arrived yet? That they were still growing spiritually and had potential to become the people He wanted them to be? Why would God "wilt" that they would *ever* be cold, no matter the circumstances? Such notions are raised when the "lukewarm Christian" comments are preached from the pulpit, and it's confusing.

But when we read this passage again with understanding of the Laodicean water complaints, we understand more accurately that the metaphor is not as much about how committed the people were, but how worthless they were in their current condition of spiritual blindness. Lukewarm water isn't just worthless, it's actually nauseating. It can be literally sickening, which denotes a negative reaction upon the body—not just a casual uselessness. It can be dangerous without purification. Jesus' words to the church in Laodicea were that they were sickening to Him—worse off than spiritually worthless, because they were willingly blind and spiritually filled with bacteria. And the reason for this state was because of what they had placed their faith in.

Because thou sayest, I am rich, and increased with goods, and have need of nothing...

They had all they needed from the Lord. Their celestial Santa Claus had provided, and they were now free to prance about in their comfortable lives with comfortable homes and comfortable dining. (Historically, every time a vast number of people are challenged with war, economic depressions, starvation, epidemics, pandemics, plagues, mass death, etc., those affected fall on their knees and suddenly develop a dependency upon the Lord. When people have what they need, they don't need God. And in a country like the US, regardless of all its issues, most of the population can say that, apart from minor, first-world problems, we have what we need. Why would our country need God? Why would we place our faith in a deity when we have what we need without one? Why would our churches be hot or cold when we are "rich" with "increased goods" and "have need of nothing"?)

... and knowest not that thou art wretched, and miserable, and poor, and blind, and naked...

In the midst of their comforts, the Laodiceans were completely complacent—oblivious, "knowest not"—that they were a wretched people. Imitation Christians. Claiming to be followers of Christ but regarding Him as marginal. Claiming to stand for something grand, something deliciously hot or cold, and wallowing in smug satisfaction of their own hollow, lukewarm achievements. Materially rich, but spiritually bankrupt. Declaring to have converted for a cause, while their hearts were unchanged. A spiritual "bacterial breeding ground." Hypocrites to the core. Counterfeits. Phonies. Fakes. Pretenders.

Dead.

Like Sardis.

They were not hot or cold, so their works wouldn't benefit the world in any way. Their works wouldn't cleanse, purify, revive, or stimulate. They were worse than worthless because they stood as a false example to the world around them of what Christ had come to do. Closing down their church would have been a better service to their community than keeping the doors open and defiling the face of the Gospel through useless, lukewarm playacting. They had all they needed in this life—every material necessity—therefore, they made it clear that they didn't need God. Church might have been a place to hobnob and meander for the sake of boredom therapy or the fulfilment of social expectations in a people group, but they regarded religion as inconsequential.

Jesus Christ saw through their façade immediately, called them "blind," and subsequently gave them a list of what they needed to have and do in order to attain real reparation.

I counsel thee to buy of me gold tried in the fire that thou mayest be rich...

The word "buy" here doesn't refer to a monetary exchange, and the Laodiceans would have been familiar with this concept if their teacher had any knowledge of the passage in Isaiah 55:1, which refers to the act of purchasing "without money and without price." (We can assume the teacher would have been familiar with this, since ancient teaching methods relied heavily on reading from the pulpit, so a sermon back then would be mostly Scripture, unlike today's sermon that preaches a whole life lesson around only one or two verses.) Gold was the most precious metal, and all metals "tried in the fire" were purified from dross and imperfection.

As such, if popular interpretation is correct, Christ is instructing them to trade their worldly gold—imperfect, temporal—for a richness that only He can provide, a richness that is purified, *true* richness of heavenly origin. The exchange of one kind of riches to another explains the "buying" reference as it represents a trade.

Consider what is being proposed of this gold trade. The Laodiceans had to stop focusing on their earthly riches and embrace the heavenly riches that had been "tried in the fire," suggesting that their faith needed to be "tried" in some way to appreciate the exchange. This concept is supported by what Christ says next, but it's also understood in other New Testament passages, such as 1 Peter 1:7: "That the trial of your faith, being much more precious than of gold that perisheth, though it be tried with fire, might be found unto praise and honour and glory at the appearing of Jesus Christ."

...and white raiment, that thou mayest be clothed, and that the shame of thy nakedness do not appear...

White garments symbolize purity/purification. In the context of the surrounding verses, however, we understand that there is an additional meaning here. When Christ just moments prior had given His instructions to the church in Sardis, He said: "He that *overcometh*, the same shall be clothed in white raiment" (Revelation 3:5a; emphasis added). When comparing these two verses and these two church messages together, we see that Christ isn't simply telling the Laodiceans to "put on" white garments, as if dressing in some kind of enlightened spirituality were enough, but that the white garments would be awarded to those who "overcame" something. Thus, we have so far an exchange of worldly comforts for purification through fire (troubles or persecution of some kind) and a subsequent donning of purity clothing for those who overcome the trial of purification.

...and anoint thine eyes with eyesalve, that thou mayest see.

Finally, only *after* a trial by fire, only *after* earning their white garments, do the Laodiceans receive the eyesalve that opens their eyes to true and undefiled religion.

It appears to me, and to *many* authoritative scholars, that Christ is alluding to an equivalent of the following: The Laodiceans were relying on worldly comforts, and therefore had become blind and wretched. What their lukewarm spirits really needed in order to understand and appreciate Christ was persecution or trial. Their comforts had to be removed so they would fall to their knees, rely upon God as more than a Santa Claus provider, get real, stop being fake, stop going through motions, and earn the white garments they prized. Only then would they be able to see the glory of all He stands for.

Bible Gateway commentary sums it up like this: "The message to Laodicea is that the congregation needs, for its own sake, to face persecution so as to shatter its complacency and test and shape its faith."[19]

Sometimes, when people have it all figured out, when they have what they need and are spoiled to comforts (such as those our country has in abundance), they need to have all of it taken from them to shake or shatter their own unappreciative complacency and return their hearts to the Provider of nonmaterial treasures. (Consider this the next time the world looks so bleak. The worse things get, the more people seek the Lord. The harsher the condition of our country socially, politically, the riper we become for the Great Awakening I believe we're on the brink of now.)

Behold, I stand at the door, and knock…

Again, we come to one of those verses that is consistently quoted just slightly out of context. Many use this verse to paint a picture of our beloved Lord patiently knocking at the doors of our hearts, willing to come in upon invitation. The verse is often given at altar calls right before the pastor says, "Will you invite Him in? Will you open the door of your heart? Will you answer the knock and let Jesus Christ into your life?"

I want to make it very clear that *I do not have an issue with this verse being used this way.* It has led countless people to the Lord, and I praise Him for that. And just as one interpretation naturally flows into another (as we discussed in our helm/ship analogy earlier), I don't think ministers who apply this verse at an altar call with this format are doing anything wrong or sinful. If Christ is willing to stand at the door of a church and knock, how much more willing is He to stand at an individual's heart door and knock? So, I do think that's a valid application and it is being used respectfully in that way.

However, in keeping with rigid exegetical practice, we have to observe that this verse lands in a charge given directly from Christ to the church in the city of Laodicea. It's a message being given to a *church body* that worships in a church building with an entrance door. If we stick solely to the immediate context, we see Christ is essentially telling the church that because of their complacency and apathy, because of the lukewarmness of the congregants in Laodicea, He isn't even in the building. He *wants to be* there, and He wants to "sup" with them, but if the church has embraced comforts and playacting and hobnobbing in trade for a real relationship with Christ, they have effectively kicked Christ out of the church where He must stand at the door and knock in order to be invited back into the very place believers would call His own "house."

If so many Scriptures instruct us that we are to "go to" or "come to" the Lord, then traditionally, *we* are the knockers asking for God's grace and intervention. *Bible Gateway* provides this intel: "These words have often been romanticized in popular religious art, in pictures of Jesus 'knocking at the heart's door.' What is wrong is that Jesus is standing outside the door, excluded from the banquet like the homeless stranger in Amos Wilder's poem. The poignant plea, though directed first to the church at Laodicea, is strategically placed near the end of the series of messages as Christ's last appeal *to any congregation that has shut him out*. The beautiful 'invitation' is at the same time a severe indictment of a church that is self-sufficient, complacent and only marginally Christian."[20]

To those who have an ear to hear: Behold, Laodicea. Behold, today's Church. Behold, today's ministers. If you are complacent, if you are apathetic, if you are lukewarm, if you use church grounds as a place of showmanship or social status or dropping verses or casually hobnobbing while you bask in the comforts of this mortal experience, then Christ is no longer in the building. It's no longer about Him. He's outside, knocking, asking to be invited back into His own home, and a ministry endeavor devoted to a Man who's not even present cannot be anointed by the Man who's standing outside.

What Kind of Church/Ministers Are We?

James continues in verse 11 to make some very wise comparisons:

[11]**Doth a fountain send forth at the same place sweet water and bitter?** [12]**Can the fig tree, my brethren, bear olive berries?**

**either a vine, figs? so can no fountain both yield salt water
and fresh.**

We are known by our fruit. What are we producing? A fig tree can't create olives. A fountain can't flow with both fresh water and salt water. The churches in Laodicea and Sardis—if left unchanged—only ever produce complacent and apathetic congregants who perpetuate the same complacent and apathetic congregants and ministers. Inviting the lost into a Body of believers who only believe a thing exists but don't treat faith like the verb-of-works that it is will only further perpetuate more bodies of believers who stand around and talk until lunchtime on Sundays but who never really, truly, deeply *reach* the lost with any longevity or nutritious meat. It's all noise. It's all clanging cymbals.

[13]**Who is a wise man and endued with knowledge among
you? let him shew out of a good conversation his works with
meekness of wisdom.** [14]**But if ye have bitter envying and strife
in your hearts, glory not, and lie not against the truth.** [15]**This
wisdom descendeth not from above, but is earthly, sensual,
devilish.** [16]**For where envying and strife is, there is confusion
and every evil work.** [17]**But the wisdom that is from above is
first pure, then peaceable, gentle, and easy to be intreated,
full of mercy and good fruits, without partiality, and without
hypocrisy.** [18]**And the fruit of righteousness is sown in peace of
them that make peace.**

Here we have a wonderful return to the value of wisdom seeking. If we passionately and zealously seek wisdom from God in our ministries *prior* to stepping up to the pulpit—wisdom, which we have already discussed, is given to all who ask for it—then the wisdom that flows into us and by extension out of our mouths will be pure, peaceable, gentle, agreeable, merciful, spiritually nutritious, impartial, and lacking of all hypocrisy. Seeking worldly wisdom with "bitter envying and strife in the heart" is a "lie against truth." This brand of wisdom, as James so avidly pointed out, is "earthly, sensual, and devilish," and leads only to "confusion and evil."

The ESV translates verses 14 and 15 with the following words: "But if you have bitter jealousy and selfish ambition in your hearts, do not boast and be false to the truth. This is not the wisdom that comes down from above, but is earthly, unspiritual, demonic."

Demonic!

What's flowing out of the spring of today's pulpits? Preachers today frequently act as if they are completely unaware of the "more strict" judgment they heap on themselves when they start opening their mouths "in the name of the Lord" to listeners. They speak with the "wisdom" of "selfish ambition," and James says such "wisdom" does not originate from heaven.

- It is "earthly," meaning that it is separated from God's grace, will, and anointing.
- It is "unspiritual," meaning that it feeds flesh and pride, but not the soul.
- It is "demonic," meaning that it draws its very origins from demons!

Preachers and teachers of the Word who approach it with the wisdom of mankind are playing with fire… And it is serious. So serious.

For where you have envy and selfish ambition, there you find disorder and *every evil practice*, according to verse 16. A modern church sermon/service carried out with selfish ambition is not *just fruitless*, it's *demonic*!

Let me share a personal illustration of how things can get really dark really fast when true wisdom "from above" is not consistently sought. I was brought up as a Pentecostal. (I still believe that the power that fell on the Day of Pentecost is relevant to believers today, but unlike some who belong to my denomination, I don't believe that Christians have to receive the gift of tongues before they can minister, even behind a pulpit.) Some of the churches I attended in my youth got a little…well, spooky, to say the least. This was especially true during the Brownsville,

Texas, and Pensacola, Florida, revivals when many signs and wonders were materializing. People outside those churches saw the manifestation of the Holy Spirit in one area or other and tried to mimic it at their home churches. Ironically, through their zeal to experience revival amidst their own congregations, they gradually removed their focus from the Gospel and placed it onto formulas and gimmicks. They built entire theologies around what was legitimate for one people group at a specific place and time, and the truth of the Gospel became less important than rituals and practices by men to prompt Holy-Spirit intervention. (Translation: The ambition became a selfish one. Churches were competing to see who could produce the biggest signs and wonders and to see who was the most spiritual. The focus wasn't on Christ or the Holy Spirit but on bragging rights.) But, to me, the more fanatic the altar behavior became, the more demonic the signs and wonders appeared to be.

As one extreme example: A traveling evangelist once visited a church I was attending and gave a sermon on the birthing pains of the church and end-time prophecies. A few weeks later, after sound bites of his sermon had been repeated and quoted around the Body without proper return to exegetical interpretation, a man was found wailing on the floor of the men's restroom following the closing altar call of a Sunday main service. Once surrounded by male leaders of the church who were understandably concerned for his strange and seemingly random sudden illness, he explained through clenched teeth that he was spiritually giving birth. He was having "birthing pains," or so he said. And if his testimony was true in any way (and I'm not saying it was), his pains were literal and physical, like a mother whose loins were opening up for the passage of a newborn.

Instead of the pastor immediately and tenaciously taking to the pulpit to correct and expel such weirdness, eradicating such behaviors from the congregants because such an experience is unbiblical on so many levels, the pastor gave a weak and timid "the Lord works in mysterious ways" kind of response the following week. He even further supported the man-gives-birth story (which had spread around the church overnight, and everyone was waiting to see how the leaders would react) by saying that he felt the church was on the cusp of the greatest revival it had ever seen, and we needed to, like those attending the Brownsville and Pensacola events, be "open minded" to the Holy Spirit's choice manifestations of glory and power, and so on and so forth.

I continued to go to this church for a short while after that incident, but in the back of my mind, I knew I had a responsibility to detect what was really going on around me in the Body I belonged to, so I got real quiet, sat in the back row, and scribbled notes about anything that sounded suspiciously off the mark for later study. (Some might wonder why I stayed at all. First, I was young, and I wasn't completely sure yet how to recognize what was from the Lord and what wasn't. Second, as a Pentecostal, I was somewhat accustomed to hearing about supernatural signs. Third, and most importantly, I know now that the Lord wanted me to see what I saw in my attendance there, as it was a learning experience in discernment.)

A few weeks later, the heresy escalated to a frightening level. Then, another man was "giving birth" in the men's room (again with claims of physical pain), and this time, the "baby" had an identity. It was "Jesus," the man said. The man was "giving birth to Christ"!

What. In. The. World.

I left that church and never went back. Not once. Not ever. It truthfully freaked me out on so many levels that to this day when I remember the retelling of that man's wailing, I just get the heebie-jeebies all over.

But it must be understood: Those "birthing" incidents did not occur as a result of overnight hype. For months on end, that church had been getting looser and looser in its tolerance of teachings that bordered on heresy (and sound-bite dropping by lay attenders). It started with occurrences that are typically appreciated within a Pentecostal church, such as baptism of the Holy Spirit. Then, people would be struck by the "holy laughter," wherein they would begin cackling suddenly and remain at the altar for hours and hours just laughing. (The first time this happened, people all across the sanctuary were alarmed, but the man's laughing was so infectious and happy sounding that, within minutes, the pastor once again endorsed the event by saying, "Look at how the Holy Spirit is blessing this man!" The guard came down, and everyone started worshiping the Lord for what He was doing then and there.)

I thought the laughter was weird, but at my age, it was kind of funny and appeared to be harmless. Sermons supporting the "holy laughter" were subsequently delivered with the impression that these men and women were only being blessed with joy. No harm done, right?

But then the laughter became the new norm, the giggles became guffaws, and slowly over time, people were just beside themselves and out of their minds with this "heavenly joy." The "holy laughter" became an experience openly referred to in that church as being "drunk in the Spirit." Even the leaders called it by those very words specifically: "*drunk*...in the Spirit." Yet, because the bar had been raised several times already regarding what was a normal movement of God, by the time people were "getting spiritually drunk at the altar" and bumping into each other and stumbling all over the place (turning the altar into a glorified alcohol bar with a few of the church leaders getting "accidentally" handsy with the women), this, too, had just become the new norm.

Then came the shaking. People started having "spiritual convulsions"—that, too, was explained away. The "Quakers and Shakers" had done it, and for them it was legit, so it must be for this church. I was getting a little nervous at this point, but the whole congregation—including men and women I had known long enough to respect (all those preachers and teachers)—was celebrating all these "movements of the Lord," so I just assumed I had a lot to learn, and they were spiritually mature.

Then came the growling. People were "involved in spiritual warfare" and as such sometimes "became possessed" (or whatever; the explanation each time was slightly different, but it was all just nonsense) and the elders needed to surround that person to "exorcise demons." (This still gets me.

It's not that I don't believe possession is a real threat. I do. Very much. But you have to understand that my reflection here is on a specific congregation whose actions were becoming counterfeit. These men and women were all smiles when they got to church every week, and all smiles when they left, but every week, the same personalities were being "cleansed" of the "demons" that had come upon them since the previous service. I can't help but shake my head. And young people my same age were starting to see that they could be the center of attention by pretending to be possessed, so they demonstrated rounds of it as well.)

And so on and so on and so on. It was not an immediate thing. It was a frog-in-the-slow-cooker image of a church that had begun sincerely and lost all discernment. By the time men were "giving birth to Christ," I knew only from a Holy-Spirit-led gut-check (I had zero theological training at the time) that this was heresy. (Brother Fuller, a prayer warrior and theological powerhouse who had been well respected for half a century in the Pentecostal Church, heard about similar things happening in his area of the state of Oregon around the same time. My sister and I were visiting him and his wife when the subject came up, and he said, "If I was the Holy Spirit and I walked up to you and saw you already had your own show going on, I think I'd just walk on by and let you keep going and put on your show." This was a telling moment, considering it was coming from a man who staunchly supported supernatural outpourings of the Holy Spirit in the modern Church.)

Were these experiences real? The laughing, the possession, the growling, the shaking, the birthing pains…was any of that real? For many, no. A lot of people were excited about taking part in what they thought was spiritual activity so they could earn their bragging rights for the week and continue in their "selfish ambition" of an appearances game. For a select few, however, I believe it could have been a real experience.

Were all of these behaviors of God? Absolutely not. God does not make men spiritually give birth to Christ. (That sentence on paper just looks so outrageous to me. Even the idea that *that* would have to be written!

Wow…) When we earnestly seek God, supernatural occurrences will happen. We can count on it. Yet, developing an entire theology or doctrine around one phenomenon—or allowing the bar to be continuously raised to the point that "speaking in tongues" becomes "birthing Christ"—is ignorant.

But—if these activities weren't from God, and they were real manifestations of…something…then from where did they originate?

The purpose behind sharing this story is to bring us back to the simple truth James shared: When *godly wisdom* is not sought, when wisdom is of "the world" ("earthly") and when ambition is selfish (and therefore "uninspired"), demonic activity is a real and present threat—*especially* when the Church is hungry for revival (and the signs and wonders that *will* occur as a result). In every Great Awakening, there have been real manifestations of God to His people, and people have had experiences they can't explain. When the next Great Awakening hits, we will need discerning leaders who uphold *only* the truth, and who are willing to use their tongues for the purposes of godly wisdom, not for selfish ambition or lofty titles or games of competition.

Who are the wise men and women—the true Christ-ians—endued with pure knowledge among us? Who among our modern Church body has asked for wisdom from the Lord *prior* to letting loose their tongues? What leaders do we have at this moment who believe in blasting a wake-up call to the sleeping congregants of Sardis and throwing a bucket of ice on the lukewarm Laodiceans? Who today is willing to take the stricter judgment of their post seriously and put a permanent end to dispirited, feel-good gospels of showmanship and false teachings within their church?

"Not many of you should be teachers." But those of us who are have a bigger responsibility than we may have thought.

Who are those endued with knowledge?

Let them stand up, today, right now, and show the rest of the world— *all* the "whosoever will" whether they "look good" to us or not—what the words of their tongues stand for in a world of spiritually destitute, starving, dying people.

Do you want to change the world?
Do you want to play a part in the next Great Awakening?

Do not seek to find teachers that alter the Gospel to coincide
with your lifestyle, seek to find teachers who only speak the
truth with heavenly wisdom, and then alter your lifestyle
to coincide with the Gospel. Do not become a teacher or
preacher of the Gospel until you are willing to take your role
seriously, control your tongue, and love the "whosoever will."

Chapter 7

The "Friendship with the World" Church

JAMES 4; 5:1–6

THE FOURTH CHAPTER of James begins with a warning against worldliness. However, from the first line, we can see (by his using the words "among you") that it isn't only about individuals engaging in worldly behaviors, but the Body, collectively (although by extension it applies to individuals as well since the Body is made up of individuals and each is expected to do their part).

> ¹From whence come wars and fightings among you? come they not hence, even of your lusts that war in your members?

> ²Ye lust, and have not: ye kill, and desire to have, and cannot obtain: ye fight and war, yet ye have not, because ye ask not. ³Ye ask, and receive not, because ye ask amiss, that ye may consume it upon your lusts.

> ⁴Ye adulterers and adulteresses, know ye not that the friendship of the world is enmity with God? whosoever therefore will be a friend of the world is the enemy of God.

⁵Do ye think that the scripture saith in vain, The spirit that dwelleth in us lusteth to envy? ⁶But he giveth more grace. Wherefore he saith, God resisteth the proud, but giveth grace unto the humble.

⁷Submit yourselves therefore to God. Resist the devil, and he will flee from you. ⁸Draw nigh to God, and he will draw nigh to you. Cleanse your hands, ye sinners; and purify your hearts, ye double minded. ⁹Be afflicted, and mourn, and weep: let your laughter be turned to mourning, and your joy to heaviness. ¹⁰Humble yourselves in the sight of the Lord, and he shall lift you up.

¹¹Speak not evil one of another, brethren. He that speaketh evil of his brother, and judgeth his brother, speaketh evil of the law, and judgeth the law: but if thou judge the law, thou art not a doer of the law, but a judge. ¹²There is one lawgiver, who is able to save and to destroy: who art thou that judgest another?

As stated earlier, the early Church did not have a New Testament. It was because of the apostolic writings of men like James that we have a canonical Guidebook to assist us in righteous Christian living. Throughout the centuries, this section of the book of James has been taught repeatedly from the pulpit, and as a result, many of the values it represents are already familiar to us. We already know what it means when we hear that the Body should not bicker and quarrel and fight amongst its members. We know we are not to speak evil of one another. We know we are not the Judge and should not act as if we are. So I don't believe a verse-by-verse analysis is needed here.

Yet, there are a few interesting points in these passages that have puzzled some readers, and I'd like to take a little time to address their context and interpretation.

First of all, were the members of the early Church *murdering* each other out of greed or lust (4:2)? Probably not in the sense that we interpret the word "murder" or "kill" today, although it would be imprudent to simply assume that's not what James was referring to. For all we know, James wrote this entire letter just after a tragic death between quarreling Church members, and his reference to "kill" was literal. However, an equally likely interpretation relies on James' familiarity with his half-brother's theological stance on murder.

Consider Christ's own words as quoted from Matthew 5:21–22: "Ye have heard that it was said of them of old time, Thou shalt not kill; and whosoever shall kill shall be in danger of the judgment: But I say unto you, That whosoever is angry with his brother without a cause shall be in danger of the judgment: and whosoever shall say to his brother, Raca, shall be in danger of the council: but whosoever shall say, Thou fool, shall be in danger of hell fire." The ESV translates this: "You have heard that it was said to those of old, 'You shall not murder; and whoever murders will be liable to judgment.' But I say to you that everyone who is angry with his brother will be liable to judgment; whoever insults his brother will be liable to the council; and whoever says, 'You fool!' will be liable to the hell of fire."

According to Jesus, then, vile hatred and slander among the members would lead to the same divine judgment as murder, though the earthly consequence is dramatically different from one to the other. And in James 2:10, "For whoever keeps the whole law but fails in one point has become guilty of all of it" (ESV). Scholars have then agreed in many instances that James' reference to the murder between the members was an admonishment of vile hatred and slander among the members. But taking one's life in a literal sense should never be completely ostracized from potential interpretive conclusions, on the count that when hatred and slander are left unchecked, murder is subsequently a natural threat. This would have been especially true in James' day when someone could kill someone else during a heated argument, and if the deed was done in a dark alleyway apart from public witnesses, there were no forensic crime scene investigators to unveil the guilty party. In fact, violence from the Zealots was not at all uncommon, and death on the basis of religious conviction was more commonplace then than it is now. Whether one chooses to believe James meant actual death by murder or simply hatred, we can safely assume that either interpretation complemented the other.

Consider, too, the party to which James is referring when he lists the verb "ask." I have heard many a preacher quote these verses in a context that suggests Christians "do not have what they want or need, because they do not pray to the Lord for it in the first place—and when they *do* pray for what they want or need, they don't get what they ask for because they're asking for something with a sinful motive, the gift of which, if given, would be selfishly utilized [to "spend on his own passions" or "consume on his own lusts"]." But in James chapter 4, the entire emphasis is upon communication between members. Are modern preachers twisting Scripture when they use this passage in this way? The breakdown of that relies on consideration of the context in the *whole* book of James, and not just on the fourth chapter. The question is raised: "Does 'you do not ask' mean the early Church was guilty of refusing to ask fellow congregants for what they wanted to see happen in their church? Or that they were guilty of trying to work out their problems via mere human logic instead of asking the Lord for His intervention in a quarrel?"

Think about these two factors:

- If James, in 1:5, was so completely convinced that asking the Lord for wisdom is necessary and that wisdom absolutely will be given to all who ask, then we know he was passionate about "asking God" for "wisdom" in *all situations*, obviously including situations involving dissention among members.
- If the "asking" was to be from member to member, meaning from human to human (neither of whom had any supernatural gifts to bestow), it isn't logical that any man "getting what he wanted" could use that gift to "consume on [or "spend on"] his own lusts," unless the object of exchange was money or some other mate-

rial item, which naturally limits James' words drastically and no longer makes sense in the context of the surrounding verses that address spiritual maturity and health.

Thus, the best logic to apply here is that James is saying, "You don't have what you need, because you're not asking *God* for the things you need. And even when you *do* ask God for what you need, you aren't receiving, because you're not asking for wisdom [or spiritual maturity, or peace among the members, etc., all still relating to and traveling back to wisdom]—you're asking for selfish gain." When someone behind the pulpit says, "You have not that shiny car you want [or equivalent], because you ask not for that shiny car you want [or equivalent]," as I have heard some prosperity preachers assert in the past, this is a deliberate exchange from the object James is so passionate about (wisdom and spiritual maturity) for a material possession. Additionally, it cancels out the warning James follows with: You will not get that shiny car you're asking for because you are asking for something selfishly.

Just last night at the time of this writing, I listened to a sermon by a man who used the words "you have not because you ask not" probably ten times in a message about life prosperity. This is a clear and present misuse of Scripture. Joyce Meyer, on the other hand, preached a sermon once that quoted "you have not because you ask not" ten times or more also, and her focus was on drawing closer to Christ through the Holy Spirit and using that relationship wisely to identify with others, whether they be among the members or the lost. *This* application, in my opinion, was spot on. It's not about shiny things. (More on this shortly.)

Upon approaching verse 4, many have isolated the "friendship with the world" and "enemy of God" comparison and applied it as a finger-wag to individual transgressions. As one example, I recently heard a pastor over YouTube preach about our bodies being temples of the Holy Spirit. His sermon had a lot of value in the beginning, but it got off track in my opinion when he made the following trail his central focus: 1) If our bodies are the temple of the Holy Spirit, then we should not put harmful things into them; 2) if we choose to put harmful things into our bodies, we are being worldly; 3) if we are being worldly, we are choosing to be friends with the world; 4) if we are friends of the world, we are enemies of God; and 5) in conclusion, smoking cigarettes or eating too many preservative-filled Twinkies makes us enemies of God. (And yes, he did list the bit about Twinkies.) This sermon was getting a lot of hearty "amens" from the listening congregation, but I was shaking my head and growing weary by the end. This is what happens when verses are isolated and taken out of context. We simply cannot "package" Scripture in that way. When I was a girl, I heard the sermon on more than one occasion stating that anyone who isn't a Christian is a friend of the world and therefore he or she is an enemy of God. Imagine how nonbelievers feel, knowing that if they aren't *already* the believers they haven't learned to become yet, then they're *already* God's enemies! Think about the first thing that comes to mind when we hear the words "God's enemy." I personally think of demons, Satan, principalities of darkness, fallen angels, etc. To people who cannot exercise mature theology in their separation of these dark entities and a pastor's "any non-Christian is worldly and therefore an enemy of God" trail, the insinuation is drastically inaccurate.

Such conclusions as these are rendered immediately faulty by the "among you" address. James is clearly speaking to the Church here, not to unbelievers or Twinkie-eaters. This is further supported by his reference to spiritual adultery. (Consider all the references to spiritually adulterous "people of God" in the Old Testament.) By and large, the healthiest and likeliest of all interpretations for this heavily misquoted verse (in my own opinion as well as the opinions of the authors of several commentaries and biblical scholars) is the following, based on all of the surrounding context: 1) You are all members of the Church, and you are fighting amidst your-selves; 2) you're not asking for wisdom, you're asking for selfish gain; 3) as members of the Church, you are claiming to be representatives of the Gospel, but you are acting like representatives of sin while you feed hatred and dissention, which are character attributes prized by the sinful world around you, *not* by the Lord whom you claim to follow; 4) the choice must then be made as to which value system you will adopt—that of the world, or that of God—and "befriending" worldly values above God places you in opposition to the values of God.

Put more simply by the *Bible Gateway* commentary, James is "warning those who call themselves Christians that they may be false Christians who are really enemies of God.... We should accept James's terms, learn from his acute sense of moral right and wrong, and apply it to ourselves in fear of the judgment that comes to any who are not *true* Christians. Harboring bitter envy and selfish ambition, with the actions of fighting and quarreling, makes us adulterous people who are treating God with hatred and enmity."[21]

James often seems to come back to that issue of hypocrisy. In no way should his words have anything to do with cigarettes or Twinkies. The congregation of the YouTube sermon laughed at that, but I didn't think it was funny. That pastor, because of his ministerial position, was a representative of the Gospel, and whether or not he was aware of it, he was abusing Scripture.

This brings us to verses 5 and 6, which, when compared to all that we've said thus far, are easier to understand. God is a jealous God. He has given the Holy Spirit to dwell within us, and when we seek wisdom alongside humility, we will be given grace. Verse 9 (another often misunderstood verse) simply says that in taking our repentance seriously, we should not be seen in "laughter" (we should not be "laughing it off," so to speak), but in sorrowful mourning over our sin against God.

I realize that I've only addressed a few of the verses above, but the rest are self-explanatory and have been preached on for centuries with the same interpretation I would give, and have already given, elsewhere in this book. At this point, therefore, I would like to redirect our attention to how all of this relates to us today. At the beginning of this book, I outlined the problems that the early Church was facing and compared them to the problems our contemporary Church is facing. If we take all that James has said up to this point in chapter 4 of his epistle, I believe a solid conclusion to the study could be wrapped up in one simple sentence…

The Church—and all its members—needs to wake up, stop bickering, put an end to its hypocrisy, repent, choose to be representatives of God and not of the world, and start acting like the Church of Christ!

And we need to do this radically.

What, exactly, are we guilty of in these James 4 passages today, how are we guilty of it, and what can we do to fix it? Ten volumes could be written as a response to such a question, and many books have already addressed the most obvious of modern Church errors. But there is one area in which I believe we are guilty of failure that nobody appears to be talking about.

Social movements today have us redefining good and evil on an all-new scale. This social group over here says such-and-such is sinful, that social group over there says it's perfectly fine behavior, and the argument between both viewpoints requires Christians to uphold moral positions. But when this church over here doesn't agree with that church over there on the moral issue, the Body fights and divides against itself, and is therefore spiritually fruitless because it cannot stand. In the recent past, the "Hellfire-and-Brimstone" churches have driven away the lost with uncompromising and legalistic lines drawn in the sand. When the world of Christendom saw this result, churches began to embrace a new level of tolerance, and the lines in the sand were blurred. This kind of change can be wonderful when it means that numbers within the Church increase, but when the numbers are going up because the tolerance has allowed for heresy behind the pulpit to flatter people groups that hold convictions that oppose Scripture, the Gospel is profaned. To put it another way: So as not to offend people and see them leave the Church, we have essentially created churches that tolerate, and eventually embrace, heresy and false doctrines.

A conundrum is consequently presented requiring the lines in the sand to be redrawn and never again erased or blurred lest the Church become an institution of heretical offense against God. To therefore quote a popular cliché: Where *does* one draw the line?

I believe the answer can be found in the "hate the sin, love the sinner" concept. But aren't we just *sick and tired to death* of hearing that? Yes. We are. Very much so.

Why are we sick of it, though?

Ancient Psychology of Repetition

There is a fascinating psychological phenomenon called "semantic satiation." It occurs when a word or string of words has been used repetitively, one utterance after another in a short period of time, and the hearer can no longer draw meaning from the word or phrase. It lands on the brain like gibberish or a foreign language. Sounds in the air. The words have lost all meaning.

Over a hundred and thirty years before this phenomenon was given a name by the scientific community, it was described by Edgar Allen Poe in his 1835 *Berenice*. The central character in the short story explains that he is a victim of the most serious case of "monomania," a mental state he describes as the "nervous intensity of interest with which, in my case, the powers of meditation…busied and buried themselves in the contemplation of even the most ordinary objects of the universe." One of these "ordinary objects of the universe" was the intricacy of the spoken word. He goes on to explain how his monomania has forced him to "repeat, monotonously, some common word, until the sound, by dint of frequent repetition, ceased to convey any idea whatever to the mind."[22]

Some words don't have this effect as quickly as others, because we have become accustomed to the saturation of that word in our vocabularies (such as "the" or "and"). Other words that we do not use as frequently can lose meaning after only a few references in the period of a minute or two.

Chimney. Wardrobe. Fireball.

In writing those three random words, I thought of: 1) the chimney-sweep scene in *Mary Poppins*; 2) the wooden wardrobe from the low-budget *Lion, Witch, and the Wardrobe* of the 1960s; and 3) a popular, mouth-burning, cinnamon-flavored, red jawbreaker candy called the Fireball from my childhood. Any one of these words inspires immediate mental imagery based on what we personally associate with its meaning. A picture appears in our mind that further defines the meaning of the word as we remember it. However, any one of these words repeated over and over, or used many times in a short period over the course of a conversation, will start to sound like nonsensical words in the air. Sounds floating around that have no purpose.

Let me give you an example of a word that almost always has this effect on me.

Ravioli.

You have just taken in a word (whether by sound or vision through text) that you already know represents a stuffed pasta. Your brain immediately pulls from its complicated filing system a mental image that you personally associate with the sound or textual word, such as a plate with round raviolis under red sauce with fresh grated parmesan and sprinkled parsley from an Olive Garden commercial, or that box you have in your freezer of a squared ravioli cut in half with Italian sausage spilling out. Whatever the image, it appears in your mind when you hear "ravioli," because the word holds meaning to you. If you try to experiment with semantic satiation knowingly, you can likely keep that image there as a result through hundreds or thousands of repetitions of the word because you're deliberately trying to beat the odds and see how far you can go before the sound or text falls flat. If you strike up a casual conversation about ravioli in a restaurant, however, and your focus isn't premeditated, then after about the thirtieth time someone says "ravioli," the image in your mind starts to fade and the sound in the air (or word on the page) becomes meaningless. Distracting. Annoying even.

Give it a try. Don't just skip this following "paragraph." Actually let your eyes land on each instance of "ravioli" and without trying to defeat it, really let the sound and letters be seen and "heard" in your mind's receptors (if you can get that far).

Ravioli. Ravioli.

Ravioli. Ravioli.

If you're like the majority of people who don't use this word in everyday conversation, you will have noticed that by about the fifth or sixth word in, your eyes have to slow down and make a conscious effort to keep the stuffed pasta picture in your thoughts. By the tenth instance, the word starts to look weird, like something is "off" in the nature of its formation, like it's spelled incorrectly or something. (Some of you just glanced back at the word again to see how it was spelled.) By the twentieth time your brain's receptors, your mind's "ears," start to jumble the vowels and consonants together and it begins to sound like a bland and irritating mixture of *r, v,* and a long *e* sound. Ravlyorli, revlorlaylee, reeveorleeli. It starts with *r* and ends with an *ee* sound, but other than that, it's nonsense. By the fiftieth instance, the pasta and red sauce image has disappeared and the repetition starts to become obnoxious.

So distracting is this useless recurrence visually that when the paragraph about ravioli first appeared in the surrounding text, your eyes flickered over to it, your brain made note of it, and then your eyes traveled back to where you were reading before you were interrupted…but it was so disruptive to the eye that you had to really focus on the text leading up to and immediately following the textual eyesore. In the end, it only serves to be an annoyance.

But why am I talking about semantic satiation and ravioli in a chapter about friendship with the world?…

The Development of the "Catchphrase Church"

In the 1980s, the words "hate the sin, love the sinner" became a mantra of Christendom. When they were first dropped out of the mouths of Christians, they inspired a call to action. They encompassed that enigmatic loving of the "whosoever will" whilst refusing to endorse the transgression—all in six words. Upon hearing this string, believers were inspired that such a difficult but necessary feat was captured in a six-word container that simplified it into a truncated, easy-to-remember, and easy-to-memorize truth that could be carried in the heart and applied at all times. From our complicated brains' filing system, a brand-new image was created depicting people across all social, political, and religious boundaries in a big family hug—or whatever mental image each person would have concocted through personal association to the words. But however this image differed from person to person, corporately we saw peace, love, warmth, and affection. When believers were placed in a difficult position involving someone in their life whom they deeply cared about, but whose decisions they couldn't support, they took their concern to their pastor, who pulled these six words out of his pocket like a salve to a wound and pressed it on the spiritual skin of their associate fellow, and the response was, "Yeah!... Yeah, that's true! I can hate the sin... [Here the recipient pauses while it sinks in.] And love the sinner! [Another pause, a nod, a euphoric facial expression.] I never even thought of it that way, but it's so simple!"

By 1985, hundreds of "instances" later over half a decade, the words "hate the sin, love the sinner" started to sound a little overused. Our brains had to slow down and make a conscious effort to keep the hugging picture in our thoughts.

By 1990, ten years of instances later, the words started to sound and look suspect, like something was "off" in the nature of their formation, like there needed to be more to them in order to mean what they originally did.

By 1995, our brains' receptors started to jumble the vowels and consonants together with a bunch of other Church clichés, and it began to sound like a bland and irritating mixture of "sinner" and "sin" and "loving" and "hating." The phrase started with what we're allowed to hate and ended with what we're commanded to love, but other than that, it was nonsense.

By the turn of the century, the hugging, loving, and charismatic backclap images had disappeared from our corporate mindset, and the repetition of "hate the sin, love the sinner" started to become downright obnoxious to the Church *and* the secular world. (Today, for me, it inspires a mental image of a book on a shelf somewhere in the "embarrassing history of religion" section titled, *How to Offend the Lost in Seven Syllables or Less.*)

Why did this happen? It wasn't that the words were innately wrong. They weren't. In fact, they were biblical (hang with me…). It's what they became after decades of being used by the wrong wild tongues and in the wrong contexts. The words had lost all meaning from their original purpose, and thanks to religious-spirited abusers, it became pejorative terminology, and much like semantic satiation, the ring of those words in the air inspires an intrinsic "please, enough already" vibe for the "sinners" and "lovers" alike.

It became a condescending phrase we simply slipped into conversation, placing everyone who didn't live exactly how we thought they should down to the letter in the "sinner" group. Us versus them. We, the "children of God," the "non-sinners," graciously accepting our obligation to love the shocking, worldly wrongdoers. We, the "enlightened minority" and "philosophical beloveds," patting each other on the back and rising to the occasion for the Creator's duds and also-rans because the Bible says we must.

For victory! For alliance! For truth! Huzzah!

The sinner wasn't the "loved," despite the open directive of the phrase. The sinner was the lesser, the failure, the one who by golly just didn't make the cut into the fellowship of those whose lifestyles and behaviors earned titles like "the brother" or "the sister." No, they were the…wait for it… "SINNER!" Dun dun dun! (Insert audience "ooooo" here.)

People, we are ALL sinners.

What began as a profound and powerful answer to an age-old "go ye into the world" mystery was now a weapon against the very peace it called for. Any Christian alive from 1980 to 2000 could quote "hate the sin, love the sinner," but how many of these same people could quote Romans 12:9, which reads, "Let love [to all, including the "sinners"] be genuine [sincere, honest, heartfelt, unpretentious, authentic]. Abhor ["hate"] what is evil; hold fast to what is good" (ESV)? This verse tells us explicitly to "abhor" sin, but it also commands us to let our love be genuine.

Here are some others (all ESV):

- "But God shows his love for us in that while we were still sinners, Christ died for us" (Romans 5:8).
- "And have mercy on those who doubt; save others by snatching them out of the fire; to others show mercy with fear, hating even the garment stained by the flesh" (Jude 1:22–23).
- "Above all, keep loving one another earnestly, since love covers a multitude of sins" (1 Peter 4:8).

None of these verses makes excuses for sin, and the verse from Jude even says that we should "hate" the sin (the "garment stained by flesh"). Yet all three openly refer to showing great love and care for the "sinner." When "hate the sin, love the sinner" first became a pop slogan for churchgoers, I believe the intention behind it was pure and based on Scripture, even if it wasn't verbatim. But it was such a celebrated slogan that it replaced real Bible reading and scriptural meditation/memorization amongst the Body where the issue of loving the lost was concerned. *No* words uttered from the mouths of men will ever have the same life-breathing authority and power as Scripture, so no words should be as important to those who claim to follow it. Nevertheless, a string of words so charming and witty captivated generations of people who, when asked, couldn't even give biblical backing for the creed they held dear.

Although I don't blame this entire period of Christian blunders entirely on the rise and fall of a single catchphrase, the phenomenon I just outlined represents the overall attitude of the era it belonged to. Multitudes of Christians during this time shelved their Bibles and adopted substandard soundbites:

- "Name it and claim it."
- "Believe it and receive it."

- "The Bible says it, I believe it, that settles it."
- "When God closes a door, He opens a window."
- "God helps those who help themselves."
- "Let go and let God."
- "Another trial, another jewel [for the crown]."
- "The family that prays together stays together."

And so it goes. Even the phrase "man of God" was so overused it became a single word: "manaGod." Whereas these soundbites all held a level of truth and sincerity by some who said them, through the abuse of overuse and inappropriate application, these words lost all meaning as well and collectively became the cliché hat rack that Christians hung their faith upon.

Botta-bing, botta-boom. Wit. Charm. The new gospel.

Believers stopped reading Scripture for themselves and learned to speak "Christianese," a language they picked up in the organized institution we call "Church." They would listen for those pulpit-pounding, hell-fire-and-brimstone zingers, memorize them on the spot, and then wait for just that right moment later when they could deliver them to a listener or corner the lost in the interest of sounding intelligent. The clever, one-two punch of the pulpit retorts were established as preferable to the very God-breathed and Christ-inspired Word of the Lord (cf. 2 Timothy 3:16).

Progressively, Christianity became a "thing to do" and not a Person to sincerely follow. A club. A league. A bunch of meetings. The Body became "judgmental," "legalistic," "phony." Believers became Judaizers. Few knew what the Bible said anymore, but most people had an opinion or a snappy comeback, and they weren't afraid to voice it, even to the detriment of the slogan itself.

The world gradually responded with a dismissal of Christianity when the "us versus them" mentality increased, and our numbers declined when the club we were members of stopped being fulfilling.

I'm not suggesting that the "Catchphrase Church" trend was our only problem. Our decline was not limited to the magnification of zingers. I *am* suggesting it was a major symptom of the apathy disease that swept the nation at that time, and using that illustration helps me paint the over-all picture of how we developed as the self-righteously indignant—but unlearned—people we were for several decades.

As a counterattack of this phenomenon, the Church started preaching powerfully on heavy tolerance of the sin and the sinner: loving all people no matter what they've done or how they live. It was about the year 2003, give or take, when I felt we were really headed in the right direction again. Christians young and old were just as exhausted with the sound bites as I was. Our disgust for that trend, atop just coming off an enormous wave of prosperity preachers who made even devout Christians participate in the quintessential embarrassment-face-palm, led to a new and exciting era in which it felt like the focus was where it should be. Finally, we were going to *really love* the sinners and not just talk about it.

Unfortunately, however, as a result of the drastic turnabout in Church attitude, we are now quickly approaching a time when heresy will be the norm if the Church doesn't wake up.

The Development of the "Dating Christ Church"

This subhead above, for some, inspires an instant shock-and-awe reaction. However, the explanation behind it is a sound one if you'll bear with me through its breakdown.

In recent years, Christians have shown a maturity to "love on" any and all who come through the doorways of our church buildings. Enormous emphasis has been placed on letting go of judgmentalism and legalism within the Body. I *love* that change. I really do. If you've been reading everything I've said up to this point about truly loving the "whosoever will," then you know already that I would rather be a part of the "Hospital/Triage Church" than any of the others I've talked about.

But I am beginning to worry that the brakes need to be applied—swiftly and resolutely—under certain circumstances. There is a point at which accepting anything and everything into our credo of intimate interaction with others becomes a casual acceptance of anything and every-thing into our belief system as well, which profanes the Gospel.

After the regurgitation of the "Catchphrase Church," churches began to open their doors again, embracing all those treasured souls it had failed to embrace before. Ministers returned to the simple Gospel of love in exchange for hellfire and brimstone and empty sound bites. The pulpit pounders of the Satanic Panic '80s fell into obscurity, and young men and women with gentle voices took the stage. The three-point sermons about how to anger God became discussions of God's grace. Songs like "Come Just as You Are to Worship" rose to the top of the charts and took a place in worship services across the nation. New imagery popped up in sanctuaries.

I remember the first time I saw the "body piercing saved my life" poster. It was a picture of Christ on the cross with nails piercing His hands, but the caption held an obvious double meaning, and it was clear that even Christian-market merchandise was beginning to reflect a new acceptance of people from various walks of life. I visited a Christian book-store and saw that the "What Would Jesus Do?" bracelets (that, like the slogans, began as a heartfelt sentiment and became a tool of criticism) were obsolete, and in their place were cross necklaces etched with the Lord's Prayer—a signal that the "Catchphrase Church" was bringing the focus back to the basics. I drove by a bulletin board featuring a church advertisement that said, "These are my church clothes," with the man in the picture wearing jeans and a black T-shirt—not unlike the clothing I had no choice but to wear years earlier.

Tommy Hilfiger and Gap were now just as appropriate as a suit and tie to lead worship in. (I visited one church where the pastor spoke wearing shorts and a flannel long-sleeve shirt.) Senior pastors began spiking their hair. Pastors' wives were dying their hair platinum blonde and gelling it up like Marie Fredriksson of the '80s band Roxette. Teenagers were being allowed to attend services in flip-flops, and their toddler siblings were still in pajamas.

Arguments about what instruments were appropriate (piano, organ) versus inappropriate (electric guitar, synthesizer) were being let go. Squabbles about how fast a song should be played were waning. Worship started to allow for almost any sound, including rock, provided it was ultimately done with reverence.

I was thrilled!

So long had I sat in my own misery, internally grumbling about the stringent expectations of the Body and a religion built on rules. Now it looked as if all that was disappearing—not in every church, certainly, but by and large, that sensation of scorn that hung over Christianity like a dark cloud to both Christians and nonbelievers alike was dissipating.

For these items just listed, I am still thrilled.

But then something else happened. The Church, in many areas, simply became *too* relaxed. Little by little, in stages that were so subtle they were nearly invisible, the anything-goes acceptance model ushered in a faint lack of respect for what church should be. The leniency of standards for clothing, hair, and electric guitars became a leniency for things Scripture tells us have no place in worship services. We are now in an emergent phase of over-tolerance.

Some of the things I see now are extremely disturbing.

Take music, for example.

Exorcistic Praise Replaced with "Feelings"

In the yesteryear of praise, lyrics were based almost entirely on Scripture. Men and women of God took lines straight out of the Word and put them to music. When we came together and sang these lines, we were accomplishing two things: 1) committing Scripture to memory; and 2) corporately cooperating in a respectful exhortation of the Holy Spirit's presence in a building dedicated to that very purpose. Praise and worship were ways to humbly ask the Lord to enter the place we were standing in, and we were accomplishing that by using the words He had given us to begin with. As such, we went to Him fully believing that He would come to us so that we could, in turn, exalt and revere Him as Lord over our lives. It was a subjective practice that honored the Lord far above our own heads, which is as it should be. And when the presence of God came into that place, anything belonging to the darker spiritual dimensions had to leave.

Effectively, we were exorcising. I know that sounds intense, but considering why praise and worship exist, it matches this description precisely: To "exorcise" is to drive out an evil spirit from a person or place, and by using our voices in agreement of bringing God *into* a place through inspired, God-breathed lyrics, we were driving everything else *out* that had no place in a church.

Our music was exorcistic.

Powerful.

Whether or not we could see what was happening around us in the spiritual realms, we were fighting in the Lord's army during warfare when we lifted our voices in praise of Him.

I don't think what instruments are played—and at what speed—or what clothing is worn matters as much as the words coming out of our mouths, and our mental focus as we utter them. That's not to say that I only endorse worship songs that are verbatim Scripture, but somewhere, a line has to be drawn regarding what words are edifying to the Lord, and which are just pretty—but powerless—sounds. Songs that openly bring our hearts' sincerest praise to God are wonderful, in my opinion, whether or not they quote the Bible. Am I the only one who has noticed this bizarre switch to the "me, me, me, gimme, gimme, bless me, bless me, I feel, I feel" songs of today's services? Am I the only one who has noticed that our songs have little to nothing to do with correct theology?

Some would argue that as long as a song talks about our feelings regarding God, it is okay to add that one to the program list. I respectfully disagree on the count that even though those songs can be beautiful, the very definition of "praise" and "worship" centers on acclaiming, admiring, and honoring God and His attributes. Worship isn't about *us*. It's about adoring *Him*. No, I don't think we need to completely remove the "I" from all modern praise music. I know some are offended every time they hear a song with a first-person perspective, but because it can sometimes be impossible to express our personal exaltation of Him without mentioning the self ("*I* praise you," "*I* exalt thee," and so on), it becomes a petty dispute of semantics to rail against a single word. Nor do I believe that every worship song has to make complicated, theological statements, but each one should at least be theologically correct.

It boils down to this: If a worship song isn't *worshiping Him*, then it isn't a worship song, and shouldn't be one we sing corporately. We can always get together around a fire pit on weenie-roast Fridays and sing happy songs about our own feelings, but when we gather into His house, advertising to God and mankind that we are going to praise Him, then praise Him we should.

Let me give the first of a few examples. Years back, I attended youth camp where we sang a "praise" song called "Enemy's Camp." The lyrics are as follows:

> Well I went to the enemy's camp, and
> I took back what he stole from me (x3)
> I went to the enemy's camp, and
> I took back what he stole from me.
> He's under my feet (x6)
> Satan is under my feet.[23]

During the "under my feet" line, all the teenagers were instructed to jump up and down and "stomp on" the "enemy." Like the other young and innocent singers, I stomped right along with them and jumped around and burned calories and had a nice little cardio deal going on, but spiritually I believe that's all it amounted to.

Two or three days into my trip, I caught myself singing these words in the middle of lunch and stopped suddenly, taking a moment to really consider what was coming out of my mouth…

"I went," meaning I willingly traveled, "to the enemy's camp," evidently meaning some place where Satan dwells, "and I took back what he stole from me," meaning that I challenged Satan head-on and demanded he give back to me something he stole, and as a result of that act, "he's [now] under my feet."

I did? I took it back? What did he take? What did he steal? You mean Satan had the right to steal from me? And when he did, I willingly marched right up to his face in some archetypal "camp" where he dwells and just took it back? Just like that? And now, through the very power of my own self, having nothing at all whatsoever to do with God, he's under my feet?

What!?

Wow. I never knew I was so powerful.

*Sigh...

Later that night, I stood and watched as all the teens around me got right into it as usual. I took a minute to glance at the faces of both the youth and their leaders. I recognized a few in my own group who didn't regularly attend church and whose theological understanding of who God is and what our relationship with Him should look like was virtually non-existent. This one week at camp was their only real exposure thus far to the foundations of Christianity. And here they were, being imprinted, being *indoctrinated*, with this crazy idea that when we feel assaulted by the enemy we just jump and stomp around and act like monkeys until we get what we believe is owed to us. Ladies and gentlemen, boys and girls, this song most definitely did not pass the theology check.

What's worse is that the chapel speaker kept using the song in his sermons all week. "We need to *stomp* that devil down! Take *back* what he stole from us!" I don't mean to make fun of him. He was a very nice person, and I'm sure he meant well. But even if songs are not intended to be used as more than just a fun hype, people who write them have to assume that there are those out there who will take those lyrics seriously— whether it be a teacher, a congregant, or both. That preacher took *terrible* theology and cemented it in the minds of my fellow youth. To some of them (and I hope this isn't the case), the entire concept of spiritual warfare might have been for the rest of their lives reduced to a glorified *Tom and Jerry* cartoon.

In hopes of learning that this particular song was no longer being played and sung in worship services, I recently did some digging. Sadly, I discovered it's as popular today among young people as it was then.

Sure, that's an extreme example. Let's look at another.

The song "Above All" on the album "Worship" by Michael W. Smith is absolutely beautiful, and when it appears as a song on a Christian CD, I don't have a single problem with it. It's in my own collection as we speak. But again, the issue is when it is adapted into a corporate setting for church praise. Amidst its picturesque words is the phrase, "Like a rose trampled on the ground, You [Christ] took the fall and thought of me above all."[24] A person could argue theology on whose glory Christ's sacrifice was ultimately for between man and God, and that argument has been a chicken-or-egg debate for over ten years since the song was written: Did God send Christ to "take the fall" for the glory of men (the "me") "above all"? Or did Christ obediently "take the fall" to glorify His Father "above all"? As a result of this issue, some Christians have stood against the song being used in churches, as it can tend to be pinpointed far too much on the importance of mankind. However, Christ *was* thinking about how His death would redeem all men and women from that day forward, so I don't see this as an issue worthy of drawing lines in the sand.

What I do see in this song is the contribution it makes toward the "focus on me" trend in worship. We should be praising and worshiping the Lord because He is worthy to be praised, not because of the benefit His works have given us. We should praise Him because He is the awesome God of the universe, not because we get freebies. Any song that ends with the words "me above all" could potentially, if even subtly so, make the statement that a worship service is about "me, above all" and not about the One being praised. I wouldn't take it as far as some have in suggesting that "me above all" was Michael W. Smith's way of exalting humans above God. I find that ridiculous considering the first half of the sentence (and besides, he wasn't the original writer anyway; Paul Baloche was). But to a gathered Body, *especially* when there's a chance it may have new visitors whose Gospel knowledge base is underdeveloped, a song like this has the capability of giving a wrong impression about who we really should be thinking about during service.

To incorporate this song into a service in and of itself is nowhere near heretical, and I don't mean to imply that dramatic action be taken against it. But when added to all the other songs that ultimately come back around to the "me, me, me" mentality, at the end of the day, we have pretty, feel-good sounds that all focus on self and feelings.

A friend who shares this concern once told me that you could essentially take any song from today's secular pop music, remove the word "boyfriend" from it, insert "Jesus," and you would have nailed down the gist of modern worship. This is a sarcastic statement, sure, but it holds some truth. In the past, many of the songs we sang from hymn books still spoke of the benefit we gain from God, but the first focus of the lyrics was upon the wonderful attributes of God and our gratefulness toward Him for allowing us to benefit from those attributes.

For example, in the long-celebrated hymn "Amazing Grace," we were once "lost" but now we're "found"; we were once "blind" but now we "see"; we were once only "wretches" but now we're "saved." Every time we sing this, we are singing of the gifts we benefit from, but the song maintains the definition of "praise" and "worship" because the lyrics come back to the theologically accurate attribute of God's "amazing grace." In "Great Is Thy Faithfulness," we likewise list many benefits we receive, such as mercy, our needs being met, beautiful nature, pardon for sin, enduring peace, strength for today, and hope for tomorrow—but the "praise" and "worship" is present throughout each lyric as it all ultimately points to the theologically accurate attribute of God's "great faithfulness." Many of the traditional hymns only barely reflect on our own benefits at all, as they were written entirely to adore the nature of God, such as "How Great Thou Art" and "All Hail the Power of Jesus' Name."

Sometimes a modern worship song does focus on the attributes of God's character, but there are strange and problematic lyrics that don't belong in a corporate setting. The lyrics "in His presence, our problems disappear"[25] from the praise song "Jesus, We Celebrate Your Victory" brings focus to us and what's going to happen with "our problems," and people who are young in the faith may be left disappointed when their problems remain during and after the service. Another contemporary worship song specifically drawing a lot of heat right now is John McMillan's "How He Loves." There is a line that says, "Heaven meets earth like a sloppy, wet kiss."[26] (Because of the poetic beauty of the rest of the song, many worship leaders have changed the lyric to "unforeseen kiss" instead of "sloppy, wet kiss" so it won't offend people in Church.) This one was so unbelievable to me that I had to see if the original artist ever explained his rationale, and I found his response to the controversy online. After hearing so much backlash, he wrote: "Are we in kindergarten?... The idea behind the lyric is that the kingdom of heaven and the kingdom of earth converge in a way that is both beautiful and awkwardly messy. Think about the birth of a child, or even the death of Jesus himself. These miracles are both incredibly beautiful and incredibly sloppy ('gory' may be more realistic, but 'Heaven meets earth like a gory mess' didn't seem to have the same ring)."[27]

After reading the original artist's complete explanation (which is not included here but is worth reading if you're interested), I actually agreed with his defense of the song. He did well to point out that, unlike so much other fluffy Christian music, this song said something bold and thought-provoking. The poetry behind the grit and "crash" of heaven and earth is one that an artist in his position has every right to write about without having to suffer the limitations of the established and organized Church, and any person in a Christian music store should have the right to buy, enjoy, and sing along with the song. But *corporate worship* is a whole other animal.

A gathering of people in a church building who are professing to honor God simply because He is worthy of praise should not be singing about sloppy wet kisses. Period. Although I am surprised my explanation of why I feel this way would even be necessary, because of the scores standing up to defend this song as a legitimate worship song, I will respond:

- Yes, much of the Bible's content is "sloppy" in that it covers blood, gore, sex, and many other uncomfortable topics. However, just because something is in the Bible does not make it "praise." Otherwise, we would be singing to the Lord about evil kings sacrificing their children on fiery alters, King David's act of adultery, or the baker from the Joseph story who was beheaded and impaled on a pole. (We are headed there if we don't reassess the foundational concepts of "praise.")

- Yes, church services should not cater to what makes congregants "feel comfortable." In that, we are in emphatic agreement—more so than I could ever say. However, if a song has the potential to completely jolt one's mind out of worship, off of God, and onto a lyric, then it doesn't matter how justified the lyric is. It's distracting. People should be encouraged to think of God, and *only* God, when they praise.

- Yes, the song is melodically gorgeous, and the poetry is stimulating. However, there are lines that either require unorthodox theological application or deep theological training and maturity to understand ("I am a tree bending beneath the weight of his grace"; "if grace is an ocean, we're all sinking"; "my heart burns violently inside of my chest"), which is not really inclusive of attenders who can't draw meaning from the words they're expected to voice between them and God.

So, collectively, considering all prior examples as today's norm, it eventually becomes heretical when the "praise *you*" becomes the "let's talk about me and what I want and how I feel." *It's not a matter of a single song, but of saturation.* It appears as if we are always singing about our feelings about God instead of simply telling Him how awesome He is. It's as if the term "praise and worship" should be updated to "relationship and feelings."

In fact, to a degree, this has already taken place. Have you noticed how many churches today no longer refer to "worship *service*"? It has been replaced in church organizations all over the country now with the words "worship *experience*."

Think about the phrase "military service."

Now imagine it called "military experience"…

Do you see the instant diminishment of meaning here? From a connotation of *duty* to that of *encounter*? The term "*joining* the military *service*" immediately inspires imagery of blood, sweat, tears, tenacity, faithfulness, heroics, battle cries, and "those colors that never run." As a sharp contrast, "*attending* a military *experience*" sounds like a club people sign up for while they're on a kick and then leave when the honeymoon phase is over. "The Military Experience" sounds like a rejected concept-title of a laser-tag theme park in Branson, Missouri, where patrons would no more fulfill a duty to their country than to run around in fake fatigues ducking for cover in army-replica bunkers.

The idea of Christ-ians "joining" something called a "service" suggests that we are faithfully showing up at a church to fulfill an ongoing duty within that ministry, *or* going to a weekly meeting that steadily increases our spiritual maturity and accountability so that we are more useful to the lost outside of it. We Christians should be *soldiers* of Christ, not *vacationers* of Christ. Calling the "service" of our Church an "experience" appeals to the laziness that is currently deteriorating the passion that defined it when the original Christian soldiers of James' day were martyred for the cause. Even "Sunday school" and "discipleship meetings" are now being called "life groups" because we come to "do life together" instead of to be *schooled* or *discipled* (disciplined) in the knowledge of God. Can't we see how these little alterations—those that appeal to the world—are slowly changing our mission from "action" to "idling," from "giving" to "getting"? Can't we see that we are becoming "hearers only" and not "doers of the Word"?

How has all of this come about? Why are we doing this? How have centuries of praising the Lord become a trend of focusing on ourselves and spiritual benefits, and why are even the most respected churches so blind to this?

In part, I believe it's because we wish to appeal to the human experience. The world has never been as ripe with "how do you feel about that?" terminology in our faces everywhere. We believe in God because of how we *feel* about our lives. We love others when we *feel* like we should. We gave into that temptation last week because we couldn't help how we *felt* when we were confronted with something our flesh desired. We gave money to the offering yesterday because it made us *feel* good. We disregarded that lost soul at work last year because he or she made us *feel* uncomfortable. "Choice" and "orthodox" have been removed from the faith. We have largely given up on songs that only worship, because we want to think about how we feel. And when newcomers enter our buildings, they, too, are able to learn about feelings and relationships, instead of being made to feel awkward by archaic hymns that only talk to God about how amazing He is. In order to make sure that our numbers increase and new people come in, we must make sure everyone in our services are comfortable and the feelings they are receiving are gratifying.

But we are not commanded to make people comfortable. We shouldn't trade the orthodoxy of worshiping God for *friendship with the world*...

The worship and praise played from the pulpit of an adult service desperately need to be revised. If the older songs are too dated, then we should update them or write new ones that keep the focus where it should be, but we should not keep singing warm-fuzzy songs. We should *never* change how we approach the throne of God in praise to appeal to the world.

That includes teaching, as well.

Heresy from the Pulpit

Somewhere between hellfire-and-brimstone and everything-is-permissible is a sweet spot we need to strive so much harder to find. When our rules and regulations relaxed decades back, so, too, did our theology. We want to make people feel comfortable at all costs. If they get offended and leave the Church, they may be lost forever, so in the interest of keeping people in church where they belong, we have blurred the lines of right and wrong. Ironically, however, by blurring the lines between right and wrong, we have allowed for a gospel that doesn't always speak the truth, and those people "in church" might be lost forever. The idea that "getting people saved is more important than discipleship" is *dead wrong*. No church should participate in a numbers game. No church should be leading people to say "the sinner's prayer" just so they can put another notch on their belt and shout, "Another one for the Kingdom!"

Discipleship of believers is just as important as helping nonbelievers reach the point of making the initial decision to follow Christ. The Church cannot assume that leading people to say words is the goal. There needs to be right teaching beyond that point. Jesus didn't say, "Go ye therefore, and make people say pretty things about Me." He said, "Go ye therefore, and make *disciples*" (Matthew 28:19a). The word "disciple" comes from the Latin *discipulus*, "pupil, learner, student, follower." When applied to Christ, a disciple is someone who continues to be a student of Christ's teachings, and the "follow" verb embedded in the etymology indicates we should pattern our lives to be like His. As such, the goal of the Body should be about helping others live as closely to Christ's life as humanly possible. We should be growing in it to the point that we subsequently teach from it. But when the teachers trade Gospel for fluff or heresy, people live in accordance to fluff and heresy, and the students can place whatever title upon themselves they wish—but it doesn't make them disciples. It is extremely important, then, that we really consider what the Church is saying today, that we "reach the saved" (in addition to the lost) with continual right teaching, and that we are careful to monitor who takes the pulpit.

Last October, I was busy wrapping Christmas presents in my office. (Yes, I do my shopping very early.) Since my hands were busy but my ears were not, I logged on to YouTube and looked up a sermon. I don't remember the first sermon that I clicked on. As many of you know, when you set YouTube to play and then walk away from the computer, it plays the next related video and the next, indefinitely, choosing for you what you are going to see next as it relates to your initial search. When I wrap presents, I take hours and hours at each sitting, placing every paper line precisely and dressing each gift with hand-crafted bows and ribbons. Several hours into my wrapping session, another sermon began (it was probably the eighth or ninth by this point). I glanced quickly at the screen long enough to see that the pastor was not one I knew, and the congregation was very small. At the start of his lesson, the man said, "Good morning, Church of Christ," so I know for sure that he was at least preaching to a congregation of Christ-followers, and not to a congregation of some other religion. (A few other things he said strongly pointed to the idea that he was a Pentecostal.) I wish now that I had written his name down for the records (I vaguely remember his name started with a *D*, I think), because one of the things I heard him say was so unbelievable and heretical that it deserves to be cited properly as a warning for you readers. And, as you may have guessed, his sermon was met with resounding "amens."

After painting a beautiful picture of the birth of Christ on "that first Christmas morning two thousand and sixteen years ago," the preacher started to talk about who Christ was and what He came to do. He moved to focus on how Christ was the only man who could have ever done what He did. Up to this point, the preacher and I were in agreement. But then he started to say that Christ wasn't human. At all. That he was *only* God.

That He borrowed a humanlike appearance for His time here.

That we can try, but we'll never live as perfectly as He did.

That because of this, because we cannot be perfect, because we are human and not "only God" like Christ was, we should be "more forgiving of our fellow man and their actions against us this Christmas season" and "love others" whose lives are different from our own so that they, too, might "come to know the Savior."

At that moment, while I was tying a blue ribbon around my daughter's tea set, I said out loud, "I see what you did there. Clever, aren't you?" In that one moment when he focused on Christ being only God and not at all human, he placed our Lord so far out of our reach that we have no choice but to be the people who surrender to sin and therefore forgive others who also cannot restrain from participating in worldly pursuits. We have to just do a bunch of "loving" because we're all so imperfect that transgressions should be dealt with through a shrug and a hug. We all have these "feelings" that teach us we're inferior to the point that we shouldn't even strive to live like Christ did. That preacher wrapped up his little "everything goes" sermon with a prettier bow than Sissy's teacups.

In a way, he was right, because none of us will ever do what Christ did. But that is the moment this preacher's teachings on Christology stops being useful for any Kingdom purpose. It became a "friendship with the world" gospel.

Show me the verse that says Christ wasn't human.

This claim might sound like a sweet one, in that it lifts Christ above the finite man, but it backfires instantly when it places all Christ did on some lofty pedestal we mere human underlings can never relate to. The fact that He was fully human and fully God at the same time is the very truth that gives the Gospel beauty and grace. He submitted to the limitations and ugliness of human life on earth, and that's what makes God available to His people in a way He wasn't to the ancient peoples of the Old Testament. If Christ didn't completely face the human experience, we couldn't see the extent to which a Savior is capable of comprehending the brokenness of humanity.

In addition, this false doctrine raises a wall that separates man from accountability. If Christ is only God, that explains why He never sinned. Therefore, we can't really help it when we sin, because we can't be like Christ, no matter how hard we try. This spreads the poisonous logic: If He wasn't "like us," then we would be excused from having to try to be "like Him." But it's specifically *because* He was fully human and "in all points tempted like as we are" (Hebrews 4:15) that He was able to set the highest standards of human moral behavior in history, and we, as true disciples, are expected to live as closely to His model as we can.

This erred line of thinking also causes confusion about John 14:12, wherein Christ said that His disciples will "do the works" that He had done and "even greater things than these." If Christ could only perform miracles because He was God and therefore perfect in all accounts, then we, the sinful, cannot perform miracles, no matter whose Name we call upon.

Do you see how quickly the entire Gospel falls flat and becomes just another cute fairy tale the second an "essential" is compromised? No matter how "happy thought" a *part* of a teaching is, if it serves as a formal denial of core Gospel doctrine (which is the definition of heresy), it can destroy the *whole*.

The idea of Christ not being fully human is only one affront to truth. There are many others. It is not the purpose of this book to address each one, but to make the point that all who claim to be "teachers of the Gospel" have a serious responsibility to put knowledge in their heads and experience under their belts before opening their mouths and letting loose their uncontrolled tongues on a particular subject. I don't mean to suggest that a person has to have a college degree in theology before being of use behind a pulpit. I *do* mean to suggest that teachers/preachers shouldn't teach/preach on anything they haven't responsibly studied. If ministers have studied and still arrive at a belief system that directly opposes core/foundational Christian doctrine, they still have the freedom to teach, but it should not be in a Christian church.

Further, how many preachers are developing a friendship-with-the-world gospel today through their stance on tolerance? Some say anything to flatter their congregations. They avoid calling sin what it is in order to incorporate people's feelings into their sermons. They make Jesus Christ a little *too* human. They take the "come to Christ no matter what you've done" to mean "come to Christ no matter what you're doing and plan to continue doing."

Will Christ still love us if we've sinned in the past? Yes. Will God still care about us if we continue to sin? Yes. Always and forever. We will always be loved, no matter what we do, much like a human mother might always love a wayward child. But with all of the Body's modern focus on how much God loves, we're losing the very "righteousness" foundation the Church was built upon. We stop calling sin "sin" and start calling it "whoopsies."

Add that approach to the feel-good worship services we've now begun to establish, and Jesus Christ—the founder of the Church we claim to be a part of—is no longer our Lord: He's a buddy. A homie. A pal. He's only there to love on us and give us the high five of fellowship, and when we sin, He's right there giving us a wink and a nod, saying, "No prob, kiddo; we all make mistakes." The purpose of His works on earth was to let us all live the way we *feel,* as long as everyone is holding hands and harmonizing during "me, me, me" songs. His tragic death on the cross only paved the way for Christians to pop bubblegum, bake cookies, and let our hair blow in the wind.

We're not "following" Him; we're casually buttonholing Him into our own concepts, forcing His position as "leader" over us into a position of "comrade." We come to the Lord's throne with the same nonchalant, laid-back, cool-cat slant as our earthly friends and equals. The deeply resonating and wholehearted commitment we should be giving Christ is lost in waves of spiritual "Facebook likes" as we "flirt with" and "date" the Gospel when it suits us and dismiss it when it doesn't. We "try Him on for size" on Sundays and then fail to return His call the rest of the week. We become the "Friendship with the World Church."

Jesus is not your boyfriend or your homie.

Jesus is your LORD.

We cannot continue to allow this misguided, spreading mindset to limit the Church Body's power in the coming days because we have become the "Dating Christ Church" or the "Friendship with the World Church."

Sin is a deliberate action against God. It's not an accidental mistake, it's not justifiable, and it's not pleasing to the Lord in any way. Any other approach to calling sin for what it is only junks up the Church with blurred lines, adds mass confusion to how we should live, and breaks down the responsibility and accountability we hold as proclaimed Christ-ians. So what is the answer?

The sweet spot.

It's hard to find, but we have to try *much* harder than we are to find it. If there's not enough teaching on love, we become phonies to the lost world around us. If there's not enough teaching against sinful acts, we become phonies within our own buildings.

What is the answer to this "friendship with the world" conundrum?

- Call sin what it is: *sin*. We must stop compromising the Gospel and treating Christ as a marginal figure in the Church. Know in advance that there will be those who will reject God as a result, but know in advance also that they are ultimately rejecting *God* as their King (1 Samuel 8:7); they're not rejecting the messenger (the Church).

- In the meantime, however, when we go about calling sin for what it is, we must control our tongues! Remember that we are *all* sinners, and that there *is no* "us versus them." We are loving our fellow humans, regardless of whether they are fellow Christians. Speak in love. Always. Before we share our opinions, consider whether our opinion was asked for. Before sharing our opinions from the pulpit, consider in advance the knowledge that needs to be presented. This, too, is what "loving" the people we lead looks like.

- And because this all looks so much easier on paper than it is in real life, we need to remember always to seek wisdom, knowing that it *will* be given to all who ask for it.

Let's take the semantic satiation out of the phrase "hate the sin, love the sinner." Let's commit to upholding true doctrine in the Church, no matter who is offended. But also let us strive with every breath not to offend with cruelty.

And what about those sermons that, like some of today's worship songs, only focus on us and what we get out of being a part of the Church? It appears that our current world is greatly invested in the treasures of today, and whereas that can mean having material items (homes, cars, gadgets, money), it can also mean enjoying lifestyle treasures. It can mean anything finite that cannot be stored and brought to heaven.

How many "treasures" are we "heaping together for the last days" (James 5:3)? How important is our current status, money, position, shiny things? Are we living in luxury and self-indulgence? How important has our temporal life become to us? Really think about that question. How important, *truly*, has our temporal life become to each of us as we cling not only to material comforts but to customs, rituals, worldviews, standards, and routine?

Prosperity preachers have caused a *lot* of harm to our understanding of the Gospel. Even though the trend of prosperity preaching is at a bit of a cultural low right now, generations of people were affected by this misleading gospel that says all of existence will be easier and glossier if we say the right words, put our faith in certain things, and "claim" specific verses for our lives. People still believe in the idea that if we aren't blessed, if we aren't getting what we want, we're just not being spiritual enough. I'm glad that, as time goes on, more and more Christians are letting go of this concept regarding material gain, but it lingers steadfastly in other lifestyle applications (especially in the pursuit of happiness and contentment).

Once in a while, a sermon that focuses on our blessings in this life is good. It's healthy for the Church, even, because it gives the Gospel balance and allows it to address the lives we Christians are living now in this human experience. But presenting one sermon after another after another, all talking about when we will be blessed and whether or not we believe God is limitless and therefore can give us those blessings, tends to have the same effect as the "me, me, me" worship services. (And, by default, these sermons preach to the choir, not to the lost, because they don't address the story of the cross that the lost need to hear.)

Consider the following potential sermon titles:

- "When Your Whole Body Aches, God Is the Ultimate Physician"
- "When Your Heart Aches, God Is the Ultimate Counselor"
- "When You Have a Great Need, God Is the Ultimate Giver"
- "When People Come Against You, Jesus Is Your Best Friend"
- "When You Can't Pay Your Rent, God Will Get You Through"
- "When Everything in Life Is Hard, God Has the Power to Bring Ease"
- "When You Are Filled with Worry, God Has the Power to Bring Peace"

I could go on and on with that fictitious list, as I had another ten potential titles going through my head, but you get the idea. These titles have great promise, and if done right, each as a stand-alone sermon could be based on correctly interpreted Scripture and bring hope to people who need it. If done right, none of these would automatically be considered "prosperity teachings." They're simply topics that are relevant to the human condition, which, whether we like it or not, is where we are right now.

But when placed all together in a row, this entire list could be repackaged into a sermon series called, "When You Want Stuff, God Is the Ultimate Handouts Guy." And when the Body focuses on this kind of preaching all the time, continuously—when this is the "meat" from which members are fed—the entire Church becomes the "Church of the 'I Wants.'" The "Gimme Church."

Another popular catchphrase in use amidst the Body states that we "too often concentrate on the gift and not the Giver." My response is, "Why does God's name tag now suddenly read 'the Giver'"—as if that's all He's about? Yes, God should be seen as the ultimate Giver—but that is only one diminutive aspect of who He should be. When He becomes *only* the Giver, then we've turned Him into Santa Claus. We mind our manners and act like good children, stay on the "nice list," ask for what toys we want, and find them wrapped up with pretty bows on delivery day—and if the presents aren't there, it's because we were placed on the naughty list somehow and we need to be more spiritual about our requests next time. Christ should be the main focus of *Christ*-ianity, well before any "come to the Lord with your list" theology is preached.

What is it all about, anyway? Life is naught but a "vapor," James says. Like a will-o'-the-wisp that burns brightly for a second and disappears into some otherworldly destination. Eternity should be what the Church is talking about, as well as the King we will be in the presence of in the afterlife—not about this temporary assignment. Yet, because this brightly burning and all-consuming human condition we know as "lifetime" is what we are experiencing now, the Body develops tunnel vision for that space and time. When we approach the throne of God, it shouldn't be on our feet with a list, it should be on our faces with reverence and awe and worship. We shouldn't follow Christ because of what we get out of the deal, but because He is, in and of Himself, the Savior of all mankind and therefore justifiably worthy of being followed.

I have many material blessings in my life I could list. I'm thankful for all of those things, from the roof over my head to the bottle of ibuprofen next to my desk and all that's in between. But if I didn't have all those things, I could still say: I'm thankful I have a Lord who designed me with precision and who has plans to use my talents for His purpose, so that maybe, just maybe, eternity might look differently for another soul. I'm thankful that when I sin in this world, there is a Redeemer who intercedes for me outside of this world. I'm thankful I can trust Someone who knows me better than I know myself to lead my current life as a mother of two into fruition, so I can more probably see my children partake of joy forever. I'm thankful I'm going to inherit everlasting love, life, and peace in a beautiful Kingdom I could never possibly be grand enough to deserve.

Eternity. Forever and ever and ever. Life is a vapor. Heaven is everlasting. The Gospel is already "good news" enough without having to pave the way toward "getting stuff." What we need is salvation, and that happens to be free.

When did that stop being enough?

James turns his attention on this issue as he continues in chapter 4:

[13]Go to now, ye that say, To day or to morrow we will go into such a city, and continue there a year, and buy and sell, and get gain: [14]Whereas ye know not what shall be on the morrow. For what is your life? It is even a vapour, that appeareth for a little time, and then vanisheth away. [15]For that ye ought to say, If the Lord will, we shall live, and do this, or that. [16]But now ye rejoice in your boastings: all such rejoicing is evil. [17]Therefore to him that knoweth to do good, and doeth it not, to him it is sin.

To some, this looks like a flip-flop of subjects as James suddenly transitions from addressing the subject of boasting about tomorrow to speaking of "doing good" (verse 17). He's addressing the future one moment and righteous behavior the next. In its proper context, however, the connection between the two subjects is clear: Do not boast of your tomorrows and your plans (13–14) without first consulting what the Lord would have you do with your tomorrows (15), because this is the right thing to do, and if you know it's the right thing to do and you don't do it, you're guilty of sin (16–17). Verse 17, about "doing good," cannot be separated from the act in the previous verses: dedicating one's future to the Lord's will.

On the point of the Lord's will for every Christian always and in every point of life is the following *Barnes' Notes* brilliant discussion:

Therefore to him that knoweth to do good, and doeth it not, to him it is sin—That is...the forming of plans respecting the future....

If he understands what his duty is; if he has the means of doing good to others; if by his name, his influence, his wealth, he can promote a good cause; if he can, consistently with other duties, relieve the distressed, the poor, the prisoner, the oppressed; if he can send the gospel to other lands, or can wipe away the tear of the mourner; if he has talents by which he can lift a voice that shall be heard in favor of temperance, chastity, liberty, and religion, he is under obligations to do it: and if, by indolence, or avarice, or selfishness, or the dread of the loss of popularity, he does not do it, he is guilty of sin before God. No man can be released from the obligation to do good in this world to the extent of his ability; no one should desire to be. The highest privilege conferred on a mortal, besides that of securing the salvation of his own soul, is that of doing good to others—of alleviating sorrow, instructing ignorance, raising up the bowed down, comforting those that mourn, delivering the wronged and the oppressed, supplying the wants of the needy guiding inquirers into the way of truth, and sending liberty, knowledge, and salvation around the world. If a man does not do this when he has the means, he sins against his own soul, against humanity, and against his Maker; if he does it cheerfully and to the extent of his means, it likens him more than anything else to God.[28]

Thanks to James, and then to *Barnes' Notes* (as well as other commentaries), we can arrive at the following simple concept: Don't run around making plans about what you're going to do with your life if God isn't in it, and if God is in it, then you will make plans to benefit *others* for Kingdom purposes.

Then, beginning in chapter 5, James' warning carries on:

[1]Go to now, ye rich men, weep and howl for your miseries that shall come upon you. [2]Your riches are corrupted, and your garments are motheaten. [3]Your gold and silver is cankered; and the rust of them shall be a witness against you, and shall eat your flesh as it were fire. Ye have heaped treasure together for the last days. [4]Behold, the hire of the labourers who have reaped down your fields, which is of you kept back by fraud, crieth: and the cries of them which have reaped are entered into the ears of the Lord of sabaoth. [5]Ye have lived in pleasure on the earth, and been wanton; ye have nourished

your hearts, as in a day of slaughter. [6]Ye have condemned and killed the just; and he doth not resist you.

You don't have to be a theologian to understand that James is harshly rebuking those who place their focus on temporal comforts.

First of all, know that James is not speaking of "rich men" in the sense of anyone who has a lot of money. He is addressing those whose spiritual heart health is in danger as they strive to achieve temporal gains by any means necessary, including to the detriment and/or oppression of others, or simply via selfish apathy and lack of concern. This interpretation is sound, according to every commentary and scholarly remark that I've read, including the notes in the margins of my numerous study Bibles, and is backed the imagery of verse 4, which addresses the oppressor's choice to withhold the pay from the laborers.

Verse 3 is extremely poetic in nature, and the word play James uses is shockingly powerful. "Cankered" is a word that applied to corroded metals. Naturally, metals that have exchanged hands and came into contact with other objects frequently would not corrode like a metal that is kept in one of the cold and damp storage rooms the people of the New Testament used. (Gold and silver would not corrode like other metals, and probably could have withstood being stored just about anywhere for any length of time, but other metals could not, and we need to remember that James is using a metaphor, not giving scientific facts about metal corrosion.) James is saying: 1) your temporal riches and comforts are corrupt because (as we learned in the former verses of "boasting about tomorrow") they are not "doing good" for anyone if they're not being spent on (exchanging hands with) those around you who need something you have to give; 2) the "rust of them" (ugly evidence of lack of proper use) will be a testimony against your lack of good works; and 3) through the sin of laying up worldly riches while people are in need around you, you will suffer severe consequences. An interesting interpretation of this final clause comes from the *Cambridge Bible for Schools and Colleges*: "The underlying image suggested is that the rust or canker spreads from the riches to the very life itself, and that when they fail, and leave behind them only the sense of wasted opportunities and the memories of evil pleasures, the soul will shudder at their work as the flesh shudders at the touch of fire."[29]

Verse 4 requires some understanding of ancient culture. Throughout the world, as early as during Moses' day (see Leviticus 19:13), wealthy men with large properties hired laborers to harvest their fields, then often refused to pay the laborers for their work when it was done. Through lofty promises of helping hungry families, yet then withholding pay, the rich men obtained free labor and the workers had to go home and explain to their families why they had to go without dinner. By the time James wrote his epistle, the reapers/harvesters/withholders analogy had become a cultural reference to anyone who oppresses or steals from the poor, not just to workers in a field. James wasn't talking about men hiring laborers to reap wheat and then sitting on their money in a literal sense (although it would apply that way, as they, too, would be guilty of the sin he's addressing here). Once all the contextual applications in this section of the epistle are married together, we can see that James' words were about: 1) people having money or other material comforts that could be given to assist their fellow man; 2) promising to assist their fellow men by virtue of the Christianity they claimed to belong to; and 3) failing to assist their fellow men, and by extension, causing them ill. In essence, any man who is willing to carelessly boast about his tomorrows and all the temporal comforts he's going to gain in "such a city" without considering what the Lord would have him do was, in James' eyes, and through the use of a cultural reference, no different than an oppressor of the poor or needy (spiritually or otherwise). People like this were a "fraud" for the Gospel, only serving to hurt and never to heal, and the cries of those hurt by those churchy frauds would enter the ear of the Lord, he said.

The words "nourished your hearts as in the day of slaughter" have been interpreted many different ways, all of them logical, and all of them conflicting with the others in minor ways in connection to cultural contexts. However, the two leading ideas could be summarized as follows:

1) You have lived a life of luxury, eating, drinking, and being merry while the needy are in your midst and you don't care—therefore, you have fattened yourself like a lazy cow whose whole worth and spiritual value means nothing more than to be slaughtered; or 2) You live your life like every day is a "day of slaughter" (a grand feast, whereupon many animals were slaughtered for feeding), and it is upon this luxury that you nourish your hearts (and therefore your spiritual health). As such, your religion is worthless (see James 1:26 for a verbatim "your religion is worthless" comparison).

Lastly, according to the most sensible of interpretations, this final verse refers to a "resistance is futile" concept. Those who hoarded up treasures were so powerful and oppressed the needy so greatly (through both acts of literal oppression and stealing, as well as outright apathy) that they could not be resisted.

With all James' words of condemnation upon the pursuits of riches in these lines prior, how can today's Church consider the "gets" of this life so important? I asked this question earlier, but it's crucial that we think about what it's asking: How important has temporal life—our money, our homes, our jobs, our furniture, our cars, our gadgets—become to us? How much do we rely on these things? Are these things even good for us anyway? Are they the blessings we thought they would be? Every incredible technological convenience in our modern, material world has brought about electronic devices that distract us from our families and the lives around us. (We want a smartphone, so we rush out and get it, only to spend the rest of our lives with our eyes glued to it. We want an iPad, so we buy one, and then stop visiting with family after we develop an addiction to Candy Crush.) The same could be said for comforts unrelated to technology. (We want that car until we discover it's a gas hog. We want that expensive house until it forces us into bankruptcy. We want that job until we realize we have to work longer, harder hours.)

But just as vital to all of this study, especially when we consider how our tomorrows should be spent in accordance to the will of the Lord for the lost, are the immaterial—but still *temporal*—comforts that we cling to (and the subject that today's preachers of the "me, me, me" Dating Christ Church and Friendship with the World Church are so focused on from the pulpit). Our worldviews, our religion, our status, our relationships, our reputations, our in groups, our out groups, our clique groups, our social circles, our movements, our politics, our blessings, our *feelings* (for crying out loud!).

We ask for all kinds of blessings in our lives that, once received, aren't satisfying: That "perfect woman" you married ended up not being perfect. That church full of smiling people stopped smiling when they discovered that your theology was slightly different than theirs. That popular group of pretty people stopped caring about you when they caught wind of some juicy gossip. That period of happiness came crashing down when your blessing wasn't what you thought it was.

All the while, those hurting souls are not being reached by a gospel that doesn't talk about the cross because it's busy talking about blessings. Sometimes, we do need to go to the Lord with a need. That's simply part of our dependent relationship with the Provider, and, as I said early on in this book, God loves prayers of dependency. I'm simply stating that the Dating Christ Church, the Me Church, and the Friendship with the World Church have a much skewed concept of what our relationship to the Lord ought to be.

If it's wisdom you want, ask! If it's spiritual maturity you desire, ask! If you're looking for the ability to love others whose lifestyles are offensive to us, ask! If it's anything that ultimately comes back to a Kingdom purpose, ask!

If it's money, material luxury, shiny things, toys, popularity, reputational security, or anything that ultimately comes back to a self-promoting purpose, proceed with caution.

He is not our servant, we are His.

The Gospel is not about getting stuff. It's about choosing to spend the vapor of life we have as if every day is our last, knowing that there is no guarantee of the tomorrows we boast about in a world of dying people who need something we have. God is the Giver, but He is not *only* the Giver. He is worthy of real praise, worthy of all honor and public fame, no matter whom that offends, and worthy of seeing His sons and daughters upon the earth take their jobs as Christ ambassadors seriously as they seek to love the "whosoever will" as the topmost priority.

The sweet spot. We've got to find it. And it's not in the "getting." It's not in the "me."

It's on our faces before the Almighty Creator. It's in the radical approach to love, whilst upholding the truth of Scripture at all costs.

It's in the "You, Lord."

Do you want to change the world?
Do you want to play a part in the next Great Awakening?

Love all sinners, just as you, too, are a sinner and always will be in this life. Hate all sin, including the trespasses you, yourself, have committed and are capable of committing again. Love the lost, always, and pray for those who hurt you or rub you the wrong way. But be always ready and willing to state, like Paul, that you "are not ashamed of the Gospel" (Romans 1:16).

Conclusion

Live Ready

JAMES 5:7–20

NOW IT'S TIME to take the concerns we have discussed up to this point and bring it all together. James' closing words are sweet music, and when his whole epistle is studied line by line as we have done, the last of his letter comes to life with fresh meaning. Nobody could have planned a better ending than his.

Yet, before we look at his charge for the last time, I have one of my own that I believe is pertinent to completing the big picture James began painting two thousand years ago.

The Three "Choice" Verbs

Christians are told to love, but one thing I've noticed is that for finite people, we have a much harder time loving others when we aren't happy. Sad and miserable people find loving others much more difficult than those who walk in joy every day. At the root of our choosing not to love certain people is our "feelings": It *feels* hard, because that person is belligerent or difficult. It *feels* weird, because that person's lifestyle is shocking. It *feels* unnatural, because it's within our human nature to love only when that love isn't complicated. And it *feels* impossible, because we're so caught up in the troubles of our own lives that we can't extend mercy unlimited while our own joy is compromised by trial.

But, being a Christian isn't about how we feel; it's about choosing to follow Christ's example.

It isn't impossible to love without joy, but if we as the Church are going to place so much emphasis on loving others, then there needs to be an emphasis on internal joy as well, since it plays such a crucial role in loving. In Scripture, there is evidence that joy and praise can and should often be treated as synonyms for believers. As such, joy, praise, and love (like faith) must all be considered by the Body as verbs that require diligent and immediate action at all times. Then, through the application of these three elements, faith-by-works is a natural and beautiful consequence.

First, we need to realize that our three prized verbs here are only feelings *after* they are choices—choices that have been practiced and exercised, like a muscle.

Consider a muscleman in a gym. An onlooker might observe as he easily bench presses a bar encumbered with enough weight to equal another human being, and to the spectator, it's a feat of incredible strength. But the muscleman didn't get there by following "feelings." In fact, he had to completely and deliberately ignore his feelings. He had to start with a small weight and gradually increase the strain over time, and continue to be devoted to the practice and exercise. In the beginning, as he was pumping his arms for the first time, he would have had days where he said, "This burns! This is a *sacrifice*! This isn't easy!" The muscleman didn't start off with a six-pack and enormous pectorals. He had to endure the burn—a sensation that after practice is appreciated as an aerobic rush but at the beginning produces an unfamiliar and unpleasant response in the muscle. Then, through diligence and devotion, he arrives on the other side, saying, "This is easy. I could do this all day." He has learned to appreciate the burn, embrace the pain, and plod through it, knowing that the discomfort he experiences is an essential step to greater health when he's carried out due diligence.

A man cannot become a muscleman until he's become a successful muscle *builder*.

Such is also true for the "muscles" at the center of our three verbs. Each must be exercised, even when our "feelings" are in conflict with the choice. But following through with due diligence produces greater spiritual health and maturity on the other side, and the exercise of these verbs becomes easier over time. Joy, praise, and love are choices before they are feelings, and I don't think we as Christians should be catering to our feelings before we've made proper choices.

When I look at my husband, I *feel* love, and I have from the beginning. He will attest that he felt, and continues to feel, the same about me. But, thank God, my husband understood when he married me that he would at times have to love me by *choice*, because there are days that I'm hard to love. (Seriously.) The older I get, the more my hormones can make me taxing to be around. Sometimes I walk in after a challenging day at work and I'm *not* quick to listen, and I'm *not* slow to anger or slow to speak. I wear my frustration on my shoulders. On these occasions, I can't even explain where the feelings are coming from. I'm just raging on the inside for a few hours, and it takes immense effort not to be a negative or moody person. But it is on these occasions that my husband *chooses* to love me. It's a choice for him in those moments. It's not a feeling. He doesn't look at me while I'm freaking out and having a fit, and think, *I'm just so attracted to her right now.* No. He looks at me while I'm freaking out and having a fit, and says, "Lord, I'm *choosing* to love her, I'm *choosing* to love her, I'm *choosing* to love her…" repeating it like a mantra until the hours of hormones are over. That is why, no matter what I put him through, we are so in love today. Our marriage is awesome. I have the Lord to thank for matching me up with a man who not only loves me when I don't deserve to be loved (thus modeling Christ-like behavior toward me), but who also sets an example that I find myself following in my relationship with him when the tables are turned the other way, as well as with others.

Happiness and love cannot be found in cars, houses, money, fame, food, or any other material possessions, because it's within our nature as fallen people to only have increased desires of our flesh once we've been given what we want, and the plate always returns void. Happiness and joy also must begin as choices.

I happen to know a thing or two about finding happiness in food. I weighed 315 pounds at one point in my life, and although I was generally happy, my body was in a great deal of physical pain related to a leg-length discrepancy I had been born with. I had no idea that my left leg was thirty-six millimeters shorter than my right, which is a huge difference. To make a very long and complicated story short, I went to many who that didn't spot the discrepancy (or pretended not to in order to ensure that I'd be back for further treatment) until I was thirty-one years old. Only then did one chiropractor tell me that he could see "from a mile away" that one of my legs was significantly shorter than the other. As a result, I have had to endure a lot of acupuncture therapy, and I limped for years.

Since the age of sixteen, I had been in pain from my shins to my rib-cage. (My left leg was so much shorter that it caused a curve in my spine from my hips upward, which placed imbalanced pressure on my whole skeleton, and because of the way I was naturally shaped above the navel, my whole body was jerked to the side wildly with every step. I didn't know that, though, and I couldn't feel it, because it was how I'd always walked.) I became so used to pain that I had my own way of "treating it." Good tasting food was my medicine for (and distraction from) my pain. By the time I reached 315 pounds, even though I had a happy life, my only escape from physical pain was a plate of nachos or pizza or pasta or some other calorie-heavy indulgence. The extra weight added to my frame made the pain worse, so I was only feeding the problem. I could go into a ten-year story about the ups and downs of my weight and the struggles I had while I "committed" to diets or exercise plans, but all those ever did was cripple me further and make me miserable because I "felt" like the only answer was when happiness came on a plate.

Today, I weigh 174 (every pair of shoes I own has a custom-tailored lift on the left side to compensate), because I dedicated my life to better eating habits and got the physical help I needed. But even though the pain in those areas of my body is almost completely gone from my life because of shoe-lifts and therapy, I had to deal with the habit of treating feelings with food before I lost the weight. I still have that little devil on the shoulder tempting me to seek happiness in food. There are so many days when I still "feel" like having a plate of nachos. *Oh* do I "feel" like having a plate of nachos! But it is in those moments that I must exercise the choice to say, "This is the day that the Lord has made. I *will* rejoice and be glad in it" (Psalm 118:24), rather than going to the refrigerator to see what junk food will give me temporary smiles.

Why don't diets work? Because people eat their feelings. They eat what they're feeling to compensate for other larger, deeper issues, "treating" their symptoms with a medicine that never reaches the root of the injury. Why does loving and having joy and happiness not work so often? Because people rely on their impulsive feelings to tell them those sensations are present, instead of bringing them into existence through choice.

Choosing to follow Christ *cannot* be about feelings. God cares about our feelings, He wants to nurture our hearts, He wants to be there for us, and He wants us to "feel good" about life…but read the Bible from cover to cover and you'll find that a lot of men and women in the service of God went where they were supposed to go and did what they were supposed to do as commanded by God, *regardless of how they felt.*

Look at the book of Jonah. It's a marvelous example: God tells Jonah to go to Nineveh and preach a message of repentance. Jonah doesn't like the Ninevites, and he doesn't think they deserve redemption, so he doesn't *feel* like doing what God has told him to do. He gets on a boat headed to Tarshish instead. God brings a huge storm to the sea where the ship is sailing, and the waves are crashing all over the place. When lots are cast, Jonah owns up to the crew that it is he who has run from his God and angered Him, and the only chance for survival they have is to throw him overboard. The crew reluctantly agrees, and as soon as Jonah's off the ship and submerged in the waters below, the storm stops. Jonah is swallowed by a great fish and spends three days in its belly. When he's vomited back up by the fish days later, God does *not* say, "Well, okay, you've paid well enough for your disobedience. Go home and scrape the digestive acids off your clothes, put your feet up, and drink a restorative cup of fig juice." Not a chance. God picks right back up where he left off. He says, "Go to Nineveh."

Straight back to square one: God's directive.

When my family and I were studying the book of Jonah together, I used the following example with my six-year old. "Joey, it's like this," I said. "If I tell you to go clean your room, and then you go off in another direction and piddle around because you don't feel like obeying me, I might make you stand your nose in the corner for not doing what I said to do. But then, once you've stood in the corner, I'm not going to say, 'Well, your punishment is over and you paid your price for disobedience, I guess you can go play.' No, I'm going to say, 'Now that you've stood in the corner and you've been punished, go to your room and clean it up!'" I went on to explain: "After we're done suffering for not doing what God told us to do in the first place, God is going to say, 'Okay Jonah, get up, go where I told you to go and do what I told you to do.'"

The message doesn't change. The directive of God doesn't change. The commands given to followers of the Word don't change when we disobey them because of our feelings.

No matter how many times you begin a sentence with "But God, I *feel…*" it's always going to come back to the same command: "Get up. Go where I've told you to go. Do what I've told you to do."

When Jonah completed God's directive, the residents in the entire city of Nineveh turned from their wicked ways and were saved from the destruction of the Lord. Jonah, however, sat outside the city and grumbled because he didn't like the idea that the evil Ninevites had received the same grace from the Lord as the prophet. He didn't want to believe in the idea that all humans were equally important to their Creator, when some had shockingly divergent lifestyles. They didn't act or live righteously, and the culture Jonah was raised in didn't appreciate that the people of Nineveh would have been anything more than a scab upon the earth that needed to be destroyed.

Jonah didn't believe in the redemption of the "Rahabs."

God raised up a shade tree that Jonah settled himself under, and God allowed it to be devoured the next morning by a worm. When the hot sun and scorching winds beat down on Jonah, he had a new reason to complain: The shade was no longer available to protect him. God asked the prophet if he was justified in his angry feelings, and Jonah responded, "I do well to be angry, angry enough to die!" (Jonah 4:9; ESV). Instead of rejoicing that souls were saved for eternity, Jonah is still thinking about his own feelings. God then gives Jonah the following breakdown: "You pity the plant, for which you did not labor, nor did you make it grow, which came into being in a night and perished in a night. And should not I pity Nineveh, that great city, in which there are more than 120,000 persons?" (10–11; ESV). Contemporarily, this could be reworded: "You pity this plant, and yet you cannot pity the Ninevites? *I* grew this plant, and *I* created mankind. Your hand had no part in it, so you do not understand My position as Creator over the things My hands have made. If you can pity a plant, then can you not see how I would pity the 120,000 people of Nineveh whose importance eternally outshines a plant?"

What if Jonah had followed God's directive happily from the beginning? What if he had "considered it all joy" that the "trial" of preaching to the Ninevites would have made him stronger (James 1:2) so that his Kingdom use would have been "perfect" and "left wanting nothing" (James 1:4)? What if he had withstood the heat of his own oven while the Master Baker was completing a good work in him (Philippians 1:6)? He never would have been thrown overboard, he never would have spent three terrifying days in the belly of a fish. And when all the people who lived in the city of Nineveh turned toward God, he would have rejoiced and praised the Lord at their conversion, because at the onset of God's commands, he would have been committed to carrying out the three verbs of joy, praise, and love through *choice*, not *feelings*. But even when he didn't obey, even when he fled from God and followed his feelings on the matter, he was never going to be off the hook as a true follower of Yahweh until he went where he was told to go and did what he was told to do.

The Gospel never changes, and its directives are solid. Christians are never "off the hook" from having to love the "whosoever will" joyfully and with praise.

Let's look at another example from Acts 16: Paul is sleeping when God gives him a vision of a man calling for him to travel to Macedonia. Paul takes this vision as a sign from God that the Macedonians (just like the Ninevites) need deliverance. Paul obeys the directive without hesitation, taking Silas with him. Soon, a slave girl with the "spirit of divination" (16) is following Paul and Silas around making public proclamations about them, and it "greatly annoyed" (18) Paul. He casts the demon out of her, but this act angers the slave girl's owners, because they have been cashing in on her ability to tell fortunes. They take Paul and Silas before the magistrates and have them beaten and thrown into prison on the claim that they are "Jews…disturbing the city" (20). One specific jailer is chosen to guard them carefully, so he takes them to the deepest cell of the prison and clamps shackles around their feet as an extra security precaution.

Paul and Silas should be freezing because the prisons are not heated and their clothing was torn from them during the violent beating by the angry mob outside. Fresh wounds and bruises were the result of "many blows upon them" (23). So there they sit, cold, bloodied from head to toe, publicly humiliated and shamed, and probably starving, as it is now midnight.

They probably *feel* like grumbling, weeping, cursing the Macedonians, and asking God why He has sent them to this wicked city in the first place if they are only going to rot in jail. They probably *feel* a lot of things at that moment; nobody could blame them for that. But, despite all the suffering and anguish, they make a *choice* to ignore feelings, sensations, and emotions. In verses 25–34 (ESV) we read:

> About midnight Paul and Silas were praying and singing hymns to God, and the prisoners were listening to them, and suddenly there was a great earthquake, so that the foundations of the prison were shaken. And immediately all the doors were opened, and everyone's bonds were unfastened.

When the jailer woke and saw that the prison doors were open, he drew his sword and was about to kill himself, supposing that the prisoners had escaped. [Quick side note: For anyone wondering why this man was about to kill himself, it was because of "dereliction of duty." If prisoners escaped a Roman jail on a guard's watch, the guard was executed, and as anyone familiar with the story of the cross knows, that the Romans were capable of unthinkable cruelty when carrying out execution.] But Paul cried with a loud voice, "Do not harm yourself, for we are all here." And the jailer called for lights and rushed in, and trembling with fear he fell down before Paul and Silas.

Then he brought them out and said, "Sirs, what must I do to be saved?" And they said, "Believe in the Lord Jesus, and you will be saved, you and your household." And they spoke the word of the Lord to him and to all who were in his house. And he took them the same hour of the night and washed their wounds; and he was baptized at once, he and all his family. Then he brought them up into his house and set food before them. And he rejoiced along with his entire household that he had believed in God.

First, Paul and Silas have every reason (based on human reasoning) to wallow in their own feelings of misery, but they make the *choice* to praise the Lord with hymns. They don't praise because they "feel like it." They don't say, "We've been beaten, we've been unfairly imprisoned, and now we can't think of anything else to do...so we may as well praise." It isn't an act of boredom, it is a deliberate act of *sacrifice*. They do it because they have been *told to* by the Gospel directive. They are capable of this because they had chosen to praise over and over again, even when it doesn't feel natural.

Second, despite all of the human-reasoning that would have supported them hiding from the guard or fleeing the prison and letting the man kill himself, Paul and Silas make the *choice* to love him, care about his soul, and witness to him about Christ, even though this could easily mean a second round of imprisonment, should the guard decide to lock them up again—or worse, it could mean death by execution if the Romans decide they are fed up with the "Jews…disturbing the city." They don't say, "Well, we could run for our lives and escape to freedom, but we're suddenly and inexplicably overwhelmed with love for this pagan soldier." This, too, is a deliberate act of *sacrifice*. They do it because they were *told to* by the Gospel directive. They are capable of this because they choose to love over and over again when it doesn't feel right to the pagan, when it doesn't feel right to the Roman, when it doesn't feel right to the Gentile.

Their verb-muscles are strong through repetitive exercise.

And the result of these decisions?

- The *choice to praise* broke the chains that bound them, and the prison doors were opened.
- The *choice to love* the very guard who was stationed to keep these men secured in their misery led to the conversion of the guard and his whole household.
- Then the guard, having been an eyewitness of these choices, showed them love in return, and after his baptism, they all praised and rejoiced together.

When someone decides to love and praise and have joy internally regardless of his or her circumstances, eyewitnesses are inspired to return that treatment, and lives are changed—but it always begins with a choice, even when that choice is a sacrifice.

Hebrews 13:15 says, "By him therefore let us offer the sacrifice of praise to God continually, that is, the fruit of our lips giving thanks to his name." The Merriam-Webster dictionary gives the following meaning of the word "sacrifice": "surrender of something for the sake of something else."[30] Applied here, we could reword this: "surrender of feelings for the sake of obedience to the Gospel directive and blessed interaction with the Divine." Using a thesaurus to look up synonyms of the word "sacrifice," I compiled two other words: "forfeiture" and "relinquishment."

Why would a subject like praise be related to concepts of forfeiture and relinquishment?

A sacrifice costs us something. Something has to be surrendered for the sake of something else, like a muscleman who pushes through the cost of pain or forfeits his Saturdays to go to the gym knowing that it will lead to the better outcome. If a sacrifice doesn't cost us something, then, by definition, it's not a sacrifice. This verse in Hebrews doesn't *just* say to "offer" something we have or feel in abundance, it denotes the deliberate act of accepting a cost and faithfully paying it.

In Mark 12:41–44, Christ observed as many rich people donated large sums of money to the offering. Then a poor widow arrived and donated two small copper coins worth the equivalent of only a penny. Christ then told His disciples that the widow's offering was even greater than the riches given by the wealthy because they had given out of their abundance while she had given out of her poverty. She gave the least monetarily, yet she went down in history as giving the most. Why? Because it cost her. It was a sacrifice. If we allow this same, Christ-given logic to apply to the verse in Hebrews, we can understand the difference between 1) praising when it feels natural because we're happy and we have good feelings in abundance, and 2) praising when it doesn't feel natural and the cost is the sacrifice of our own feelings and desires.

When Paul and Silas praised God in that jail cell, they were "bringing the sacrifice of praise" as a result of exercise and practice. An act that couldn't have felt natural the first several times they carried it out became buried in their hearts as a natural instinct through repetition. They made the unfamiliar become familiar; they made the impossible become possible. When we Christians continually and repetitiously praise the Lord even through dire circumstances, we are engaging in spiritual warfare. *We are telling the enemy that what Christ has done for us is sufficient.* And we see miracles. Our shackles shake loose and the doors of our own internal prisons of emotion open wide. Others see Christ in us because we model Him. It doesn't matter how we feel; we model Christ because we choose to.

It doesn't do the world around us any good if we don't strive to become expert at something that ultimately benefits the Kingdom of God. If the most important of all Gospel directives is love (1 Corinthians 13:13; Matthew 22:37–40), and if love is bolstered by praise and joy, then love, joy, and praise must always be a choice, even when it involves a sacrifice.

Prepare yourselves, Church. A Great Awakening is coming. Be well exercised and ready for that day.

James' Final Send-Off to the Church

Some of the most beautiful and inspiring words in the whole of Scripture come at the end of James' epistle. But, just like James, amidst all his beautiful words is underlying instruction.

> [7]**Be patient therefore, brethren, unto the coming of the Lord. Behold, the husbandman waiteth for the precious fruit of the earth, and hath long patience for it, until he receive the early and latter rain.** [8]**Be ye also patient; stablish your hearts: for the coming of the Lord draweth nigh.**

It's difficult to be patient for the coming of the Lord when we know that these words of James were written two thousand years ago and we are still waiting for Christ's return while watching for the signs. Yet, consider the words of Peter: "But, beloved, be not ignorant of this one thing, that one day is with the Lord as a thousand years, and a thousand years as one day" (2 Peter 3:8). When James said "draweth nigh," I'm sure it ignited a feeling within the early Church that the coming of the Lord was likely to be any second. Perhaps they looked up every time they walked outdoors, scanning the clouds for any unusual activity. It's probable that some pastors of the fledgling Body used James' words from the pulpit as they railed passionately about the fact that their listeners should get their things in order, sit at home, and wait in prayer because Jesus was going to appear in the next few days. Maybe followers said their prayers extra fervently each night, reverent of the notion that it could be their last prayer before something split the heavens apart with a mighty roar during their slumber.

And here we are now, today, and He has not yet come back.

Hundreds of thousands of books have been published over the last two centuries discussing the signs of the coming of the Lord. Many interpreters of Scripture have claimed specific dates or years with confidence, only to face embarrassment when their predictions were incorrect. Others have made prophecy charts, showing that most if not all of the signs have already been fulfilled, and are warning the world that Christ's return will be this year or the next—especially considering all the headlines regarding Jerusalem's temple today alongside such heavy, global persecution against Christianity. Whether any of these calculations are correct is anyone's guess. I have my own opinion, but because I have just as much a chance as anyone to be wrong (and I am certainly no prophecy writer), I figure it's best to leave the day and hour to the Lord (2 Peter 3:10).

But with all this waiting, it's easy to understand why most of today's Body has stopped acting as if it could happen any second. That, to me, is a tragic misuse of time, energy, and resources.

Everywhere I look today, I see apathy within the Church. A universal and grand proverbial shrug applied to the Second Coming. We attend, we sing, we listen to words, we go home, and we live out the rest of the week as if we've met the quota of expectations upon us by the righteous club. We treat religion like our Scripture came from a shampoo bottle: "Wash, rinse, repeat." Where is the passion anymore? Where are the D. L. Moodys and the Billy Grahams and the Kathryn Kuhlmans of this generation who will take to the platforms and rouse our sleeping Sardis Church with a mighty shaking through the power of the Holy Spirit? Where are the John Wycliffes and the Martin Luthers of this generation who will challenge the organized establishment of today's lukewarm Laodicean leaders?

Have we given up on the vow of Christ's return? Are we, the Body, guilty of being the scoffers mentioned in 2 Peter 3:3–7 who shrug and say the promise of His coming is old news and things are never going to change? Are we the scoffers who "deliberately overlook [the] fact that the heavens existed long ago" (ESV), and that we belong to a space and time segregated from the unfathomable workings of heaven that could manifest themselves on earth in a twinkling of an eye (1 Corinthians 15:52)? We will not know the day or hour. We never will. We're not supposed to (2 Peter 3:10). But we are commanded: "Therefore, beloved, since you are waiting for these, be *diligent to be found by him* without spot or blemish" (2 Peter 3:14; emphasis added). This means we have to keep ourselves ready at all times, diligently. By extension, if we are to keep ourselves ready, to "be found by him" at any moment, we should be radical about keeping ourselves without spot or blemish while we diligently strive toward reaching the lost.

Maybe we do believe the promise, but our actions just don't reflect that belief. If so, in this alone, we stand guilty of hypocrisy. Either way, simply belonging to clubs and going through motions might mean that we believe a thing exists, but we are not practicing faith as the verb with works attached. We are ripe with a religious spirit, but we don't appear to be on fire through the power of the Holy Spirit. If our "works" mean we participate in the functions of a lifeless organization, we may as well admit that our religion is worthless (James 1:26).

We *must* stop living as if the verses regarding Christ's return don't exist. He is coming back, and He is coming soon. "Soon" or "nigh" might be another hundred years, for all we know, but I care enough about the generations ahead of me to make my footprint *now*! What if Martin Luther had simply shrugged his duty as a radical reformer on grounds that he didn't believe Christ would return in his lifetime? Everything we know about Protestant faith today would be different. No, Martin Luther refused to be a member of a religious club. Whether or not he believed Jesus was coming back during his lifetime, his *actions* were those of a man who followed the teaching that we should always walk as if it could be any moment. Don't just "get" ready, "live" ready. At all times. Our current generation depends on this if Christ returns in the next couple decades; the future generations of our children's children depend on it if it's farther away. But whether we live ready for the return of Christ because we believe He's coming tomorrow or we believe we have to prepare the future for His later arrival, the instruction to live ready applies to all generations.

If the Church *did have* some for-sure way of knowing Christ is absolutely and undoubtedly coming back, say, on February 21, 2018 (which, I assure you, is a date I literally pulled out of the air), the entire Body would be exploding into action all across the world. Every choice made, every conversation held, every single action taken would reflect a people preparing for February 21, 2018. True Christ-ians would be separated from the Laodiceans. True Christ-ians would make themselves known outside the church of Sardis. The world would ignite in a flame for the Gospel. A spiritual earthquake would shake the foundations of our exhausted Church. A true return to theological study would replace the sound bites. Praise and worship would become about *Him* again. Sermons would become about *Him* again. Men and women would "count their trials as all joy" until that blessed day when they would become "a perfect work wanting nothing." Ministers would embrace the tests of the faith. Scriptural interpretation would be carried out with extreme care. People from all backgrounds would come out of the woodworks and fall on their faces before the altars of the Lord in repentance. The "tough guys" would weep openly. The "loose women" would strive for innocence. The "rough teenagers" would turn their focus from peers to Christ. The modern "Rahabs" would leave their pasts behind.

An earth-shattering revival would take our world by storm and *it would never be the same again.* It would be, as revival leader George Whitefield once said, "the whole world in a flame"![31]

But it doesn't happen, because we *don't* have a February 21, 2018. We become Sardis. We become Laodicea. We don't have a date, we never will, and we're not supposed to according to Scripture, so that enigmatic commandment of "diligent" living is traded for lackluster lump-on-a-pew motions.

Remember, however, that this on-fire scenario above has happened before, via revival-hungry young men and women throughout history who didn't just "get ready," they "lived ready." It didn't matter to them if they had a date, because it wasn't about a date. To them, it was about following 2 Peter 3:14 with a diligence to always live in a state of glorious expectation with or without a date. As a result, the whole world was aflame.

Whether *we* have a date or not—and we never will reliably—we have a duty to live in the expectation of "any day," knowing that whether Christ comes or not on any given day, it is through the very commandment of expectation that we keep the Church alive and on fire *today, right now*! There is a reason living ready is biblical, because *by living ready, we remain on fire*, and the lost is irreversibly reached!

Is anyone else as hungry for this as I am!?

I beseech you all. Live as if there really is no guarantee of tomorrow, whether that be on a personal or a global scale. Live as if that next conversation may be the last you ever have with that man or woman. Live as if the next ministerial move you make—the next song you pick for your roster, the next sermon you put on schedule—is the last one you will ever sing or preach. Live as if the next action you take is in preparation—personally or for others—for the return of Christ.

In the meantime, while you live in expectation of the beautiful Savior in the clouds, have patience, James says. Apply your patience to your fire, knowing that "patience" doesn't mean tranquilly staring at a clock; it means carrying out your passion for the Gospel whether you have reason to believe the Second Coming is soon or far away in your own limited concepts of the time/space relationships heaven employs here on earth.

[9]Grudge not one against another, brethren, lest ye be condemned: behold, the judge standeth before the door. [10]Take, my brethren, the prophets, who have spoken in the name of the Lord, for an example of suffering affliction, and of patience. [11]Behold, we count them happy which endure. Ye have heard of the patience of Job, and have seen the end of the Lord; that the Lord is very pitiful, and of tender mercy. [12]But above all things, my brethren, swear not, neither

by heaven, neither by the earth, neither by any other oath: but let your yea be yea; and your nay, nay; lest ye fall into condemnation.

It amazes me that, even though James has spoken at such length about the wildness of the untamable tongue and the dissention among the Body, he feels it necessary to reiterate the thought again here: Don't fight with people in the Church. Don't hold grudges. Know that the Judge is watching what you do. Embrace endurance. Don't open your mouth with utterances of promises and then fall into the condemnable act of not following through. Watch what you say. Let "yes" really mean "yes" and "no" really mean "no" when you speak. And on the heels of the previous verses, do all of this in the light of Christ's "nigh" coming.

Now, for the final words of James' epistle, regarding what I believe could be the prayers that usher in the next Great Awakening. For all the wonderful things James has said in his letter, this is the moment it all comes together. This is that point where all the other parts fall under the authority of the whole. When all previous points of study culminate into a crescendo from charges to application. When the question of what to do becomes the answer of how to do it.

When it gets serious for the Body, if the Body will take it seriously.

[13]Is any among you afflicted? let him pray. Is any merry? let him sing psalms. [14]Is any sick among you? let him call for the elders of the church; and let them pray over him, anointing him with oil in the name of the Lord: [15]And the prayer of faith shall save the sick, and the Lord shall raise him up; and if he have committed sins, they shall be forgiven him. [16]Confess your faults one to another, and pray one for another, that ye may be healed. The effectual fervent prayer of a righteous man availeth much. [17]Elias [Elijah] was a man subject to like passions as we are, and he prayed earnestly that it might not rain: and it rained not on the earth by the space of three

years and six months. [18]And he prayed again, and the heaven
gave rain, and the earth brought forth her fruit. [19]Brethren, if
any of you do err from the truth, and one convert him; [20]Let
him know, that he which converteth the sinner from the error
of his way shall save a soul from death, and shall hide a
multitude of sins.

Verses 13–14: If we are suffering (afflicted), or if we're sick, we should pray; pray in church, pray at home, and let the leaders of the church know we need help; let us rely on each other in the coming days to lift one another up in fervent intercession! If we're not afflicted or sick, however— if we are happy—let us sing praise to the *Lord,* for it is *He* who has given us everything we have, and therefore it is He who stands as the Source of our happiness.

Verse 15: And the prayer "OF FAITH!"—that enigmatic "works" verb, manifesting itself from a mere belief into an *action*—will heal the sick, relieve afflictions, and sins will be forgiven.

Verse 16: Be accountable to each other for the wrongs we commit, treasuring friendship and love above all other acts of holiness. Intercede for each other, not just so we can put a checkmark down on our duty list, but until we see the prayer answered and people are healed of physical, emotional, and spiritual malady! Don't let "I'll pray for you" become the indifferent and trivial "let's do lunch" line that stands for nothing more than frivolous cordiality with no intention of corresponding action. Start praying, and DO. NOT. STOP. until real change is achieved. "The effectual fervent prayer of a righteous man availeth much." It availeth…*much*! It not only makes a difference, it makes a *huge* difference. When we pray for someone else, fervently, it can do the following incredibly powerful things: 1) Real, tangible change occurs; 2) we begin to believe in miracles; 3) the recipient begins to believe in miracles; and 4) *everyone involved* grows in their relationship with God and experiences radical overhauls of faith…

From slumber to FIRE!
The world in a FLAME!

Verses 17–18: Elijah believed in miracles. He didn't just pray hoping, he prayed knowing. He directed his words to the Lord unwaveringly, not like a man who is double-minded or unstable in all his ways. Such a man as this can expect to receive nothing from the Lord (James 1:7–8). No, Elijah prayed *knowing*. As such, rain didn't fall for three and a half years as a result of his fervent prayer (1 Kings 17:1–18:46). Believing in miracles equals the occurrence of miracles. True belief only comes through spiritual maturity and relationship with the Miracle Worker. Spiritual maturity and relationship with the Miracle Worker relies on diligence of the Body, both independently and corporately.

We cannot live unstable, double-minded, religious-spirited lives as members of organizations and clubs and expect to receive miracles or awakening or revival. The Me Church and the Catchphrase Church and the Dating Christ Church and the Friendship with the World Church all have to die away completely and become revived through radical reformation of these social and finite endeavors. Only *then* will people return to faith through works centered on the true Gospel. Only *then* will people become diligent about living as if every day is the last before Christ's Second Coming. Only *then* will revival blast our world like an uncontainable brushfire of Christ-passion across all nations and all social/lifestyle barriers.

And then, we will see miracles.

We will see angels. We will witness with our own eyes the sick healed, the lame walk, the deaf hear, the blind see, the dead arise! We will observe the very powers of the Almighty God like nothing our planet has ever seen before! Our current generation will raise leaders of the Church whose legacies will be documented as changers of the world, and every generation in the future will be inspired to keep the on-fire, heart-on-the-floor, sold-out, *radical* energy of revival every day every minute and every hour that we exist in this human condition until the sweet Messiah blazes down upon the earth, parting the clouds with a roar!

Can you hear it? Can you see it? Do you feel it? Do you want it? Is it pulsating within your blood like it is in mine?

When you close your eyes, do you hear the cheering of uncountable masses who are falling to their knees with weeping and laughter and testimony of the power of God like they did in James McGready's tent revivals of Kentucky in the 1800s? When you close your eyes, do you see the potential future droves and masses of precious people rising out of wheelchairs and jumping across stages like they did in Kathryn Kuhlman's church, or the fifteen thousand teenagers in one single service surrendering their lives to Christ like they did all over the country during the Jesus People Movement of the counterculture era? When you close your eyes, do you, like millions of others talking about it today, "sense" something is in the wind, like an invisible harbinger of conflagration sweeping over the people, preparing to separate the "Christians" from the Christ-ians, the passionate from the apathetic, the sleepers from the leaders, and the phonies from the faithful like the Holy Spirit did in D. L. Moody's day?

Are you ready for it? Are you "living ready" for it?

Verses 19–20: Here we have the simplest of instructions to carry it all into fruition. To make it all happen. To see the revival winds become the revival fire. To see lost souls enter the pearly gates of heaven where they will spend eternity in the presence of the King. To see those who are already saved finally harness the true potential within them through the direction of the Holy Spirit and make momentous, lasting difference on earth for this generation and all who follow.

The ESV renders these verses: "My brothers, if anyone among you wanders from the truth and someone brings him back, let him know that whoever brings back a sinner from his wandering will save his soul from death and will cover a multitude of sins."

Here, as written by James, as promised in Scripture, is the proof: Whoever kindly loves a lost soul holds the key to bringing that person into the loving hands and ever-pardoning grace of God. That soul *will be saved from death*. Sins pardoned. Forgiven. Redeemed. Name written in the Lamb's Book of Life. A nod of welcome from Peter. Pearly gates opening wide. The throne of God ahead. Walking down a street of pure gold. Listening to the deafening praises of the angels over their entrance. Bowing to the King…

And inheriting eternity among the saints.

Where there will be no danger.

Where there will be no physical pain.

Where there will be no emotional hurt.

Where there will be no night.

Where there will be no fear.

Where blessing and honor and glory and praise will be lifted to the Giver forever and ever, amen.

Home…at last!

Is your heart beating as fast as mine?

The worse things get in the world around us with dissention between members of the Body and quarrels between social groups and kingdoms unable to stand as they fight against themselves, the closer we get to the day Jesus Christ comes to take us all home.

If this moment in time and space is the moment Christ has positioned you in, then believe that God knew you have what it takes to be here, and God has a mission for you. Yes, the world is filled with sinners. Yes, you are one of them. And *yes*, it is the very experiences you've had in your life—including your mistakes—that make you the likeliest to reach the lost in your arena of expertise.

Don't "get" ready. "Live" ready.

So when the time comes, we can be the New Church.

Reformed.

Awakened.

Radical.

Notes

1. As quoted by: David Malick, "An Introduction to the Book of James," January 17, 2014, *Bible.org*, last accessed October 4, 2016, https://bible.org/article/introduction-book-james.

2. David Malick, "An Introduction to the Book of James," quote derived from note number 9, https://bible.org/article/introduction-book-james.

3. Hegesippus, "Fragments from His Five Books of Commentaries on the Acts of the Church," *Early Christian Writings*, last accessed October 5, 2016, http://www.earlychristianwritings.com/text/hegesippus.html.

4. "Christian Persecution," *Open Doors*, last accessed October 19, 2016, https://www.opendoorsusa.org/christian-persecution/.

5. Ibid.

6. David deSilva, *Honor, Patronage, Kinship, & Purity: Unlocking New Testament Culture* (InterVarsity Press, Downer's Grove, IL: 2000), 23.

7. Ibid., 24.

8. "Sweetcakes" court testimonies and minutes, *Oregon Bureau of Labor and Industries*, archives, last accessed January 11, 2017, https://www.oregon.gov/boli/SiteAssets/pages/press/Sweet%20Cakes%20FO.pdf.

9. Ibid., page 6, line 8.

10. Ibid., page 6, line 14.

11. Ibid., page 16, lines 21–25.

12. Keith Green, "Asleep in the Light," *The Ministry Years: Volume 1* (Sparrow Records: 1987), track 18.

13. "James 3:2 Commentary," under "Barnes' Notes on the Bible" heading, last accessed January 16, 2016, http://biblehub.com/commentaries/james/3-2.htm; emphasis added.

14. "James 3:4 Commentary," under "Gill's Exposition of the Entire Bible" heading, last accessed January 16, 2016, http://biblehub.com/commentaries/james/3-4.htm.

15. Ibid., under "Barnes' Notes on the Bible" heading; emphasis added.

16. "James 3:6 Commentary," under "Barnes' Notes on the Bible" heading, last accessed January 16, 2016, http://biblehub.com/commentaries/james/3-6.htm.

17. Ibid., under "Matthew Poole's Commentary" heading.

18. Ibid., under "Gill's Exposition of the Entire Bible" heading.

19. "The Message to Laodicea," *Bible Gateway*, last accessed January 18, 2017, https://www.biblegateway.com/resources/commentaries/IVP-NT/Rev/Message-Laodicea.

20. Ibid.

21. "Don't You Know the Choice to Be Made?" *Bible Gateway*, last accessed January 20, 2017, https://www.biblegateway.com/resources/commentaries/IVP-NT/Jas/Dont-You-Know-Choice-Be-Made; emphasis added.

22. Edgar Allen Poe, *Berenice*, 1835. This short story can be read on *The Literature Network Online* at the following link, last accessed January 18, 2017, http://www.online-literature.com/poe/23/.

23. Richard Black, "Enemy's Camp," lyrics and chords available at *Higher Praise*, last accessed January 19, 2017, http://www.higherpraise.com/Lyrics4/EnemysCamp.htm.

24. Michael W. Smith, "Above All," from the album "Worship" (Reunion Music, 2001), track 6.

25. Billy Funk, "Jesus, We Celebrate Your Victory," from the album "See His Glory" (Integrity Media, 1995), track 2.

26. See John McMillan's personal blog about this controversy here: John McMillan, "How He Loves, David Crowder, and Sloppy Wet Kisses…" September 14, 2009, *The Promenade*, last accessed January 20, 2017, http://johnmarkmcmillan.blogspot.com/2009/09/how-he-loves-david-crowder-and-sloppy.html.

27. Ibid.

28. "James 4:17 Commentary," under "Barnes' Notes on the Bible" heading, last accessed January 24, 2016, http://biblehub.com/commentaries/james/4-17.htm.

29. "James 5 Commentary," from the Cambridge Bible for Schools and Colleges, under the "James 5:3" heading, last accessed January 24, 2017, http://biblehub.com/commentaries/cambridge/james/5.htm.

30. "Sacrifice," *Merriam-Webster Dictionary Online*, last accessed January 31, 2017, https://www.merriam-webster.com/dictionary/sacrifice.

31. Harry S. Stout, *The Divine Dramatist: George Whitefield and the Rise of Modern Evangelicalism* (Eerdmans, Grand Rapids, Michigan: 1991), 117.